ONLY FOR THREE MONTHS

*This book is dedicated to the Basque children
who came to Britain and to all those who helped them.*

ONLY FOR THREE MONTHS

The Basque Children in Exile

Adrian Bell

Photographs – sources
We are grateful to the following picture libraries and archives for their cooperation in the illustration of this book: Hulton Deutsch (pages 50 and 63), The Illustrated London News (pages 58 and 59), Trades Union Congress (page 84).

Published in 1996 by
Mousehold Press, Constitution Opening
Norwich, NR3 4BD

Illustrations by Caireles Martínez

Cover design by Patrick Loan
Cover photograph courtesy of Illustrated London News Picture Library

ISBN 1-874739-05-6

Printed by Watkiss Studios Ltd., Biggleswade

Contents

Preface

My initial interest in the 'Basque children' came from reading Hugh Thomas's *The Spanish Civil War* where, in a brief paragraph, he mentions the evacuation of some 4,000 children from Northern Spain to Britain in 1937. It is a tantalising reference: no details as to how it came about or how the children were supported, nor what ultimately became of them. Intrigued by this, I wrote to Professor Paul Preston, who kindly directed me towards Dorothy Legarreta's book, *The Guernica Generation,* which would, he suggested, answer all my queries. Well, it did and it didn't. It deals with the entire evacuation of children from the Basque area in the aftermath of the destruction of Guernica, when a reported 20,000 were sent to safety in half a dozen countries and, for the most part, it is concerned with events up to 1940. Like all good books, though, it serves to raise as many questions as it answers; it clearly indicated that, when the process of repatriation was completed, some 250 children had stayed behind in Britain and it certainly stimulated my curiosity about the actual experiences of those children.

In the two years that followed I succeeded in meeting a good number of the 'Basque children' (for so they continue to be called), thanks especially to Helvecia Hidalgo who introduced me to many of them. I travelled often to London, where half of those who remained still live, to other parts of Britain and eventually to Spain. Looking back over those two years, I am amazed at their willingness to admit me, a stranger, into their homes, and to recount, so openly and fully, the story of their lives, even though this often involved revisiting painful memories. 'There are some things we have forgotten,' said one of the boys, and then, as an almost silent afterthought, 'and some things we have deliberately forgotten.' Yet, not only did they give freely of their time and patiently answer my questions, on many occasions the full generosity of Spanish hospitality was extended to me. This was a memorable period and often I returned home deeply moved. My only regret is that I embarked too late upon this project because, sadly, some of those I met, who contributed to this book, are no longer alive.

Every book, it is said, has several authors, but never more so than in this case. To all of the following I remain indebted: Jesús Alcón, Enriqueta Brooks, Joseba Campo, María Luisa Charlton, Josefina Delgado, Amador Diaz (dec.), Emilio Espiga, Federico Espiga, Rafael Flores, Valeriana Flores, Antonio Gallego, Elvio García, Fausto García (dec.), Rosa García, Leno Guerrero, Oscar Guerrero, Helvecia Hidalgo, Caireles Martínez, Feliciana Martínez, Herminio Martínez, Javier Martínez, Rodolfo Molina, Virgilio Molina, Amelia Montero, Salomé Moreno, Antonio Murga, Pilar

Murga, Eliseo Ochoa, Laureana Puerta (dec.), Caridad Rodriguez, Marina Rodriguez, Palmiro Ruiz, Luis Sanz, María Sanz, María Luisa Silov, Juanita Vaquer, Alvaro Velasco, Carmen Villegas, José Mari Villegas, Ascensión Wakeman and Mario Zornoza.

There were several others who made substantial contributions but who expressed the wish to remain anonymous.

In addition, I was privileged to talk with a few of the many men and women who had voluntarily worked to support the Basque children after their arrival in Britain: Inez Benham, Sister Ignacius, Walter Leonard, Eric Pittman, Cora Portillo, Ronald Thackrah (dec.), Poppy Vulliamy (dec.) and Charlie West. Every one of the children spoke with gratitude and with great warmth for those who, 50 years earlier, had given so much to them; meeting just these few made it easy to understand the abiding strength of that affection. Most especially I wish to thank Poppy who was my first contact. I visited her several times in the nursing home to which she had retired and, alert and witty to the end, she was a constant source of encouragement.

I had only one conversation with Jim Fyrth whose book, *The Signal Was Spain*, contains a chapter about the Basque children, but it taught me a lot about the background to the evacuation. He also passed to me the papers of the late Wilfrid Roberts MP, who, for many years, was Secretary of the Basque Children's Committee. They provided an invaluable fund of material and I am therefore especially grateful to Joanna Matthews, Mr Robert's daughter, for allowing me unlimited access to them. I must also thank Jo Clements and Jane Fardon for the time they spent in the British Library's Newspaper Collection, searching for relevant reports of the evacuation of the Basque children, and of their stay in Britain.

Herminio Martínez was kind enough to read an early draft, and his detailed comments and factual corrections were unfailingly helpful. My warm thanks go also to Sue Mullard for her sympathetic editing of the text, and to Caireles Martínez for readily agreeing to provide the illustrations that accompany it.

Lastly I want to thank Marilyn, my wife, for her support throughout, and for her gentle but persuasive reminder at a critical moment that the time had come to stop gathering further information for this book, and begin the task of writing it.

DEPARTAMIENTO de ASISTENCIA SOCIAL
DEL PAIS VASCO
EXPEDICION
A INGLATERRA
Nº 3.917

1 POINTS OF NO RETURN

Really I suppose, if you listen to the Gods, that storm we went through in the Bay of Biscay was a sign of what was going to come.

One morning in the spring of 1938 Luis rose from his hostel bed early. He dressed quickly and silently, and slipped out of the dormitory. In the pantry he filled his pockets with enough food to last him the day and then, taking two bottles of milk from the doorstep, he walked away to hide in the New Forest.

The hostel was one of 70 or so that had been set up to care for refugee children from the Basque region of Northern Spain. This one, organised and financed by a committee of local Southampton people, was the third one Luis had lived in since his arrival in England the year before, but he remembers it fondly. It was supervised, he says, 'by a kindly woman and her two daughters', and 'she made it feel like home'. But it was not home. Home was in Baracaldo, five kilometres north of Bilbao. He had left there in May 1937, one of some 20,000 children to be evacuated from the perils of the Civil War. The largest contingent of these young exiles went to France, others to Belgium, Switzerland, the Soviet Union and Mexico; and 4,000 came to Britain, including a reluctant Luis:

> We didn't come we were sent. I didn't want to come. I grumbled a lot.

But evidently his grumbling was to little avail. Today, in his home in North London, the slow shrug of the shoulders, the touch of a smile are the silent acknowledgements of the futility of such protests. His parents were resolved: Luis was to join the 'expedición a Inglaterra'.

Parents do not readily separate themselves from their children at moments of acute danger or abandon them to the unknown mercies of strangers in a foreign land unless they have cause to feel desperate. Luis's parents had cause enough. Six years earlier, after alternating between years of dictatorship and monarchy, Spain had become a democratic republic. Democracy, however, was always likely to prove a fragile creature in a

1

nation rent by centuries-old class antagonisms, fierce religious and anti-clerical enmity, the centrifugal yearnings for regional autonomy, and near-feudal conditions throughout much of the countryside. Furthermore, the times were scarcely propitious for so brave a step towards modernisation, with a world economic slump and fascism rampant across Europe. The generous hopes for social and political reform, invested by so many in the birth of the Republic, were soon to be thwarted.

In July 1936 a caucus of army officers, eventually to be headed by General Franco, orchestrated an armed rebellion against the constitutionally elected Republican Government. Confident that they commanded the loyalty of the army, the generals had anticipated a rapid *coup d'état*; but it was not to be. Their rebellion was countered by a spontaneous uprising of popular resistance throughout much of Spain. All the latent hostility which had been simmering for so long now erupted into a civil war that was to last for nearly three years.

It was, as so many were to remark, a peculiarly passionate war. In its first month nearly 100,000 people perished, not on the battlefield, but summarily and without trial, on the doorsteps of a thousand towns, and villages as all restraint was abandoned to ideological fury. There were repeated scenes of extraordinary cruelty and brutality, enacted by men who, from the bottom of their hearts, saw their actions as sanctioned not by the mere exigencies of conflict but by reference to some higher ideal to which they ardently adhered.

After the confusion of the first few days had settled it was apparent that the Republican forces of the elected government held control in two separate parts of Spain: Madrid and the area south to the Mediterranean, and east through Aragón and Cataluña to the southern end of the Pyrenees; and a narrow strip along the Cantabrian coastline from the Basque provinces of Vizcaya and Guipúzcoa westwards into Asturias. The Basque region had remained staunchly loyal to the Republic and it would remain so, pledged José Aguirre, the leader of the Basque Nationalist Party, 'until the defeat of Fascism'. On 1 October 1936 the Basques were granted regional autonomy by the Madrid government and, a week later, municipal councillors met in the sacred town of Guernica to elect Aguirre president of the new Basque Republic.

Of greater significance both for the prospect of defeating fascism and for the future of Basque autonomy was another meeting which had taken place in London three weeks earlier – the inaugural meeting of the Non-Intervention Committee. Formally proposed by the French, although with strong encouragement from the British Foreign Office, the international

2

Non-Intervention Agreement was a pact designed to prevent the escalation of the Spanish war. All military support, and the sale and shipment of armaments to either side was to be strictly prohibited. From its inception and through to the very end of the war the pact was never more than a threadbare masquerade, flagrantly and knowingly flouted by Hitler and Mussolini, and eventually by Stalin. 'An improvised safety curtain,' admitted Foreign Secretary, Anthony Eden, 'tattered and full of holes no doubt, but better than total war in Spain and a European war out of that.'[1] This was a point of view, but not one with which many on the Republican side of the Spanish conflict would have concurred. The agreement prevented the elected government from legally buying arms while doing nothing to prevent thousands of Italian and German troops, and substantial quantities of military equipment flowing to assist the Nationalists' cause. Of the very much smaller amount of Soviet aid which reached the Republican forces little saw its way to the north. There, the material support of the Fascist powers was soon to prove a decisive factor in the tide of events.

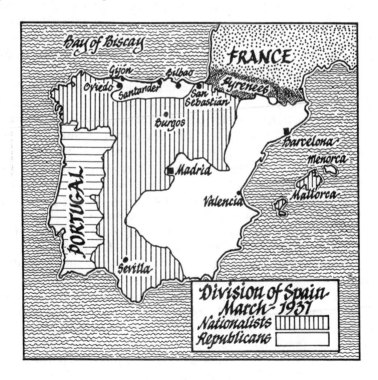

Contrary to the Nationalists' expectations Madrid did not immediately fall. In March 1937, after a first winter of stalemate, General Franco, by then Commander-in-Chief, ordered his forces to direct attention towards the north. Already the attempt had been made to starve the Basques into submission by means of a blockade of the ports along the northern coast, but now the process was to be accelerated. General Mola, placed in charge of the northern campaign, at once proclaimed:

> I have decided to terminate rapidly the war in the north...if surrender is not immediate, I shall raze Vizcaya to the ground, beginning with the industries of war. I have the means to do so.[2]

There was no surrender, nor ever any likelihood of it, and, within a matter of days, the means at his disposal had been put to work. In the early morning light of 31 March a detachment of the Condor Legion – the German squadrons that were serving with the Nationalists – bombed the small town of Durango: a total of 127 bodies were collected from the wreckage of the town; a further 121 died later in hospital.[3] Systematic aerial bombardment of undefended targets which had no military significance – a rationally calculated move to undermine an enemy's morale by terrifying its civilian population – was warfare of a new kind.

A month later the target was Guernica, again a place of little military importance, but of inestimable symbolic relevance – the ancient seat of Basque government, the emblem of its culture and aspiration for independence. The day chosen was 26 April, a Monday, and therefore a market day. For three and a half hours, wave after wave of bombers, arriving every twenty minutes, rained high explosives, followed by incendiary bombs, while fighter planes machine-gunned those who ran through the streets, and into the surrounding fields and hills in the hope of escaping the inferno. General Mola's boast was not idle: the town was razed completely and an unknown number perished in the flames. Throughout the following night the sky to the east of Luis's home town glowed its forewarning.

Set against what was soon to befall cities such as Coventry, Rotterdam and Dresden, where this frightful horror was to be amplified beyond measure, the saturation bombing of Guernica may now seem almost trivial. But it was the first – 'the first blitz of the second world war', Eden was later to remark – and, being the first, it had the power to provoke revulsion.[4] In the days that followed the town's destruction Franco's command issued a shifting series of verbose denials of responsibility, finally attributing the total devastation to retreating Republican arsonists. But this was scarcely

4

convincing when set against the graphic eye-witness accounts which began to be reported in national newspapers everywhere. George Steer's measured reconstruction of the event and his description of the inferno, made more agonising by its subdued, unsensational tone, filled a whole page of *The Times* on 28 April, and carried the news to the world:

> At 2 a.m. to-day when I visited the town the whole of it was a horrible sight, flaming from end to end. The reflection of the flames could be seen in the clouds of smoke above the mountains from 10 miles away. Throughout the night houses were falling until the streets became long heaps of red impenetrable débris ... In the form of its execution and the scale of the destruction it wrought, no less than in the selection of its objective, the raid on Guernica is unparalleled in military history. Guernica was not a military objective.[5]

Anticipating the questions he would receive in the Commons, Eden called for whatever information could be provided locally. The British Ambassador to Spain, Sir Henry Chilton, from the temporary embassy set up across the French border at Hendaye, at first repeated the Nationalists' denials, but a report filed by Ralph Stevenson, His Majesty's Consul in Bilbao, also arrived at the Foreign Office, and Stevenson had walked among the ruins and the ashes:

> Nine houses in ten are beyond reconstruction. Many were still burning and fresh fires were breaking out here and there, the result of incendiary bombs which owing to some fault had not exploded on impact the day before and were doing so, at the time of my visit, under falling beams and masonry. The casualties cannot be ascertained and probably never will, accurately.[6]

To substantiate his account, he later sent two German incendiary bombs that he had picked out of the ruins to the Embassary in Hendaye.[7]

There is no doubt that Eden put great store by this report, from a man whom he described as 'well balanced and impartial'.[8] Stevenson, in fact, had his partiality: he was emotionally attached to the Basque people – too attached, in Chilton's view. But this was a personal sentiment which the Foreign Secretary himself shared with Stevenson: he was pro-Basque rather than pro-Republican. In the House of Commons, only a week earlier, he had expressed his view that it was the Basque Government rather than that of either Franco or the Republic which would more closely resemble

British notions of democracy.[9]

Stevenson's report also detailed an extraordinary attempt he had made, completely on his own initiative, to persuade President Aguirre to offer surrender. 'Resistance against overwhelming odds was useless', he had argued and surrender was now the most prudent course, in fact the only option that could offer realistic hope to the non-combatants of Bilbao. All this had been to no avail. Surrender, he had been assured, was impossible, whatever the consequences of continuing to resist. Stevenson could only indicate, in his report to the Foreign Office, the slim straws to which they were clutching:

> The official denials of Salamanca [Franco's headquarters] respecting the bombardment of Guernica lend colour to the belief that whatever the physical courage of the rebels they will not have the moral courage to carry out their threat to raze Bilbao. Many people build fresh hopes on this slender chance.

But he ended with a plea:

> I have, though, strong views on the question of evacuation of women and children, even if it is only a few thousand and if anything can be done in this respect before it is too late, so much the better.

This was to reiterate an idea that he had first proposed some weeks earlier. Although he had been able to report the willingness of the French Government to cooperate in evacuating non-combatants from the northern war zone, he had been firmly instructed by the Foreign Office not to pursue the idea.

At the same time, the National Joint Committee for Spanish Relief was also discussing the idea of evacuating women and children from the worst danger zones. This committee had been formed at the end of 1936 to coordinate all the voluntary relief activity being undertaken by a plethora of political and non-political organisations. Although its inspiration was the Liberal MP Wilfrid Roberts, it contained every shade of political opinion and a wide range of humanitarian interests, and it was on Roberts's suggestion that a Conservative MP, the Duchess of Atholl, chaired the committee. She and another of its leading members, the Independent MP Eleanor Rathbone, had visited Madrid in April 1937, and been deeply affected by the plight of the children they saw. They returned to Britain determined to devote their energies to organising whatever relief could be provided to these young victims of war, but, within a fortnight, Guernica had seized their attention.

Were it not for what happened in that small and hitherto unknown Basque town, it is unlikely that Luis would have been wandering alone, seeking his hiding place in the New Forest just one year later. In all probability he would not have been evacuated to England and nor would any of the 4,000 who came to be known as 'the Basque children', for, up until that moment, the British Government had resisted all requests for non-combatant refugees to be permitted to enter the country. In the immediate aftermath, however, in the two or three weeks when the frightful agony inflicted upon Guernica was still vivid in the public imagination, the National Joint Committee was able to take the initiative and obtain approval for a limited evacuation from the region. The approval was extracted, only with difficulty, from a reluctant British Government determined not to be seen to be stretching the terms of the Non-Intervention Agreement.

It was not until 18 May that the Government's agreement was finally obtained and cabled to Stevenson in Bilbao, and even as late as 13 May the Prime Minister was still expressing his disapproval of the entire idea. By then, however, the process that was to lead to the evacuation had built its own momentum: Leah Manning, another of the resourceful and indefatigable women on the National Joint Committee, had been in Bilbao for several weeks, arranging details with members of the Basque Government; two English doctors were there, medically examining the children; back in London the National Joint Committee had announced the impending evacuation in *The Times* and successfully appealed for funds; and the first large-scale evacuations to France had already taken place. Outright rejection of the Committee's proposal would, at that stage, have been difficult.

Nevertheless, the Government's final approval was subject to stringent conditions. It insisted, principally, that the responsibility for the children's maintenance, welfare and eventual repatriation would be borne entirely by the National Joint Committee: no public funds of any sort were to be made available. The Committee accepted that stipulation: for some children, at least, the agreement opened up an avenue of escape from the bombs that were then falling daily upon Bilbao; and from the acute shortage of food in the city. To administer its responsibility, the Basque Children's Committee (BCC) was established. Although scarcely imaginable at the time, it was to remain in being until 1951.

In Bilbao, swollen now by 100,000 refugees from other parts of the Basque region, Stevenson was being inundated with requests from thousands of parents. 'The public has come to look upon British destroyers as a public utility', he had earlier reported. Unaware, as they must have been, of the protracted negotiations that were taking place in London, their concerns were far more immediate. For Luis, the facts can be put very simply:

> My parents sent me because of the bombings. Bilbao is an industrial town and we were also very hungry. It was mainly the bombs and the lack of food.

So he was signed up to be evacuated to England. He came as one of 3,826 children, together with 95 maestras (teachers), 120 señoritas (young women who had volunteered to accompany the children) and fifteen priests. They left Spain on the morning of 21 May 1937, packed aboard an ageing liner, the *Habana*. Escorted by two Royal Navy warships, they weathered a storm in the Bay of Biscay to arrive in Southampton Water in the early evening of the following day. They formed the largest single influx of refugees into this country and the only one to consist almost entirely of children. For all his reluctance, Luis was, at least, reassured by his certainty that the stay would be brief, probably for no more than three months.

Three months was, in fact, most people's estimate. During the days before their departure, parents and children had been able to comfort themselves, and each other, with the belief that their separation would be short. And, finally, on the night of their departure, on the blacked-out, teeming platforms of Portugalete station as anxious parents said their farewells and saw their children into the trains which were to carry them to the docks at Santurce, that consoling prediction was constantly heard through the noise, the confusion and the tears – 'Don't worry. See you in three months.'

Virtually everyone remained far longer. The first repatriations did not occur until the beginning of November. In April 1938, nearly a year after their arrival, more than half the children were still in this country. In June 1939, on the eve of World War II, 1,150 remained. Then, with war known to be inevitable and imminent, the process of returning the children to Spain was greatly accelerated. Until the early part of 1940 contingents of exiled children continued to cross the Channel to be reunited with members of their family in French refugee camps or escorted to the Spanish border. But, following the fall of France, that route was cut off and then, since nobody was prepared to risk sending children across the Bay of Biscay by boat, some 470 were stranded in Britain for the next five years. Only after the war did repatriation once more became feasible and then, some did leave, either for Spain or to join relatives in exile in France, or in various parts of South

America, but about 250 never did. For a variety of reasons, they remained in England.

For those who have seen 'only three months' stretch out beyond 50 years, and what was to be a brief respite from the bombing become the best part of a lifetime, the memory of those words now invariably provokes an ironic laugh, and repeatedly – 'Oh, yes, yes, definitely. We all thought it would be only for a short time, a few months at most.'

For Luis there is the further irony that, despite his objections to leaving Spain and his previous grumbling, when he slipped out of the hostel in Southampton to hide in the woods it was expressly to avoid repatriation:

> I was told in Southampton to get ready because on such and such a date there was a boat leaving for Spain. So I stole a couple of bottles of milk when the milkman arrived and ran into the New Forest. I knew which date, of course. I knew when the boat was leaving and I came back to the colony later that day, only when I knew the boat had left.

By any standards, here was a striking act of independence. This was a boy of sixteen, a young exile, shunted from one place to another during his short stay in England, and with none of the confident grasp of another's language which enables one to feel at least some measure of command over one's fate in a foreign land. Now, whether he wanted to or not, he was being instructed to pack his bags ready for the return journey. He was the first, but not the only boy, to attempt to resist repatriation in that way. Soon after, when he had been moved to yet another colony, in Margate, he learned of two others who had entertained the same idea:

> They had tried to do as I had done, only they had bicycles and so they rode away. Since their geography of this country was nil, they rode south and of course they were caught very near Newhaven, and they were put on the boat.

In their innocence they had pedalled directly towards the very thing they had sought to avoid. Luis, however, had not been so geographically naïve: his father had been something of an Anglophile and regularly used to receive an illustrated magazine from England. So, he relates his own success with a self-deprecating laugh, but it cannot disguise the fact that here was an act that required considerable courage to execute. Not just the running and hiding, but the calculated, solitary walk back later to the colony

9

to explain his defiance and face the consequences. Like any such public display of moral strength it had the capacity to influence wider events. As a result of his example, the Basque Children's Committee successfully persuaded the Home Office to accept the principle that those above the age of sixteen should, in future, be allowed to choose for themselves whether or not to remain in England.

Paradoxically, perhaps, this act of defiance was also an act of obedience, for he carried with him into the New Forest instructions not to return to Spain at that moment. His father had sent him a newspaper cutting which reported a speech by General Franco, demanding the return of all the exiled Spanish children to their homeland, which contained mention of a repatriation ship that would shortly be leaving from England. Across it he had written in ink the single word 'OJO' – caution. Ambiguous enough to confuse any Spanish censor who might perhaps have opened the envelope, it left Luis in no doubt as to his father's meaning. Not surprisingly, he still has that cutting – one column wide and an inch long: it was to govern his life.

In retrospect we can see his flight into the New Forest to avoid the repatriation boat as a point of no return, but it didn't seem that way to him at the time. The realisation that the Republic was losing and would lose the war was gradual, and even with its dawning, Luis says, 'We were still going to go back. There was no question of that.' But there was a question. His day in the forest first posed it and determined that he would be marooned in England throughout the years of World War II. Afterwards, when returning to Spain next became a possibility, he would already have been in England for nearly ten years. Today, he and the Basque girl he later married are still here, and even now the question is not finally answered.

For others, too, it was a coded letter from home which shaped their destiny. María, one of the señoritas who had accompanied the children, remembers her initial difficulty in deciphering the meaning of what her mother had written:

She used the second name and I didn't catch it at first. 'Tell María Teresa,' she said. In the Confirmation, you know, with so many Marías – María this and María that – they put in a second name. I was María Teresa, and she wrote in the letter, 'We are so very pleased to hear you are coming back, and tell María Teresa' – that was me – 'tell her that if she comes back she couldn't stay for long. We are very poor now; we've got nothing. If she comes, she will have to go and live with Granny.' Well, my Granny was dead for twenty years!

They used to tell you things like that. They couldn't say anything else. They couldn't say the real thing.

Fear of retribution if their letter were to be opened by a Nationalist censor did not inhibit everybody. Some sent an unambiguous message, hidden behind no disguise: 'Don't come here! You'll be only a burden to me', was the instruction Palmiro remembers from his mother just as the Spanish war came to a close in 1939. He was just fourteen at the time, and if the rejection and its peremptory tone sound unbearably harsh, he recollects it without any trace of rancour:

So we had nowhere to go, actually, when the Civil War ended – my brother and I. My mother was working hard to keep my three older brothers alive. 'Don't come here! You'll be only a burden to me', she said. She was able to write to tell us that conditions there were impossible – she couldn't take care of us. Both my sisters were in prison as well as my brothers. She was working hard to try to take them bits of food, because in Spain if you didn't have food brought in, you starved in prison. Or it was only through the generosity of the other prisoners who had families who brought some in, which they shared there, you know. That was the political life in Spain.

He was the youngest of a family of seven, and even before the *Habana* carried him and an older brother off to England, he had already known the upheaval and the loss that evacuation brings. They came from San Sebastián, and had joined the westwards exodus of much of its Republican population when the town was taken by the Nationalist army and their Italian allies early in the war. Crowded aboard a tramp steamer with whatever few belongings they could take with them from their past, they were carried down the coast, first to Baracaldo – but there was no accommodation there – and so on to Bilbao. Then the bombing started:

You could see them overhead – squadrons of them – so you never knew where they were going to hit you. All my parents thought about was to send us to safety – for a period of three months, perhaps. That's what they thought it would be. We came away, of course, thinking it was going to be a holiday!

How wrong they were, although the tents they were to occupy on their arrival in England may have suggested a holiday. A 30-acre field at North

Stoneham, just outside Southampton, had been loaned to the Basque Children's Committee by a local farmer and in one week had been transformed into a campsite capable of accommodating the 4,000 children. Hundreds of volunteers, responding to appeals in the *Southern Daily Echo*, together with contingents of Southampton Scouts and Guides, had prepared the area, laid on mains water, dug latrines, put up the perimeter fence, and, finally, erected tents hired from the War Office.

Although Palmiro was to stay there until the end of August, North Stoneham was only ever intended to be a brief transit camp. Gradually, through the summer, groups of varying sizes were moved out into the more permanent hostels. The Catholic Church offered to accept 1,200 in its existing orphanages and convents; the Salvation Army took 450 to its hostel in East London; the remainder were to live in what came to be known as 'colonies' – hostels run by local voluntary committees. By the end of September the children were dispersed across more than 70 colonies from Plymouth to Montrose.

Many of these, in fact, turned out to be as temporary as the original camp. In not much over a year Palmiro was living in the fourth of the five colonies he was to know and it was here that he learned of his father's death:

> It was just his bad luck that when a Spanish submarine sank the *Baleares*, one of Franco's ships, they just picked up 250 prisoners at random and shot them all. Put them all in a big grave – revenge killing, you know. My father was one of them.

His mother's letter in the aftermath of the Civil War marked his point of no return to Spain and, when the colony closed, he was offered a job:

> 'Well Palmiro,' they said, 'there is a job for you where you won't get paid anything, where you just work for your keep. It's on a farm down in Devon. You'll have to go. The colony cannot be maintained; there are no more funds and the Spanish war is over. And now it means that everyone has to go. They either find jobs or return to Spain.' I said, 'Right. I'll go to the farm.'

Although faced with such limited options Palmiro had to decide only for himself, whereas others shouldered the weight of additional responsibilities. Helvecia had arrived with a younger brother and sister; they too had believed it would be for no more than three months:

I can still see my mother when we were getting into the boat at Santurce and her shouting, 'Sólo por tres meses. Hasta tres meses.' We thought the war was going to finish and that the Republicans were going to win. Yes, we definitely thought we would win. Then we would come back – to pick up the pieces or at least to be reunited with our families. We never thought we'd stay here for ever.

Two years later they were still in England and throughout, Helvecia maintains, it had been possible to retain that hope. Only when she heard of the final desolate weeks of the war, with Republican resolve irretrievably worn down and with half a million people caught up in the last, unutterably weary retreat along the coast road and through the Pyrenees into France, did her optimism eventually dissolve. And, by then, there were no pieces left to pick up. The family was scattered beyond any hope of immediate recall: one sister and a cousin in exile in Russia; another sister alternately on the run or in hiding; a wounded brother and a cousin in prison; and she with her younger brother and sister in England. Only her widowed mother was left and she, long before that, had been firmly telling Helvecia not to go back to Spain:

So in her letters my mother used to say – because she knew we were alright – she used to say, 'Don't come here. If anything, go to your sister in Russia.'

Helvecia's older sister had volunteered to sail on the *Habana's* next voyage as one of the señoritas caring for a contingent of children bound for Russia. It was to have been a return journey, but, in Leningrad, that intention was forestalled by the news that Bilbao had fallen: she decided to remain there. Meanwhile, in England, from the moment that Bilbao was taken by the Nationalists, there were demands for the children's immediate repatriation. The city was now spared the bombing and the food supply was improving, and, so it was argued, there could be no just cause for retaining them in England. As the summer and autumn of 1937 wore on, and the whole of the Republican north was captured, Franco repeatedly insisted upon their return. This demand was echoed, ever more stridently, by his supporters in Britain who accused the Basque Children's Committee of exploiting the children and their parents for the purpose of political propaganda by unnecessarily prolonging their separation.

The Committee resisted the clamour for immediate repatriation, and insisted that it could not return any child without the explicit request of his or her parents; the problem was to ascertain what the parents' wishes were. In February 1938 there were still 2,500 children in Britain, but, the Committee pointed out, they fell into three, roughly equal categories: those whose parents were thought to be in Bilbao but who had not reclaimed them; those who had been part of the exodus from the city and who were now, themselves, refugees in France, or elsewhere in Republican-held Spain; those whose whereabouts, and even whose fate, was simply unknown.

Few of the children could have realised the full extent to which their presence in Britain had assumed a political significance. No foreign event in the twentieth century cleaved political opinion in Britain so profoundly, or ignited such passion, or provoked such bitterness in public debate. Mercifully, however, they did not read the English newspapers which would have told them how their continued presence had made them the unwitting focus of ideologically-driven spite. And, as one of the boys recalls, 'those who didn't like us, never came near us anyway'. Some of the older children, however, were aware of the calls from Nationalist Spain, and the demands from Britain, for their return. They could scarcely avoid hearing it in the colonies. But, in the colony at Carshalton, where Helvecia was living, there were señoritas willing to conspire to help those whose parents had cautioned against repatriation. In that respect, she says, they were very lucky:

We were very lucky with the señoritas. They asked everyone their situation. They knew – we showed them the letters and everything. So they said, 'Right, next week there's somebody coming from London and they're going to start asking if you've got letters.' And we arranged, each of us, what story to tell. And my story was that I hadn't heard from my mother, didn't know where she was. If they wanted me to go, to send me to Russia with my brother and sister. 'My older sister [in Russia] does write – here are the letters – and she is always saying we can go there', which was true. And I kept on like that, and they gave up in the end. They gave up.

And, because they gave up, the three children stayed. They were the only ones out of the twenty who had originally formed the Carshalton colony who did not return to Spain. Helvecia remembers a last farewell at Lyons Corner House, in December 1939, with a dozen or so children from the colony who were about to depart for Spain. Some were looking forward to returning, even if somewhat apprehensively; others were clearly very reluctant to relinquish the security, the camaraderie and moments of happiness they had known in Carshalton. It was, as she recalls it, a sadly ambivalent occasion:

> They weren't sure what they were going back to; and they weren't sure what would happen to them here either because war had been declared by then.

Perhaps it was the Russian gambit which made Helvecia's 'story' sufficiently convincing, or she might simply have told it more appealingly, or perhaps it can only be put down to the working of chance – if only once, when the papers were ready, the Baltic had not been frozen, they might surely have gone.

Fate figured prominently and repeatedly in these young lives. It was a similar intervention by the Spanish teachers in the colony at Tamworth which made Tony decide not to return. Two English ladies had visited the colony and urged the children to return to Spain:

> They said that the Quakers were going to open a home in Barcelona and they had the money, and so on. I was tempted because I was one of the older boys – fourteen or so. They came to see us in the Midlands. Whoever they were, they were trying to say it would be a good thing to go back to Barcelona and so on. And we all – I don't know, because we were young – I said, 'OK, I'll go back; my family is in Catalonia.' But we didn't know what we were saying. And just before they got back to their car, the teachers, they said, 'But you boys are mad to go back to Spain. They kidded you.'

And, in the sudden impulse of that moment, Tony ran to the car to say that he'd changed his mind. It was to seal his future in England and yet, all these years later, the events of that afternoon still remain something of a mystery. He is uncertain as to the women's identity and purpose in coming to the colony at Tamworth: 'Even to this day I wonder why they should have encouraged us to go.'

Probably they were Quakers, many of whom contributed in numerous ways to the support of the Basque children. The colony in the Somerset town of Street, for example, was located in a large house owned by Clarks, the Quaker shoemaking firm; the Quaker's journal, *The Friend*, carried news of the Basque children and issued regular appeals for their support: 'You can't say no to hungry children. Give for Spain' ran one of their numerous appeal pamphlets. Furthermore, two representatives of the Society of

Friends were always on the central Basque Children's Committee. However, the declared policy of the Friends Service Council was that children, even though exposed to the worst dangers and deprivations of the war, could best be helped by relief work within Spain itself. Accordingly, Quaker volunteers worked, principally with Catalonian agencies, to establish colonies in and around Barcelona, and its fund-raising effort was directed towards ensuring them an adequate supply of food and clothing. It was to such a colony, one can only guess, that Tony might have returned, had he followed his first instinct.

Where it might eventually have led him, there is no knowing. His parents were then near Barcelona; they had followed the route taken by many Republican families who fled from Bilbao – by sea to France and then back into eastern Spain. Like so many, however, they were eventually to join the final exodus back through Cataluña, and over the border into a French refugee camp. And, like many, they never returned to Spain. In the years after 1945 there was to be one compensation, both for them and for Tony – family reunions were that much easier to arrange. But, at that moment, all of this was still buried in the future. Only years later was he able to see the finality of the decision he made that afternoon in Tamworth.

For others, however, the decision was simply not theirs for the making. Mario, for example, had received no instructions from home, and when he and his younger brother were told to pack their few belongings, so as to be ready for the journey back to Spain, there were no doubts in their minds: they were both willing to return. Furthermore, they knew – it had been made abundantly clear – that this was likely to be a final call. It was December 1939 and there might well not be another chance until the war was over, and those that were left behind were likely to be stranded. It wasn't that Mario was unhappy in England: quite the opposite, he had enjoyed the life of the colony at Keighley. The premises had been ideally suited: an old house on the edge of the moor, it had been a military hospital in the First World War and then a sanatorium. And he remembers the chairman of the local committee, the Reverend Balmer, as having discharged his responsibility with a broad vision:

He genuinely tried to do things, that man, and to get the people of the town to accept that. They were very kind and probably didn't need his assistance, but he tried to organise them in a very wide way. He was instrumental, for instance, in bringing people in from the town to teach us English.

16

Later, he would speak of all this as having been a 'marvellous experience', but, at that moment, he simply wanted to go home. In any case, the colony itself was closing: the house was being emptied of Basque children and put to a more urgent need as a military hospital once more.

> So we said we wanted to go to Spain. I know we wanted to go back very much because we remembered what Spain was like.

What he remembered, of course, was the small industrial town in which he had been brought up and through which he rode his solid-tyred bicycle while local peasant farmers walked their cows; and the house the family occupied, together with his grandparents, and the two girls in service, such that never fewer than a dozen people sat down to meals; and the busy café-bar his mother ran, to which all manner of people – doctor, teacher, and factory workers – congregated every evening; and he remembered his quietly-spoken father and the respect he had commanded in the town. But when Mario indicated his eagerness to return, the Revd. Balmer knew that this would be to a Spain which no longer existed, except in the memory of this twelve-year-old boy and his brother. He told them:

> 'But you can't go to Spain; there is nobody there for you. Your father's not there; your mother's not there; your family's not there. I don't think you should go.' We said, 'Well, we want to go.' I said, 'I want to go very much.' ⁂

The vicar explained again, carefully, that there might be nobody to look after them, that even their uncles and aunts who might still be there would be living now in considerable poverty, and facing great difficulties. None of this made any difference. The boy was not interested in hearing a catalogue of adult reasons as to why he should not return to Spain; he simply wanted to get back and that was that. In the end, Balmer was adamant and Mario recalls their struggle:

> He said, 'Well, I'm not going to let you.' And I said, 'Well, you must. You must. We're going to Spain.' And when he finally said, 'No, you're not going', I remember crying and saying, 'We're going anyhow.' And I remember going to the bus and he wouldn't let us go in. It was like that, almost, children fighting him to get on a bus. … He obviously knew and I didn't. Of course I had no means of knowing. I didn't read the newspapers and, anyhow, as a child

you're not interested. It wasn't important enough, somehow, as a child – the fact that people told you that things were bad, no food or whatever, it wasn't relevant. There was the need to go ... So, anyhow, he barred us from going and quite rightly too.

Quite rightly too? Today, Mario has no doubts about that. The hardships – no food, no money, no work – which had failed to make an impression upon him then, were, as he was later to discover, even worse than Balmer had described. The small Basque market town to which the two boys fought to return would not have been as they fondly remembered it. Their imprisoned father had been shot dead without trial; the house commandeered and everything confiscated; their mother exiled in France and, then, on her return, prohibited from getting work, and forced to eke out a living doing favours for friends; their sister dying in childbirth for want of an injection:

After Asturias fell in October 1937, that's when the real punishments had begun. And we learned afterwards that they had a terrible time during the poverty years.

He knew none of that at the time. Then, all he knew was that he and his brother wanted to go home and here was the adult bulk of an Anglican vicar standing in the doorway, preventing them climbing into the bus that would have begun their return journey. For these two boys there was to be no return.

But why these two especially and not others? There certainly were others in a similar situation, who, on their return, would find themselves having to confront the same deprivations. Such were the inevitable anomalies that Federico, for instance, and his twin brother, found themselves disappointed, reluctant travellers on the very train that would have taken Mario and his brother back to Spain. They returned to parents living then in extreme poverty and who, Federico insists, had never reclaimed them:

Other parents did, but our parents, no. It was the one in charge of the colony [Caerleon] who sent us. They told us we would be sent in three lots and we were due to go in the first shipment. We said, 'No, please. Don't send us at this moment. Leave us here.' We didn't want to go you see? The second time, it happened the same, but the third time they said, 'You must. You have to go.'

Despite their pleas they crossed the Channel just before the Christmas of 1939 and were taken by train to the Spanish border. In Caerleon there was no Reverend Balmer. But Mario has a theory as to why he and his younger brother, unlike Federico and his twin, were prevented from returning. It was because of an older brother who had been with them in the first few months at Keighley:

Balmer took a liking to three or four boys who were distinctive from the rest, including my brother, Esteban. There was an intelligent person, very quick. I mean, he learned English in about three months and he managed to get himself out of Keighley in Yorkshire, to London, and into a job in an office where he was earning about fifteen shillings a week. And he managed – again, how a child of fifteen does this! He managed to get himself together in such a way as to persuade a relative of our mother, in Chile, to sponsor him to go there. And, better still, he managed to leave here after war was declared, which was unheard of. Now Balmer was a very good friend to my brother in that he helped him. My brother – he was trying to surmount these difficulties and for a person of fifteen, that's quite something. Balmer helped him to get himself enough English to get to London and into a job; he probably helped him to arrange his passage to Chile. And, anyhow, my brother must have said to him, 'Will you look after my two young brothers?'

And the Reverend Balmer pledged to do so? That, at any rate, is Mario's belief and he tells of it with no sense of having been abandoned. His brother would write to him from Chile, 'very good letters', as he recalls them, 'letters full of hope and full of encouragement, and love', but there can be no certainty that Esteban, the older boy, had spoken to Balmer: he died, only a few years later, in Chile. The only certainty is that, for Mario, this proved to be a point of no return.

There might, perhaps, in the months that followed, have been further opportunities for him to return. During the spring and early summer of 1940, when it still remained safe to cross France, contingents of Basque children continued to leave England. They were reunited with their families in the sad camps that had been set up for Republican exiles in France or taken to the border town of Hendaye, to cross the bridge back into Spain. The last children to be officially repatriated left Manchester on 26 July 1940 aboard a Spanish cargo boat.

Living in Manchester, at that time, were Juanita and her sister, María Angeles. Three years after their arrival in England they had still received no word from home. It was to be another two years before any news would come through. But, by then, it was the middle of the war and there was no question of them going back. Only afterwards could their mother write to ask them to return to Spain. Juanita, sixteen years old by then, and uncertain whether to return or not, sought the opinion of the Basque Children's Committee. The advice was to wait and Juanita did, for several months. 'They were', she says, 'still careful, even then in 1945 and '46.'

In fact, they were considerably more careful. Free of any governmental pressure for immediate repatriation, the Committee was able to investigate each case with a thoroughness which had been impossible in the frantic last months of 1939. Eventually they were able to inform Juanita of the conditions to which she would be returning:

I decided that I would not go back. I can remember writing to my mother and telling her that I'm not coming back, that I didn't want to go back, that I wanted to take a chance here. I was sixteen and after everything that had happened to me – you know, you don't trust people. You lose all the trust that you … you wonder if you might be going back to something worse and at least then I'd started a career here, and I was very English. My sister wrote to me – 'Are you going back?' and I said 'No.' So she said, 'If you're not going back, I'm not going back.' And that was final. I mean my mother did try, but no.

Eight years before, their mother, widowed in the war, had been reluctant for the girls to be evacuated, but they had persuaded her.

We lived in Santurce, so we were just taken down to the harbour and put on the boat. Really, you know, I thought it was a great adventure – going on a big boat – but I suppose, if you listen to the Gods, that storm we went through in the Bay of Biscay was a sign of what was going to come.

Loneliness, unhappiness and a penetrating sense of rejection was to come. They had been sent to one of the colonies organised by the Catholic charity, the Crusade of Rescue, although the reason for that still remains something of a mystery to Juanita. Their father, she recalls, had been a staunch Republican, but it is possible that their mother had indicated that the

20

family was Catholic when she filled in the registration forms in Bilbao. The colony was a convent which contained an orphanage for English girls, and there Juanita and María Angeles found themselves among 24 Basque refugees:

> It was like a dream really. One minute you're on a small farm, then you're on a boat, then you're in a camp, then you're among nuns. And very strict Catholic, Irish nuns.

Almost all of the other Basque girls there were to return, many within a short time. This was normal, for the children in the Catholic colonies were among the first to be repatriated in large numbers. Their parents were, for the most part, the supporters of the Basque Nationalist Party. Conservative and staunchly Catholic, their principal aspiration was for Basque autonomy. This divided them irrevocably from Franco but, even so, they were not viewed with the same passionate enmity as the Socialists and varieties of revolutionaries within the Republican coalition. Furthermore, few of them had left Bilbao to continue the war in the south and east of Spain. So, some months after Bilbao had fallen, they began to reclaim their children, hopeful they would not be subject to the pitiless revenge that was to befall others who had been ideologically committed to a secular Spanish (rather than Catholic Basque) Republic.

But Juanita was not among those who were reclaimed. She had expected to be, imagining, like so many others, that 'it was definitely only going to be for three months – that was the maximum'. But, from their moment of departure, she and her sister had heard nothing from their mother. There was never a letter, only increasingly miserable silence. They and only two other Basque girls were left in the colony when they learned that the Civil War was over:

> Three nuns came out into the play-yard and one of them announced that the war in Spain was finished and that the Republic had lost. And I remember we all started crying. You know? We started crying at the idea because we realised that we weren't going anywhere. We were told that we would stay there. To them we represented orphans. We had no parents, and we were just the same as the others there and, even if we had one parent, obviously we were not wanted because we hadn't been reclaimed. They told us that.

Then Juanita and María Angeles were separated, and forbidden to speak to each other, so that they would learn English more quickly. It was a desperately unhappy time with no foreseeable end. There was no means of knowing what had happened to their mother or young brother, and, not knowing, there remained only the enduring suspicion that they themselves had been abandoned. But, in 1942, a stranger, a Spanish doctor who was working in Manchester, arrived to see them in the convent. It then became possible to piece together what had happened throughout the years of silence. Their mother, it appeared, had never known where the daughters were; nor had she known how to contact them. Almost from the time they had left for England, she herself had been carried like flotsam on the tide of the Civil War, to France, back into eastern Spain, and then, in the final retreat through Cataluña, back towards France once more:

> When she got to Barcelona it was just as bad. So she and half a dozen other women started walking to the Pyrenees and over, and on the way they collected children who had been abandoned. That was in February 1939 when the Franco troops were advancing. They were walking for months collecting children and when they got to France, the Red Cross took them over.

She then endured the misery of a French refugee camp for eighteen months, and remarried before returning to try and resurrect her life in Bilbao again. It was through the fortune of a connection that her second husband had among the exiles living in London that she learned, finally, in 1942, that her daughters were still in an orphanage in Manchester.

Like most of those who remained in England Juanita speaks with feeling for her mother's hardships during the Spanish war and her continuing trials in the years that followed – trailing back and forth over the French frontier on the migrant workers' route, with the family house in Bilbao confiscated, and her possessions gone. 'It was through no fault of hers,' she says. Nevertheless, the filial affections which might have taken her back to Spain could not be recaptured. The trust, she says, was not there. Such damage is casually wrought by civil wars:

> I mean, I left when I was eight. Then the next time I saw her I was twenty-three. It was such a big gap. Really, she was my mother, but she wasn't. She couldn't be, could she?

When her mother wrote, asking her to come home, Juanita had already left the colony and was training at night school and day release classes in the bomb-torn East End of London to become a nursery nurse. With so many mothers working, post-war England was going to need nurseries and nurseries required nurses. She could glimpse the possibility of another kind of future for herself:

> I thought, 'To hell with everything. I'm going to try and make it here.'

As far as one can ever know anything for sure, she knew in that moment that the decision was final. Nine years after her arrival in England, this was truly a point of no return.

For the others, that point came and went without the same sense of irreversibility. There were, in fact, to be other moments when they might have gone back to Spain, to what would have been a completely different life. For most of the other 250 children who remained in Britain the realisation that they were destined not to return came much more slowly, as expectation turned to hope, and hope, always coloured by all the longings and ambiguities which exile brings, gradually faded. 'We were never certain,' says Luis, more than half a century after that decisive walk into the New Forest took him away from the repatriation boat. 'We always thought we were going back.' But Juanita's stubborn determination – 'To hell with everything. I'm going to try and make it here' – was to prove characteristic of almost all those children who had been sent away for a brief escape from the bombing and the hunger, and who were to see three months respite turn into a lifetime's exile.

2 FROM BILBAO TO SOUTHAMPTON

It's very difficult to tell people what went on in the North because the fight was all-enveloping; it affected us all. It was going on only a few miles away – you could sometimes hear noises – but it was coming to you every day in waves of bombing.

Bilbao, in the last days and weeks before they left, lives vividly in the memories of all but the youngest children who were evacuated. As the front line retreated its population doubled with the influx of refugees from other parts of the Basque region. Almost completely surrounded on land, blockaded for much of the time by Nationalist warships, and fully exposed to the air raids from the Italian and German bombers, Bilbao was a city under siege, a city in which the exigencies of civil war had penetrated every aspect of life: schools were closed; there was next to no public transport; families lived in over crowded and make shift accommodation; hotels had been converted into hostels, and dining rooms for refugees and orphans, the old, and the poor; strict food rationing was in force and still there was perpetual queuing for what little was available; factories had been turned to armaments production, making bombs out of tin cans, while, constantly, in the streets and squares of the city, the militia was drilling. It was that kind of improvised irregular army in which it was not uncommon for milicianos to go to the front line in the morning and then return home in the evening.[1] By April 1937 this was perfectly possible: the front line was just beyond the encircling mountains, so close that the noises of battle could sometimes be heard. And, most days, squadrons of bombers carried the war to the women, and children in the city: Joseba remembers the shock of the first raid:

It was September 15th, 1936, three o'clock in the afternoon. Us kids – well there was no school – and we used to go outside, near the station in the back streets of Bilbao and we used to play pitch-a-penny, and as we were playing, the siren went. Well, we knew nothing. We knew nothing about sirens or planes: we were innocent. And the siren went three times. Three times – the warning. And I remember a soldier, a miliciano, and he says, 'Come on, you kids.

Come on!' And we went for the tunnel. The line had to go into a tunnel through the mountains to Derio and those villages, and he took us in. And I shall never forget it. As we went in – Boom! Just on the top of the tunnel. It didn't hurt us because the tunnel was well into the rocks, but those houses on top. That's when we got scared.

It was not long before he knew how to interpret the siren's shrieks: one meant that planes had been sighted; two was for danger; and three told you they were overhead. After the first raid the Government extended the tunnels deeper into the mountains and constructed an extensive network of bomb shelters; sandbags were everywhere. At first, some minimal air defence had been offered by a handful of Russian fighter planes. Small, bi-winged and very manoeuvrable, they were known as 'Chattos' (snub-nosed) because of their blunt radial engine, but one by one they were shot down. Then there was nothing, all except one ancient aeroplane known affectionately as 'el Abuelo' (the Grandfather); it was so slow that boys like Eliseo used to race against it through the streets:

We had no protection in Bilbao – just a couple of Chattos and the old Abuelo. We used to run faster than that damned thing. We did. We used to dare each other – 'See who can run faster than el Abuelo!' And we used to run along the street, you know. And on the hill they put some field guns – not anti-aircraft guns – fixed guns to keep them out. Keep them out?

But they had nothing that could keep them out. The German and Italian bombers could come and go as they pleased, sometimes as often as a dozen times in a day, beginning at first light with the raid that came to be known as 'the Milkman'. The blessing of a low cloud ceiling, keeping the bombers on the ground, provided the only relief; the only hope was that the fighter planes, forever promised by the Republican Government in Madrid, would one day finally arrive. Eventually, a few did; one of the boys watched them come in:

Finally some aeroplanes arrived from France, and can you believe they landed, and on this cinder, bloody aerodrome, we saw them come in. And as they landed and they grew heavier on the ground, the cinders would suddenly sink in, and over they would go. And, oh, you could almost cry. And this happened to three or four of them. And I mean there was nothing else. There was no concrete to put on the cinders.

25

In fact they'd come, not from France, but directly from Barcelona, having made the perilously long flight over Nationalist-held territory where one had been shot down. Two previous attempts to route them safely through France had failed: they had been ordered back by Non-Intervention Committee observers and their guns confiscated. In Bilbao those planes that had not crash-landed survived only a week before being caught on the ground, bombed and destroyed.

In the end, when the raids became so frequent, mothers and children spent whole days sitting on the steps of the 'refugios' ready to take cover when the siren wailed. The alternative was the constant dash to safety that Feliciana recalls:

> The shelter was any tunnel or under any bridge. I can remember running to the tunnel, with my mother holding on to my younger brother and me holding on to her – scenes like that. It was very frightening because the bombs were dropping left, right and centre.

In their anger and frustration militiamen would sometimes fire futile rifle shots at the roaring black shadows above. Similarly, Jesús speaks of his mother's outburst of impotent fury:

> The day after Durango, that's when I heard my mother swear for the first time in my life. They made a horrible massacre and that's when I remember my mother looking up at the sky at this aeroplane that came down low, and shouting 'hijos de putas' [sons of whores] ...
> I never heard my mother swear before.

That was the beginning of April 1937 and, before the month was out, the process which was to culminate in Jesús himself, and almost 4,000 other children leaving Bilbao for Southampton had begun. 'It all happened so quickly,' he says, but, for those who had embarked upon the mission of securing the evacuation of these children, it was to be a long three weeks, beset with obstacles. 'It seemed as if we were never going to get away,' Leah Manning later recorded in her autobiography.[2] An ex-Labour MP, and official of the National Union of Teachers, she had been sent to Bilbao to represent the National Joint Committee. Arriving, unannounced at the British Consulate, late in April, she had informed Stevenson that she was there to supervise the evacuation. Stevenson, surprised and sceptical – he himself had been the first to propose the removal of women and children as early as 8 April, and been curtly rebuffed by the Foreign Office – advised her to leave Bilbao. Far from leaving she remained for a month, negotiating with President Aguirre and other members of his Basque Government, broadcasting regularly on Bilbao Radio to publicise the evacuation, and energetically coordinating the details of its organisation with the Asistencia Social, the agency responsible for all refugees. While understandable, her exasperation with what must have seemed like interminable delay in the midst of her own hectic round perhaps understates the equally determined, if less flamboyant, efforts that were being made in London to wring final approval from a reluctant British Government. For all her zeal and apparent confidence that the evacuation would be achieved, it was, at this stage, no more than a possibility.

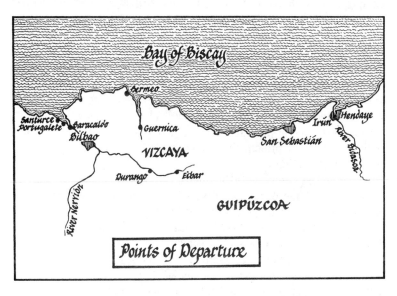

Replying to a proposal from the National Joint Committee for evacuating children from Bilbao, the British Government had granted approval on 29 April, just three days after Guernica's destruction. But it was approval only in principle, subject to the Committee producing a convincingly detailed plan that would satisfy the Home Office, and then only for that number of children whose support could be wholly ensured by voluntary means. As for the cost, the Committee had estimated that it required one shilling per child per week; the Home Office calculated the cost at ten shillings (far more realistic, as it turned out) and insisted upon their figure being guaranteed by the Committee.

In the Foreign Office there were plenty of opponents to what became patronisingly referred to as 'our Bilbao babies policy'. On 2 May, Sir George Mounsey, Assistant Under Secretary with responsibility for Spain, protested against the idea of using British naval vessels to escort evacuation ships.[3] Relations between Britain and the Nationalist authorities had already been soured over the question of the legality of Royal Naval protection for merchant ships attempting to carry food supplies into Bilbao. This had culminated in a British merchantman, the *Seven Seas Spray*, steadfastly ignoring the Admiralty's advice and single-handedly running the Nationalist's blockade of Spain's northern ports. She steamed up the River Nervión on the morning of 20 April to an enthusiastic welcome from the quayside, with cries of 'Long live the British sailors' and a civic reception for her master. With the blockade once broken, other merchant vessels, now with British naval support, were quick to follow in her wake.

The British Ambassador, Sir Henry Chilton, an enthusiastic apologist for Franco, also expressed his unequivocal disapproval of any civilian evacuation. He warned of foreign journalists, hovering in Bilbao, waiting to seize upon any British violation of the principle of non-intervention. Even after the children had arrived in England, he continued to argue that 'the removal of useless mouths' (as he put it) from the area of combat around Bilbao was liable to prolong the city's resistance and thereby to constitute an act of intervention.[4]

Nevertheless, Anthony Eden, almost certainly influenced by Stevenson's report on the effect of the saturation bombing of Guernica, and perhaps by his repeated plea for the evacuation of women and children, ignored these protests. On 3 May 1937 he informed the House of Commons that British warships would be instructed to escort any civilian evacuation from northern Spain through international waters, to wherever was their destination. But whether this meant any would be arriving in Britain was still, as yet, another matter. 'No final arrangements have been made for the admission of Basque children,' he added.

Three days later, on 6 May, the escort policy was put to work when British destroyers accompanied the first major evacuation (consisting of 1,000 women and 2,300 children) to France. It produced an angry reaction from Franco, exactly as was predicted by those who had objected to the idea. His Minister for Foreign Affairs protested at this 'insult to the prestige of the Spanish navy and attack on the sovereignty of Spain'.[5] It also marked the beginning of a sustained campaign of opposition to the evacuations in the Nationalist press: 'They steal our children,' ran the front-page headline of *Unidad*, arguing that this was not a voluntary, but a forced, evacuation:

The red-separatist cruelty stops at nothing. Now (after trying to break the Unity of Spain) it is destroying the unity of the family. Here are Spanish children who are pulled from the arms of their mothers by English 'humanitarianism' so they can be put under the protection of the French popular front.[6]

In Britain another objection to the evacuation proposal emerged from a much less predictable direction: immediately following Eden's announcement in Parliament, Mr Golden, the Secretary of the Save the Children Fund, wrote to inform the Foreign Office that, on the basis of its substantial experience, his organisation was 'absolutely opposed in principle to the removal of young children from their native land'. As for himself, he volunteered the view that he 'would sooner see them die in their own land than rot slowly in exile where they deteriorate physically, morally and mentally'. He went on to offer his conclusion that the members of the National Joint Committee were moved, not by any humanitarian motives, but by political partisanship. Ironically, although in the end this view was not to prevail, it emphatically reinforced the Government's resolve that public support should never be made available to these young exiles, thereby making more austere the conditions under which they were eventually to live in Britain.

On 6 May, the very day that the first evacuation was leaving for France, the Duchess of Atholl, Chairman of the National Joint Committee, wrote to Prime Minister Baldwin asking that the Government should 'do more than merely give its approval to the voluntary care of the Basque children evacuated to the United Kingdom'. Her principal request was for the Government to reverse its previously stated position and contribute financially. 'A pound for every pound privately subscribed,' she proposed. The letter was handed to the Foreign Office for its comment and there, as it was passed from one desk to another, the view hardened against any further governmental support, particularly the provision of public money.[7] The example of the French Government, which was already providing substantial financial assistance, was judged to carry no weight, whereas Golden's opinions were cited as authoritative. Above all, it was argued that such active participation by the Government in humanitarian work would compromise its non-intervention stance. The Prime Minister replied to the Duchess of Atholl on 11 May, turning down the Committee's request. Furthermore, even at this late stage, Baldwin expressed his dislike of the whole idea of evacuating any children to Britain: the climate would be unsuitable, he maintained.

But, while this request for Government assistance was circulating through the Foreign Office, the National Joint Committee was preparing its own detailed plans for how the children would be supported in England. Wilfrid Roberts, joint secretary of the Committee, had submitted these plans to the Home Office on 10 May, before receiving the Prime Minister's rejection. By then the Committee had received donations of £12,000 in response to its appeal published in *The Times* on 1 May and a promise of a further £5,000 from the Trade Union Congress. On 13 May he wrote once more to the Home Office arguing that the Committee's financial position justified it proceeding with an initial evacuation of 2,000 children.

Meanwhile, in Bilbao, parents were already signing up their children for the 'Expedición a Inglaterra' which Leah Manning had been widely and enthusiastically proclaiming throughout the city for more than a fortnight. Ten thousand applications had been made for the first French evacuation and Stevenson reported that he too was being besieged by similar numbers. Within the Foreign Office there were fears that the National Joint Committee was planning the *fait accompli* of 'several shiploads of refugees at Portsmouth, whom it would then be impossible to turn away without a public outcry'. Stevenson was therefore instructed to make the position clear to the Basque Government: there would be no evacuation of anybody, until and unless the British Government gave its approval.[8]

Even before this cable from the Foreign Office reached Stevenson, a British medical team of two doctors and two Spanish-speaking nurses was in Bilbao examining each individual child destined for evacuation. They had been sent there by the National Joint Committee, early in May, to calm the anxieties voiced within the Ministry of Health regarding the possibility of contagious infections being imported into Britain. The contrast between the Committee's imperative to act quickly, and the tempo in Whitehall, was never more keenly felt than by that medical team. Despite what might be thought of as their premature arrival in Bilbao, their task was immediately rendered almost impossible by the incessant air raids. On his return to England, Dr Richard Ellis described their efforts:

> On the first morning, a group of children was assembled in the building of the Asistencia Social. The examinations had hardly begun when the sirens sounded the alarm, and the children scattered to the nearest 'Refugio'. The air raid lasted 40 minutes. This happened four times during the morning, by which time only about sixty children had been seen and the rest had all dispersed.[9]

The following day there could be no examinations at all. Nobody dared leave their improvised air-raid shelters – there had been a leaflet drop from Nationalist planes announcing that, because this was Coronation Day in England, the opportunity would be taken to bombard Bilbao from land, sea and air. The third day was as frustrating as the first: although they had, by then, moved into a hospital which had a bomb shelter in its garden, their work was still constantly interrupted. Thereafter, Ellis concluded, all the examinations would have to take place at night when the bombers didn't fly:

And so a continuous queue filed by each night until 2 a.m., without the slightest complaint, children often attending alone or with an older child, and not infrequently unable to get home that night.[10]

Dr ELLIS.

That same sense of urgency and uncomplaining humility was conveyed by the report of two observers for the Friends Service Council who were also then in Bilbao. They were frequently finding themselves engulfed in the sudden tense rush through the streets, triggered by the sirens' forewarning. There they would stand with the mothers, their children and the old in the refuges, 'laughing and joking till a silence falls, broken by the drumming of the aeroplanes overhead':

These people did not willingly ask for help, but here and everywhere else there is one poignant appeal – 'Take our children away. Save them at least from the horrors of this war.'[11]

The constant bombing was not the only trial with which the beleaguered population was having to contend each day. Food was now in very short supply throughout the city. For weeks previously, the diet had consisted largely of beans, rice, cabbage and a rough, black bread. All of this was strictly rationed and, even then, you had always to queue for it, and, as Jesús remembers, queue early:

> We had to queue for everything. If you didn't go to the shop early enough or queue up early enough, that was it. Somebody before you had it and there was no more left for you, and there was nothing else you could do about it.

Meat was almost unheard of and there were said to be no dogs, or stray cats left in Bilbao. Occasionally, though, word would get around that an animal, a donkey perhaps, was being slaughtered, and then families would start to queue two days ahead. Virgilio and Rodolfo remember their father giving them a little money each morning with the strict instruction that if they saw a queue they were to join it: 'If there is any queue, stay in the queue, and buy whatever there is. You buy it!'

These two boys were, in fact, lucky: they had an older brother who occasionally provided some extra food. The family had escaped on the day before the final Republican collapse in San Sebastián; they had walked until they could walk no further and then managed to catch a train to Bilbao. There they lived in one of the hostels established by the Asistencia Social for the tide of refugees that was flooding in from the surrounding towns and villages before the advance of General Mola's army. The oldest boy was a sixteen-year-old militiaman. He would be ferried by lorry to the front line outside Bilbao each morning and brought back to the hostel in the evening. If he had any of his rations left, he would share them. Or else, Virgilio himself would go up to the barracks:

> In the hostel they gave us chick peas and rice, and they used to put a bit of salted cod on, to give it flavour. And I swear they took it off, and used it again the next day – a bit more flavour. But I used to queue up at the barracks in the evenings to see if there was any food left. There would be twenty to thirty of us kids there, waiting. And as soon as there was any left, they used to go and give you a ladle each. And I used to be so happy, and take it back, you know.

Mario, just like Virgilio, was another who did not see much of his older brother during that time:

> He seemed to spend most of the time roaming about the countryside, gathering a potato or an egg. I don't remember him around much, but he often used to come with a little sack of bits and pieces because the food – well, food! Bread was not just strictly rationed, it was more like brown sawdust mixed with bread. And you were lucky if by the time you got to the end of the queue there was enough.

Yet, when the British doctors conducted their medical examinations, they were surprised to find that nearly all the children were in reasonably good health. Despite the physical deprivation that the population was living through, few of them showed serious signs of malnutrition. 'In many cases,' reported Dr Ellis, 'it is obvious that mothers have starved themselves to provide for the children':

> One pregnant mother who brought up five healthy looking children for examination was herself so weak she could hardly stand, and said, smiling, that perhaps she could find 'time' to eat when her children were safe in England.[12]

That time would be imminent, for, in London, on 15 May, after further discussions with Roberts, the Home Office finally accepted the plans he had submitted on behalf of the National Joint Committee, five days earlier. The Foreign Office immediately telegrammed Stevenson that approval had now been officially granted for an evacuation to Britain of 2,000 children, between the ages of six and twelve.[13]

But, in Bilbao itself, not 2,000 but 4,000 children were being signed up for the evacuation to England and many of them were older than twelve. They were all being medically examined; individual registration cards were being written out for each one; and the Basque Government was issuing them all with passports.

With many more applications than could possibly be accommodated, the process of determining which children would be evacuated had also become somewhat bizarre. An essential condition that had been laid down by the Government as early as 29 April, when it first granted its approval in principle for the venture, was that the selection of children should reflect no political favouritism of any kind. To meet this requirement evacuation places had been allotted to the political parties in Bilbao in proportion to the voting pattern of the last election. As each child was signed up, the parents' political affiliation was written in the top corner of the child's record card.

There is no way of knowing whether the Foreign Office officials in London seriously believed this impartiality to be feasible; perhaps the stipulation was intended merely as a prepared defence against any accusation that Britain was contravening the Non-Intervention Pact. Either way, it was a quite unrealistic demand. Bombs and starvation do not discriminate between the children of Communists and of Fascists, but it was hardly conceivable that, in the fiercely partisan atmosphere of besieged, blockaded, and bombarded Bilbao, supporters of Franco would willingly declare themselves before the Asistencia Social. Equally, it was Republicans, particularly those on the political Left, who had most to fear if the city was to fall to the Nationalists: they had heard Mola's boast; they knew of the brutal reprisals that had accompanied Franco's advances elsewhere. It was they, therefore, who would be most eager to see their children removed to safety.

The Consul, Stevenson, as ever, did his honourable best to ensure that the injunction was adhered to, in spirit, if not to the letter. He had already received one irritable cable from the British Ambassador, Sir Henry Chilton, complaining that many of the first contingent of children to be evacuated to France were said to have given the Communist clenched fist salute as they disembarked; he had been instructed to ensure a more equitable distribution next time![14] The likelihood of accomplishing that, however, was highly improbable: invariably all the evacuations contained far higher proportion of children whose parents had sided with the Republic and fought against the Nationalists. Even within that distribution there were some peculiar anomalies: Rodolfo's registration card was marked 'Anarchist', about which, to this day, he remains scornful:

Anarchists! What Anarchists? There were no Anarchists to speak of in the north. In Barcelona, yes, but not where we came from. What happened was that when my father went to register us, he said that he was a Republican Socialist. They said that there weren't any more places for Republican Socialists, but there were still some places for Anarchists. So he said, 'All right then. Put me down as an Anarchist. What the hell difference does it make?'

In the end, of course, it was to make no difference.

With the required medical examinations of 4,000 children nearly completed, Dr Ellis flew back to England. He had been deeply moved by all that he'd seen during those days and nights in Bilbao: the quiet stoicism in the queues, waiting through the night for the medical examination; the staff in the hospital where he was based, bereft of basic dressings, and operating without anaesthetics; the resilience of the officials of the Asistencia Social, coping with an ever-increasing tide of refugees with constantly diminishing resources. Above all, he said, it was the humble trust of the parents that had affected him most:

> It was impossible not to be touched by the absolute faith the parents had in handing over their children to the care of England. It will surely be the desire of everyone to see that their faith is justified, and that those children who have parents still living return to them under happier circumstances safe and well.[15]

Although he could hardly have foreseen it then, a few of those children he examined during the nights spent in the clinic were destined to live through the longer night of the blitz on London or the Midlands. They were to know bombing which, in its scale, was far more horrific. Yet many of those who did so comment that nothing they encountered later strained the nerves so much as during those last weeks in Bilbao. There, the bombers came by daylight; they came constantly, wave upon wave; and, unimpeded by any air defences, they flew so low. And, of course, they themselves were that much younger.

Shortly after they arrived in England an aeroplane flew innocently over North Stoneham, intending to take an aerial photograph of the camp. It caused an instant panic among many of the children; they threw themselves to the ground and covered their heads as their parents had once taught them. Even two years later, the wail of a siren could bring the memories rushing back: one Sunday morning in the summer of 1939, Laureana, one of the teachers who had accompanied the children to England, was escorting some of them back from church to their colony in Redhill. Suddenly, without warning, a practice siren started up:

> We came out of church and the siren went for the first time. That first Sunday, September '39. And the siren went and they went wild. We couldn't control them. They went right to the Common – miles away. They ran. Fear. They remembered the other sirens. You couldn't convince the kids that the Germans and Italians weren't coming.

It was a couple of hours, Laureana says, before all those who had fled were finally collected and returned to the colony. This was the same uncontrollable panic which had previously seized a few of the children in Bilbao. Enriqueta remembers the terror of her twelve-year-old sister:

> She really suffered that child did. She cried and cried. She wanted to go to France. She wanted to get out of Bilbao. She was terrified of the bombs. She really used to panic to such an extent that as soon as she heard the sirens, she would just run like mad, anywhere, wherever there was shelter, as long as she felt safe. She was the first to go.

Sadly, but with some relief, her parents put her name down for the first evacuation of children: she left for France on the *Habana* at the beginning of May. Barely a fortnight later Dr Ellis was on his way back to London expressly to impress upon the National Joint Committee and the Home Office the need to accept all 4,000 children immediately. He returned to Bilbao having argued that 'the ship could have been filled many times over with children whose parents would prefer to be separated from them for an indefinite time rather than let them face existing, and imminent, conditions in Bilbao'.

The existing conditions were known only too well and they went beyond the shortage of food, and the danger from air raids, or the fear induced by them. There were other horrors visible to the children. Amelia can recall the rows of dead bodies, stretched out on the floor of the hospital, even as she was waiting for her medical examination. Joseba remembers something similar, while standing in a queue on the day after Guernica had been obliterated:

> There was a poor old lady next to me, with a black shawl on. She'd be about 70 and she was crying. 'Excuse me, lady,' I said. 'Qué le pasa a usted?' – What's the matter?' – 'Ah, hijo. Hijo' – you know, like they do – 'Son. Son. You don't know what's happened?' 'What's happened?' I asked. 'Guernica. Guernica's been bombed flat.' And as I was talking to the lady – she was still crying – a lorry came by, like a sand lorry, and it was full of dead bodies. Dead bodies they were taking to be buried.

So, in Bilbao, on the night of 17 May 1937, Leah Manning persuaded the proconsul to cable the Foreign Office with her request that the permitted number be doubled, to 4,000, and that the age limits be extended. The following morning the Duchess of Atholl sent a similar telegram to Eden, stressing the Committee's concern at the fate of 'girls of about fifteen' should Bilbao fall and foreign troops be allowed to run rampant through the city. Later that day the Government acceded to the pressure. Four thousand children, aged between five and fifteen, with a higher proportion of girls amongst the older age group, would be allowed to enter Britain. This decision was promptly cabled to Stevenson.[16]

Ten days earlier, when the Duchess of Atholl's request for additional Government support was circulating through the Foreign Office, Sir George Mounsey had advised the Government to make up its mind between the conflicting pulls of humanitarian concern and adherence to the letter of non-intervention:

If they are going further, they ought to make their attitude clear publicly beyond all doubt, and thus show at least that they are acting on their own initiative and not in response to outside pressure, and that they regard humanitarian work as more important than Non-Intervention.[17]

His advice was ignored. Although the cynical farce of non-intervention was to be stolidly maintained through to the bitter end of the Civil War and although no public funds were ever made available to the Basque refugee children (which was later to prove a mixed blessing to the National Joint Committee), the Government's attitude was never made unambiguously public. Only in the privacy of the Ministerial Committee on Foreign Policy, which met on 19 May, was it conceded that the Government's reluctant agreement to admit the children from Bilbao had been wrung from them by outside pressure. The following day the process of embarkation began in the port of Santurce. A total of 3,826 children were to be released from the 'existing and imminent conditions' in Bilbao.

What the imminent conditions were, of course, could only be guessed at, although the example of Guernica tormented everyone's imagination, just as the Nationalists intended it to. Throughout the month of May a rumour was running wild that General Mola had made a radio speech, threatening Bilbao with the same frightful treatment. 'And its bare and desolate site shall make the British people regret for ever the aid they made to the Basque Bolshevists,' he was said to have proclaimed. In response to an inquiry from Foreign Secretary Eden, the British Ambassador was unable to confirm that these words had actually been spoken.[18] Nor was

Steer, the journalist whose report in *The Times* had broken the news of Guernica to the world, but, living in Bilbao, he could confirm that the rumour was alive, and those words, whether uttered or not, were having their effect:

> But they had their currency in our city, and it moved from hand to hand as quickly as any fearful inflation. Bilbao was trembling.[19]

Understandably so, for the alleged threat conformed to the pattern of the war. At the outset of the northern campaign the General had stated his aim to 'raze Vizcaya to the ground unless surrender was immediate' and the Condor Legion had demonstrated the means. What conceivable purpose was served in fire-bombing Guernica, other than to provide a further, more terrible demonstration to the population of Bilbao itself? Throughout the war to that date, terror, and the portentously broadcast promise of it, had proved to be an effective military tactic against an enthusiastic, but un-trained, citizens' army. It had characterised the Nationalists' advance everywhere.

The threat was not only of immediate violence rained down from the air, but also of the subsequent campaign of graceless reprisal and savage, revenge executions in captured territory. Many of the children who were destined to remain in England speak of their parents' political views, and their fear of the retribution this would incur, as having spurred their determination to see them evacuated. If the ladies of the National Joint Committee in Britain were fearful for the safety of young girls, Spanish mothers felt they had cause to worry also for their sons. Antonio's mother was terrified by what might befall him and his brother:

> She was worried by Franco's continual advance and she said 'I'm going to get you out of the country somehow. Lots of other children are going.' So she put us down to go to Russia, even though it was said at that time that they were only taking boys. Mother felt she could look after the girls; her concern was for the two boys. 'You two, I want you out. I know what's going to happen to you. They didn't get hold of your father, so they're going to get hold of you.' We were going to go on a certain date, but, before that, she heard of the one to England, and she put the five of us in for that – two brothers and three sisters – and we were gone within a few days.

And yet, if Bilbao was trembling, not all of its children were. While some were petrified by the perpetual bombing and others awed by the mutilations to which they had paid unwilling witness, there were others who had adapted to such realities of civil war. They could live for the day and for the adventure it offered, sometimes to the point of growing indifferent to its horrors. In particular, those who were already evacuees from elsewhere in the Basque region had often seen far worse than Bilbao revealed. Nothing had been hidden from the eyes of boys like Virgilio, who had watched the furious fighting and the public executions in the first month of the war in San Sebastián:

> You get hardened to all sorts of things. We had seen a lot of street fighting and dead people about. We used to go to the cemetery and see all the bodies with the labels, saying 'Republican', 'Communist', 'Fascist'. They used to be buried in different ditches.

On the hill above the army barracks, where the militia was pinning down a Nationalist battalion, he and his younger brother, Rodolfo, had found themselves a job, earning a few pesetas by picking up empty cartridge cases which could be refilled, and reused: 'As kids, we did things like that; we didn't seem to mind.' He says that now, as if scarcely able to believe his twelve-year-old insouciance. Only later in life was he to be disturbed by the full impact of those scenes:

> I'll tell you something: I have very vivid memories of the Civil War when I was a child – we used to be in the streets most of the day. I can see it all, over and over again. It haunts me sometimes.

Similarly, when Rodolfo speaks of that time, now in the tranquillity of an English suburb, his voice seems equally full of incredulity:

> We used to walk anywhere and watch it – street fighting, executions. I'm amazed at the things we were allowed to see, to witness – bodies picked up and thrown on a lorry and taken away, in front of everybody. When you're a child, you don't think of death, It doesn't mean anything. You don't think it's going to be your turn, ever.

But then, released from the restraints of school and often free of any adult supervision, the two of them roamed fearless through the streets of Bilbao. Or else they would cross the river and go up the mountainside, close to where abandoned mines provided emergency refuges, and look down upon the town, watching where the bombs were falling: 'We were not afraid; we walked anywhere.' Only when they were nearly killed by a collapsing building, did their father decide that the boys should be evacuated to some place, any place, of greater safety.

Enriqueta tells the same story – 'We knew no fear; we just wanted to see.' Caught out by her own rash inquisitiveness on that same mountainside, too far from the disused mines, she had barely escaped with her life when a stray Junkers had released its bomb load. Her curiosity then took her to visit her father at the front line. The intention had been to stay for a few days, but, she surmises, 'they must have found me so handy they wouldn't let me go'. She remained for a month, helping to clean the house where her father and the other militiamen were billeted, until the retreat was called, and the position abandoned:

> I saw some horrible sights really. When we were in the hamlet, just before the retreat, I happened – again you see, nosey, looking to see what was going on – I happened to be on the balcony, and everybody, even the soldiers were trying to take shelter somewhere, wherever they could. But I was watching them on the balcony. Somebody – I can't remember who it was – grabbed me by the scruff of the neck and pulled me inside and shut the door. Oh dear, but afterwards, when the all-clear went and I went out again. Oh dear, the sights were pitiful. The wounds were dreadful. They had been machine-gunned. And yet, somehow, it didn't seem to have much effect. I must have been a pretty tough egg.

Somewhat later they learned of the expedition to Britain. Another adventure, or so it seemed, and Enriqueta and her middle sister, Carmen, persuaded their mother to allow them to go. It took all their powers of persuasion,but she believes her mother was silently relieved that her two remaining daughters were going to be removed from the imminent dangers, and thankful also that it was they who had proposed the idea. It was not something that she herself could easily have done:

> No – she wouldn't. A mother doesn't like to be parted from her children and naturally she wanted to keep us under her wing. But things were beginning to get tough – very tough. She probably thought it was in our favour, for our benefit, that we should leave for the time being.

It was the urgency of the moment and the need to register the children quickly that perhaps rendered this anxious decision somewhat easier to make. 'There was precious little time to agonise over it,' says Helvecia:

> Probably they didn't have time to think too much about it. I suppose, if they had been for weeks thinking about it deeply – but, you see, the bombs and the shortage of food, and came this opportunity, and believing it was only going to be for three months. You could hear everyone calling, 'It'll only be for three months.'

Virtually each one of those children heard that confident prediction in the final days before departure and, almost without exception, they believed it. But the parents? Did they believe their own optimistic forecast or were these just the sad words of hope, spoken without conviction? Spoken bravely, of course, but spoken only to give courage to their children and, perhaps, to themselves.

There were some adults who could not bring themselves to say it. Alvaro's parents, for example, could not summon those words of assurance: they told him he had to go so that 'there will be at least one of us left alive'. He remembers walking away from them, on the station platform at Portugalete, past the barrier beyond which parents were not permitted to go, and looking back with the sudden realisation that he might never see them again. But they seem to have been exceptional, a family which had been brushed too often by the war's perils to be anything other than fatalistic:

> The first house to be bombed in San Sebastián was our house. My sister, she was pregnant at the time, she was in the house, and she moved from the kitchen to the bedroom and that way she was saved. The front of the house was intact; the back was completely destroyed. Then, in Bilbao, exactly the same happened: my sister was still expecting the baby. Well, good God, just the same. The sirens went and they said, 'Margarita, come on. Come down!' 'Oh, I'll be there now. I'll be there now.' Then, boom! Another bomb. She was alright again. Then the baby was born. A beautiful baby, so they say. Caught pneumonia in the boat to France and died.

Although it is impossible to be sure, most of the parents, it would seem, said their final goodbye with some faith in their own promise that the reunion would be soon. This is what their children still believe although, with the knowledge of hindsight, it is difficult to understand how that optimism could have been sustained. The mothers who spent days forever waiting at the mouths of the bomb shelters, the fathers who fought in a front line that was always retreating closer to home, must surely have realised that the resistance in the north was collapsing. What was it which sustained a belief that the war would be over in so short a time, Franco vanquished and Bilbao peaceful once more?

In many cases, the children's parents were already preparing for their own eventual flight from the city knowing that the war would be carried on elsewhere, knowing they faced personal peril if they stayed. This was one reason, in fact, why some were so anxious for their children to be taken to safety, anticipating they would travel more easily if they travelled alone. And, whether westwards with the retreat, or eastwards by boat to France and then back into Republican Cataluña, their own exile could perhaps be borne with a lighter heart knowing that their children were safe elsewhere. For some it made no difference whether they were in Britain, France or Russia: many children came to Britain only because they had failed to be accommodated aboard the previous evacuation ships to France; others were registered to go to Russia and came only because their parents seized the earlier opportunity that Britain afforded.

And yet it is equally difficult to view the optimism of those final calls – 'It'll only be a short while' – as simply a spontaneous adult conspiracy to reassure the children. Somehow, despite the reverses of the war, there was hope, built out of shared deprivations and a common experience of suffering. Even in retreat the spirit of 'No pasarán!' (they shall not pass) was everywhere. Mario speaks passionately of that atmosphere:

> They fought terribly hard, and they marched and they sang and they created solidarity to such an extent, the like of which I have never seen, and I never shall see again. All right, I was a child and I was impressionable, and all those things, but, I was in London during part of the war and there was that then. But, in Bilbao, it was sort of ten-fold, because all the time the soldiers were drilling around you. We were living then as refugees already, in a ten storey building with what seemed like thousands of small apartments – but it was a neighbourhood. And it was a very happy neighbourhood. If there was a siren, everyone would call, 'Oye, María. Que viene!' And everyone would run out, and go under the bridge. So it was a terribly sad, but also a tremendously elating experience because of this enormous togetherness of people.

Laureana also knew that experience and she was not a child. She had qualified as a teacher the previous year, one of the first to graduate from the reformed and liberalised colleges established in the early years of the Republic, but the Civil War had broken out immediately, and closed the schools. It was a college friend who had encouraged her to reply to the call, printed in the Bilbao papers, for volunteers to accompany the children to England. 'Let's go with the children,' her friend had said. 'Oh come on, let's go with them.' Laureana did and she too was to spend the war years in London:

In Bilbao, mostly we spent half of the time in the shelter. It was such – well, it reminds me a bit of war in London, because I spent the war in London too. It was such an atmosphere of – oh, I don't know – friendship and love between the people. Everything was shared, though there was not much to share. Oh, no.

Soon the children were to know that sense of togetherness once more, in the Basque children's colonies which were to be set up throughout Britain and where many of them were to spend the next two years. Friendships that were destined to last a lifetime were to be formed there and, for some who were not to make the return journey, the fraternity of the post-war Basque network in England was to provide a vital source of constancy in their lives.

But, at dusk on the evening of 20 May 1937, nobody could have been so far sighted as to have guessed any of that. It was raining then in Bilbao and rain had come to be regarded as 'lovely weather' because it dissuaded the bombers from flying. At about six o'clock, in Portugalete station, groups of children, 600 at a time, began to board the special trains that were to take them to the quayside at Santurce; there, the *Habana*, cleaned out and disinfected after discharging its first cargo of refugees in France, was waiting. Inevitably it was an emotional parting: reports speak of 'parents waving their tearful but uncomplaining farewells'. For the children, the emotions varied from one to another; and they could be very mixed – sorrow, relief, and inevitably the excited anticipation that accompanies any travel into the unknown. For Virgilio 'it was just another adventure; it was the war wasn't it?' But, in the same carriage, he remembers three distressed girls:

I remember there were three girls, three sisters sitting in front of us, and they were crying and crying. And we tried to make them happier by chatting with them: 'It'll be alright; you're going on a long sea voyage and it'll be fun, you see.' And when we arrived it was dark, and they picked up our luggage – our little cardboard boxes and things like that – and put them in the hold, and we went up. And we stuck together in the beginning.

These girls were not the only ones to weep; there were others who were similarly affected, including some whom one might least expect, like fifteen-year-old Eliseo:

I didn't want to come. I was crying my heart out. My father took me to the *Habana*, in Santurce, and on the gang-plank I was still trying to get away. And he said, 'Don't be silly. It'll only be for about two or three months, then you'll be back.' To sweeten me up he gave me a duro, a five peseta coin, and said, 'Go on. Now get up there.' A silver coin – I've still got it.

He has also still got the official papers that discharged him from the Republican militia for being under age. Perhaps growing bored with chasing 'el Abuelo' through the streets, he had applied to play clarinet in the

band of a newly formed Bilbao battalion. Armed with a letter of recommen-
dation from his music teacher and with sufficient self-assured cheek to
persuade the recruitment sergeant that he really was 'going on eighteen', he
had enlisted in the militia band. The band had played to the troops along the
front line, in Durango the night before it was bombed and in Guernica two
days before its destruction. That ought to have been enough, but Eliseo
requested to be transferred into a machine-gun section. It was then that his
true age was revealed and it was that which resulted in him being discharged, and eventually led him to the gang-plank of the *Habana*. There, on
the evening before the departure for England, his tears had flowed.

Early next morning, on 21 May, they left Spanish territorial water, 4,000
young passengers squeezed like sardines aboard a ship built for 4,000, they
were accompanied by the yacht *Goizeko-Izarra*, carrying refugees to
France, and two cargo vessels. Laureana remembers sighting another ship
in the vicinity, 'that awful ship that wanted to sink everybody was waiting
for us in the bay. It was outside, waiting.' Presumably it was the Nationalists' cruiser, *Almirante Cervera*, but it remained sullenly silent as the
convoy was picked up by its British escorts, HMS *Royal Oak* and two
destroyers. One of these, HMS *Fearless*, remained with the *Habana* until
they reached the Isle of Wight the following evening. It was a voyage best
forgotten, said Dr Ellis, who had returned to Bilbao for the final stage of the
evacuation:

> ...four thousand wretchedly seasick children crowded into an old
> boat whose very latrines are apt to regurgitate in sympathy, are not
> a pretty sight.

The combination of excitement, overcrowding, food suddenly in abundance and a gale in the Bay of Biscay proved too much for most stomachs.
Many children who had endured the privations of the previous weeks of
poor diet and often hunger, were very soon to regret the food they had
devoured so eagerly. It was the first good food they had eaten for months,
Rodolfo recalls. Clearly one of the better sailors, he only regretted the sheer
squander of it all: 'All that good food gone to waste!'

Pilar sailed with two younger sisters and one of them had an idea about
defeating seasickness:

> My middle sister stuffed herself with eight boiled eggs. I'll never
> forget it. She said, 'That's the way you don't get sick.' So she had
> eight boiled eggs.

Her theory turned out to be fallible, but they were lucky in another respect. Their father had known one of the stewards on the boat and, through that connection, the three girls had been allocated a small cabin, and a bunk each. It was here that Pilar, just ten years old, began to assume the responsibility for the welfare of the younger members of her family. This was a duty that had been impressed upon her by her parents in the days leading up to their departure and she started with the most practical of concerns: 'I made them change their underwear. One day on the boat and it looked like a lifetime.'

Perhaps this was just the natural outcome of Spanish family life, for the fact is that amongst all those who came to Britain in family groups, the eldest child, boy or girl, understood that responsibility, and accepted it, even if not always uncomplainingly, for sometimes it was a heavy burden for young shoulders to carry. It was honoured through their years in the colonies and often long beyond that into adulthood. Whether or not they recognised it at the time, those who lived under the caring eye of an older brother or sister, have invariably come to acknowledge their good fortune. Ascensión was six years old, the youngest of a family of four; Oscar was the oldest:

> Oscar became head of the family. He was the oldest and he always looked after us. He took us over; he was a father figure, I suppose, to us. I've always had a soft spot for Oscar.

That, too, had begun as the *Habana* pitched through the storm:

> It was very rough and I was very, very sick. I remember Oscar putting me, carrying me, on to a big coil of rope and telling me to stop there, and not to move. And I hadn't any shoes on; I remember that because it hurt to walk anywhere.

But the storm that accompanied them across the Bay of Biscay subsided in the Channel and from early morning light the port rail was always crowded with children seeking their first glimpse of England. Dr Ellis was inundated with questions: more than anything else, he recalled, they wanted to know whether there would be white bread in England? At 6.30 on the evening of Saturday 22 May, the *Habana* dropped anchor off Fawley, at the entrance to Southampton Water.

Awaiting them in England was the reception camp – 500 Bell tents on a 30-acre site at North Stoneham, a few miles out of Southampton on the main Winchester Road. It was barely a week since Mr G. H. Brown, a farmer in Eastleigh, had responded to the National Joint Committee's desperate plea, reported in the *Southern Daily Echo*, for a suitable location: he offered them three adjoining grazing fields. 'I am only too pleased to be able to do something for the unfortunate children,' he told the reporter on 13 May, and 'the field is an ideal one for the purpose':

> It is on gravel soil, and very dry. It could rain night and day there without much effect and it is well sheltered.[20]

A torrential downpour within a few days of the children's arrival was to prove this a somewhat exaggerated prediction, but nevertheless his offer was made with the same spontaneous generosity that had brought an army of volunteers there to prepare the camp to receive, as they first thought, 2,000 children. Piped water and gas had to be laid on, latrines dug, the perimeter fence made secure, all the tents and three large marquees erected, field kitchens assembled, and huge quantities of straw brought up to the field to fill matresses. Much of this endeavour was coordinated by a hastily formed committee of the local Cooperative Society. Appeals for specialist help were posted to trade union branches and Labour Party ward associations, and carried in the *Southern Daily Echo*. Throughout the week its front page contained a progress report, notice of meetings in Southampton's Guildhall to raise funds and more immediate appeals for practical help:

A special bus or buses will leave the Civic Centre at 8.45 a.m. tomorrow for the camp. Volunteers for manual labour are wanted, and in addition at least 12 joiners, who are asked to bring their tools. Other tools, for digging etc., are being supplied.[21]

It also requested donations of equipment:

Urgent needs of the committee are: beds, bed linen and blankets, household china and cutlery, kitchen utensils, carpets, tea and kitchen cloths, furniture and packing cases suitable for adapting as furniture, trestle tables, toys and books.[22]

Then came the abrupt news that the number of children to be evacuated had doubled – now it was to be 4,000. Perhaps this was not entirely unexpected. There had been hints of it earlier in the week when the local paper reported that Dr Ellis had return to London to urge the Home Office to accept the increased number. 'Conditions in Bilbao are now intolerable,' he was quoted as saying. But it was not until the evening of Tuesday 18 May, two days before the departure, that it was officially confirmed that twice as many children were to be evacuated.

The final few days were frantic as the camp was reorganised to accept double the number originally envisaged; even the Duchess of Atholl dug trenches. 'No urge to work hard was needed from the "foreman",' reported the *Echo*. 'All carried on strenuously, making up their minds that the camp must be got ready as soon as possible.' In fact, the work carried on through the night until the Sunday morning when the first bus loads of children were already being ferried from the docks. Extra tents and field kitchens had been hired from the War Office (hired, since no public funds were to be spent on the refugee children), at a rate of £340 for the first 30 days and £170 for each subsequent 30 days, and hurriedly set up by volunteer contingents of local Scouts, Guides, and the Boys Brigade.

On the evening of 21 May, as the *Habana* was bucketing across the Bay of Biscay, there was another public meeting in the Guildhall to raise funds. It yielded £157 and various individual offers of help, like a baker who promised 50 loaves per week. It was largely through gestures of this sort, from thousands of people, that these children were to survive over the next two years, first in the Basque Children's Camp at North Stoneham, and then

The transit camp at North Stoneham. Left to right: H. W. H. Sams, camp organiser; Capt. J. R. J. Macnamara MP and Wilfrid Roberts MP, joint secretaries of Basque Children's Committee

Sometimes the generosity had a political edge: for those on the political left, the arrival of the Basque children presented a unique and practical opportunity of expressing some human solidarity with those who were seen

49

to be standing up to the menacing belligerence of European Fascism – how could they not offer aid to its most recent and innocent victims? For others, the response was purely compassionate – these were, after all, just children. Their photographs were about to appear on the front pages of the nation's newspapers, some grinning broadly from the rails of the *Habana* and waving with the optimism of the young towards England and the future, and others, dark-eyed, sorrowful, huddled in upon themselves. And there were stories to be collected, and told, of their continuing, spirited resilience, or the sadness of their loss, all equally able to touch the heart.

The Habana *in Southampton Docks*

Early on the Sunday morning, as they steamed up towards Southampton, the City's Medical Officer, immigration officials and the National Joint Committee's representatives, together with Mr Sams and Mr Henry Brinton, appointed to take charge of the transit camp, were brought aboard. Another round of medical examinations for each of the children and accompanying adults commenced. Shortly before eight o'clock, with all the children on deck, the *Habana* was docked. There, on the quayside, together with hundreds of spectators, a band of the Salvation Army, whom many of the children mistook for 'lady policemen', was playing. Within a couple of hours the first children were setting foot on English soil.

Throughout the remainder of the day and part of the following morning they were taken in bus loads through the city, past the Coronation bunting which had been deliberately left flying for the occasion, and out to the camp at North Stoneham. A few, however – those suspected of being verminous or who were still in a particularly uncomfortable state because of their sickness at sea – were driven to the Corporation Baths. There they were given a hot bath and a change of clothing. Helvecia's eight-year-old sister was one of them, and it was here that they became separated:

> My little sister had been terribly sick so that – well, unless I tell you that we were all on the floor and being sick on top of our clothes, you wouldn't believe how she was at the end. They took her to be cleaned and to have a bath, and I lost her. They didn't let me go with her and I didn't find her for two, or maybe three days. You can imagine, in that very big camp, me looking for her. The poor girl, she was so relieved and so was I when she found me. I took her to my tent.

Amid the chaos of the first few days it was hardly surprising that one small girl should go astray. The camp organisers and their voluntary helpers, few of whom spoke any Spanish, were initially overwhelmed by the enormity of the task that had descended upon them. But the children were in England, all 4,000 of them. They were safe from bombs and assured of a reasonable diet, even if the first breakfast did take four hours to prepare, and distribute to the hungry mass that swarmed excitedly and vociferously around the field kitchens.

'Four thousand refugees arrive safely at Southampton', read the front-page headline of the *Southern Daily Echo* on Monday 24 May, and it offered a bilingual 'sincere and hearty greeting':

> We appreciate the trials through which they must have passed in recent weeks, and hope that here in the quiet, green fields of Hampshire, they will find rest, contentment and – more important still – peace ... The public of this district will do all it can to bring them happiness in their new surroundings.

The sentiment reflected the widespread sympathy throughout the district, at that moment, for the plight of these child refugees. The story of one of the young survivors from Guernica featured prominently on the same front

51

page. She had greeted Southampton, the report read, 'with a brave and friendly smile', and now her only complaint was with the flat contours of the green fields of Hampshire: 'Where I come from,' she said, 'everything is mountains. We shall miss our hills.'

Almost certainly she imagined that her separation from them would be brief. So, perhaps, did the immigration officer whose stamp on her passport had permitted her entry to Britain, subject to the condition that 'the holder does not remain in the United Kingdom longer than three months'.

3 LIFE IN THE COLONIES

In the colony he really educated us – the four oldest boys and two oldest girls – to do things for the community. We did a lot of the work there.

As the convoys of corporation buses left the docks and drove through Southampton, the children could only guess at what was awaiting them, but even the most far-seeing could scarcely have envisaged a farmer's field full of tents. Amador recalls the simultaneous gasps of astonishment from everybody aboard his bus as it turned off the country lane in North Stoneham and drove under the high banner which proclaimed 'National Joint Committee for Spanish Relief – Basque Children's Camp', and one girl crying out, 'I can't sleep there! I'm not a Gypsy.'

Camping was something quite foreign to these children, the majority of whom had lived their lives in the densely packed, high-rise flats in the working-class districts of the most intensely industrialised city in Spain. Like most others, Alvaro had never so much as seen a tent other than on the cinema screen:

> When we arrived there – a huge camp full of tents – I'd never seen a tent in my life, only in the films with the Indians and cowboys. And there were piles of straw you see. And we were talking among ourselves, and I said, 'Good God, they're not going to give us the straw to eat, are they?' We were very ignorant in those days.

Somehow, across the barrier of language, one of the many Boy Scouts who had been drafted in to help managed to convey the idea that the straw was only for filling the canvas mattresses. So Alvaro filled his and, in his ignorance, filled it so hard that he was forever rolling off it. But at least he had a mattress, which was more than many had.

That first week in the camp was chaotic: at times, children were left waiting for hours for their meal; on occasions there was simply not enough food and voluntary helpers had to scour Southampton for extra supplies. The sanitary arrangements proved to be inadequate as well as alarming for the youngest children: Herminio, for example, is still haunted by his recollection of the sight of one small boy who had fallen into the deep trench of the latrine. There was a clothing depot – two tents full of donated children's clothes – but, with nobody in charge, much of it was eventually wasted, literally trampled under foot, and few of the children ever recovered the small cases or cloth bags into which their mothers had packed a few belongings.

Regulations to control the entry of visitors to the camp were also quite haphazard: visitors often appeared to outnumber the children themselves. The lack of any sense of order was demoralising to the local volunteers, upon whom so much depended. They complained that instructions were not given, or, if they were given, were changed and changed again, as on a whim.

To make matters decidedly worse the long dry spell which had preceded the children's arrival suddenly broke, with two ferocious thunderstorms during the first week and, contrary to farmer Brown's confident assertion, the field became a quagmire. One hundred tons of clinker, brought in by the local borough authority, made some difference but, even so, wet blankets, bedding and groundsheets lay around in disarray. And, in one dripping wet tent, Palmiro became ill:

It rained – oh, a deluge – and the water was coming round and underneath the tents. And, actually, I had no mattress. There were some mattresses, canvas filled with straw for some of them, but I had nothing and I was tired from the long journey and I got soaking wet, and I had no clothing, nothing much. My overcoat had disappeared on the ship coming across. I don't know what was the matter with me, I was too young to know, but I was in a bad way and I never even saw a doctor. My brother took care of me – he was two years older than me. I was spitting blood; I don't know if I had pleurisy or what I had. I recovered and, you know, it hardened me, I think. Well, it hardened most of us.

Such desolate isolation amidst the noisy, undisciplined turmoil of 4,000 excited and bewildered children, and hundreds of well-meaning but inexperienced volunteers, speaking mutually unintelligible languages, is not impossible to imagine. At the end of the week, the local *Eastleigh Weekly News* complained: 'The camp is not the triumph of organisation which some people would have us believe.'

Mary Sutherland, Chief Women's Officer of the Labour Party, was more sharp-tongued after visiting the camp on the first Wednesday after the children arrived:

I would like to emphasise that in my view the major part of this week's muddle at the Camp is due essentially to the fact that last week there was no one down there capable of sitting down and trying to envisage the problems of organising the Camp and seeing that 4,000 children were adequately fed etc. Had any attempt been made to find suitable directors for the various departments and to organise the necessary voluntary labour the confusion would have been avoided.[1]

Of course that was the case, but it was a harsh judgement none the less. At the beginning of the previous week the camp had been no more than an empty field and throughout most of that week it was still envisaged that there were only going to be 2,000 children to be cared for. The senior members of the National Joint Committee were still primarily preoccupied by their negotiations with the Home Office. Nor could they accurately have envisaged all the problems they were about to encounter – the spirit of independence shown by some of the older boys, for example. On arrival in England all the children were in quarantine and had been instructed not to leave the confines of the camp, but boys who had survived the anarchy of a city in the throes of civil war had little trouble hoodwinking the English Boy Scouts whose job it was to patrol the perimeter fence: small groups were frequently escaping and being brought back in the luxury of a police car.

Although that initial disorganisation is something the children have never forgotten, for the most part they recollect it now with a smile and with magnanimous understanding. Alvaro, for instance:

> They were very disorganised. For a week we didn't have much to eat. I think we arrived much earlier than they expected. It was no fault of anybody – just one of those things. They did the best they could, but with 4,000 children, the language problem and everything...

And Luis:

> The poor Boy Scouts were very nice, extremely nice and kind, but very disorganised. They had never had 4,000 children and 200 young ladies to look after before!

Nobody had. This was the largest single contingent of child evacuees ever to enter this country. The enterprise had been undertaken in desperate haste, with limited resources, and against a back-drop of persistent government resistance. The torrential rain in the first week would probably have defeated anyone. It had defeated Mr Sams, who had collapsed under the strain, leaving Henry Brinton in sole charge. Hardly surprisingly, then, those early days were more the triumph of heart-felt good intention than efficient organisation.

Although it was not long before some semblance of order and daily routine was established, this was not enough to save Mr Brinton's position. Not only was the Committee acutely sensitive to those initial criticisms and press reports of its disorganisation, it also feared the withdrawal of support by the TUC, whose representatives were insisting that Brinton be replaced. It was a formidable threat: in addition to the initial grant of £5,000, the TUC's 'Save the Basque Children' appeal had, by 8 June, raised a further £2,840, together with a variety of material offers such as '1037 pairs of youths and maids boots and shoes' provided by the National Union of Boot and Shoe Operatives.[2] In early June Mr Brinton was dismissed and the Basque Children's Committee stiffened the management at North Stoneham by appointing an ex-Army officer to run the camp.

In response to the fears of typhoid infection expressed both in Parliament and by the Eastleigh Borough Council, they arranged for every child, and the accompanying Spanish adults to be inoculated. That is what Juanita remembers most vividly:

> They tried to inoculate you against so many things. I always remember standing in a line, crying, because we knew that at the very end there was going to be a needle waiting for us. And queuing up to go into these big tents to eat. They were the important things.

Others hint at the loneliness of separation from their parents: Helvecia, having lost her little sister for three days after disembarkation, then found that her nine-year-old brother was forever wandering out of sight:

> My brother was very homesick. We had lied to him that mother was following us in another ship. I used to lose him – I didn't know where he was. I almost always found him at the end of the camp where the barbed wire was. I used to say, 'What are you doing here, Elvio?' He said, 'I'm waiting for mother; you said mother is coming.' It was dreadful because I knew mother wasn't coming.

Eventually she confessed the truth to him – although by then he had perhaps guessed it – but not before she had written to her mother several times to grumble at the burden of responsibility put upon her. Years later, when she finally met her mother again, it was an enormous relief to learn that those complaining letters, 'selfish concerns' as she now calls them, had never arrived in Bilbao.

There were other manifestations of family concerns and loyalties in the camp. Jesús hoarded the tobacco he had extracted from cigarette dog-ends to present to his father. Eventually, after a couple of months, he threw it away. Similarly, many of the English volunteers noticed and remarked

Lunch in the camp

upon the fact that children would frequently leave the dining marquee taking something from their meal with them, half a slice of bread surreptitiously hidden in a dress, or under a pullover. There was a girl in Juanita's tent who regularly did that:

> There were about eight in our tent and one girl would come from the big tent where we'd been eating, and she'd always save a piece of bread. When she had to leave and go to the colony they found her pillow case filled up with bread – dry bread that she'd wanted to take back to the family because they'd been so hungry in Spain. It stayed in my mind. We'd been lucky because we lived on a small farm in Spain and so we were never that hungry, but to her it meant something. She was only about seven or eight.

Within a week of their arrival the first children were moved out of North Stoneham. It was only intended to be a brief transit camp from which the

Washing day

children would be dispersed to the far smaller colonies where it was intended they would spend the remainder of their time in England. It was not until the middle of September, however, that the last contingent departed and the camp was finally closed. Those who stayed longest and who saw the initial confusion turn into a regular, steady routine, retain the fondest memories of that long summer in North Stoneham.

Across the wire of the perimeter fence they learned their first words of English and formed their first English attachments with the many local people who came up to the camp in the evenings. Virgilio was one of the last to leave: he was enjoying himself and in no hurry to move. In Eastleigh he had found a playing-field with swings and roundabouts, such as he had never seen before, and in the local shop had stumbled upon the incomprehensible English idiosyncrasy of twelve pennies to a shilling; he had acquired a number of shillings:

A lot of people used to come regularly and they'd say, 'I'll come back tomorrow at five. You be here at five.' So I'd been changing

my little Spanish money into English money, and for every peseta
I had, somebody gave me a shilling, which was a very good
exchange!

He had already acquired an instinct for survival in Spain and in the camp
he found jobs for himself:

I worked for a while in the camp hospital with another boy. We used
to work in the kitchen, peeling potatoes. I resigned when I was told
to scrub the floors in front of the girls in the girls' ward. Then I got
a job controlling people going into the camp cinema.

That brought certain privileges as his younger brother, Rodolfo, found
out. Rodolfo had been removed to spend a week in the local hospital, 'a
lovely week, lovely food', as he recalls it and, on his return to the camp,
things had changed:

Virgilio had got a tent to himself – wooden floor in the tent and a bed.
A bed! An ordinary bed stuck in the tent! Goodness me, I couldn't
believe it. I'd been away one week and he'd moved from being six
in a tent and sleeping on the ground, and he'd got this tent in an area
all on its own with a wooden floor and a nice bed in there. He'd got
friendly with the people who ran the cinema. I suppose it was for one
of the English people who were running the cinema. He had another
bed put in for me and I moved in.

It was a far safer job than picking up spent cartridge cases for the militia
during the defence of San Sebastián, but eventually he became bored
watching *The Three Stooges*, three times a day. He decided it was time for
the two of them to leave North Stoneham. That was in mid-August and, by
then, the patience of the local authority was also wearing decidedly thin:
'When is the camp going to close?' they were asking in complaining letters
to the Basque Children's Committee.

The camp had been steadily emptying ever since the end of May: every
two or three days groups of varying sizes were leaving. The Salvation Army
had accepted the responsibility for 400 children and had taken them all to
its hostel in east London. The Roman Catholic Church had agreed to look
after a total of 1,200 children whose parents were practising Catholics; its
charity, the Crusade of Rescue, administered their distribution to its own
convents and orphanages. These were mostly single sex and the Basque

Children's Committee was unhappy with the resulting separation of some families. However, faced with the scale of the responsibility it had taken on, there was little option but to accept their offer.

The remaining children were dispersed as and when individual local committees were formed. First, however, they had to find suitable premises, and guarantee the Home Office's essential requirement of ten shillings per child per week. More directly concerned with these colonies, the BCC produced a set of guide-lines about their formation and running, and insisted upon the right of inspection but, again, it was in no position to be fastidious. Ronald Thackrah, who later adopted two of the boys and who eventually became chairman of the Committee, concedes: 'We had little chance to exercise quality control.'

On 20 September, almost four months to the day since their arrival, Captain Neil Hunter, then in charge of the camp, wrote to Wilfrid Roberts reporting the final exodus. The last group to leave was destined for a hastily assembled colony in Kent:

> You may believe it or not but it was quite impossible in the rush to check the children, either on the buses from the Camp or when they entrained. However, it did not matter because we carried out a very thorough check during the journey and ascertained we had with us 209 children, which is what we calculated we ought to have had.[3]

Thus, nearly 4,000 children and 200 accompanying adults were dispersed into some seventy different locations, from Plymouth to Montrose, and from Cardigan to Ipswich. Life in the colonies had begun and, for half of them, this was to be home for the next two years.

It was very much the working of chance that determined the colony to which any particular child was sent. Sometimes one of the señoritas would be assigned to a colony and would individually invite children to join the group she was taking. Alternatively, many describe a typical announcement over the camp loudspeaker: 'There will be a bus leaving for a new colony in Carlisle tomorrow. Who would like to go to Carlisle?' And those who did would report to the appropriate tent. Not that any of them, of course, would have had any idea where Carlisle was.

Nor could they, or anyone else, have had any idea what they would find there. There was enormous variation in the character and quality of the premises that housed the colonies: fine country mansions in Witney, in Street, and in Barnet; an empty hotel near the Thames at Maidenhead; redundant rectories in Pampisford – a village outside Cambridge – and at

Watermillock in Cumbria; a reinstated sanatorium at Keighley; a Victorian workhouse at Wickham Market that had been lying empty for the past year; and bleak wooden huts at Brechfa near Carmarthen, at Beydon Hole – high on the Berkshire Downs – and on the Essex coast at Hadleigh. At one extreme the colony in the Norfolk market town of Diss comprised yet another set of tents that had been borrowed from the local Scouts, while at Hurstmonceaux, in Sussex, it was a medieval castle.

The first, and largest, contingent to leave North Stoneham was bound for Congress Hall, a Salvation Army hostel in Hackney. The *North London Recorder* reported their arrival through the crowd-lined streets with the extraordinary prophecy that these 400 Spanish children might eventually become Londoners themselves:

SPANISH REFUGEES BROUGHT HERE
And Perhaps Never Will Go Home

> Perplexed Salvation Army officials told the 'Recorder' yesterday: 'We have taken on a big task. These children may never be asked to return to Spain. Whether they will stay in London indefinitely we cannot say.'[4]

Mario was among them; he was destined to spend most of his life in London:

> I wish I could describe to you the place, but it was not a complaint to say that it was like a prison, because it was a blood, thunder and water hostel. It had tiers of galleries … and a very distinctive smell of carbolic which was one thing which has stuck with me for ever after. I wish I could see this place again, but it's been knocked down unfortunately. Otherwise I'd make a pilgrimage there.

In its urgency to help, the Salvation Army had taken on more than its resources could cope with. The hostel was severely overcrowded, with virtually no playing space surrounding it; and the staff, few of whom spoke any Spanish, had been given no time to prepare any activities that might have absorbed the energies of the children. 'Congress Hall has seen many strange and moving sights,' commented the Salvation Army's paper, *The War Cry*, a week after the children had arrived, 'but nothing more than that of a handful of staff striving to bring some sense of discipline into lives from which it has been entirely absent.'[5] There had been pandemonium and, as the reporter noted, never more so than at bedtime:

One recalls the din of bedtime along the boys' corridors, with lithe forms clambering up posts and racing like the wind, pillows flying, other folks' property forcibly shared, tongues racing at full strength, couples clinched in arguments not so friendly while they last, and on occasion that swift rise of the mob fever welding the lads into unthinking, highly volatile groups.[6]

The initial difficulties were exacerbated by the fact that these young exiles, still officially in quarantine, were restricted to the hostel. Incarcerated during the first three weeks, the older or more enterprising boys were constantly scaling the wall, sliding down the corrugated iron roof, and dropping into the street outside. There they would disappear into the East End and on to the front page of the *North London Recorder*:

Another twenty-three escaped on Wednesday and returned in the evening accompanied by local residents. As the boys marched in through the gates they threw each other kisses. 'They felt they were the heroes of the day,' said one official to the 'Recorder'. When asked how the boys got over the twelve foot barricade and the barbed wire, he said, 'You can't keep them in. They climb like monkeys.'[7]

*The first children to leave North Stoneham arriving
at the Salvation Army hostel in east London*

Eventually, when the quarantine was lifted, the children were taken out on numerous excursions – often to local swimming baths and to the open spaces of Hackney Marshes – and the overcrowding was eased when nearly half the children were transferred to the Salvation Army's orphanage in Brixton. Then life in the colony became more orderly, but its militaristic, evangelical ethos persisted and that created its problems, especially with the older boys. Contrary to the perception expressed in *The War Cry*, these were not 'the victims of a war whose significance they can scarcely comprehend' and whose 'principal need was for order and discipline': many of them, in fact, had a very clear understanding of European politics. With that often went a highly developed political consciousness which included the capability of organising a strike within the colony, and a boycott of its meals. The staff, insists Mario, were very kind, but 'they couldn't cope with the fact that we were terribly apprehensive about what was happening in Spain where we knew everything in the north had collapsed'. Nothing better illustrates that gulf in understanding than the communal singing that was regularly organised for the children:

> The Salvation Army would want us to sing Salvation Army songs, which we didn't know and couldn't understand – songs about 'the demon wine'. Whereas what we wanted to sing was 'The Marching Soldiers of the 5th Ebro Battalion', or whatever – all the songs we knew, which were very meaningful to us because they were not only catchy tunes but tunes which had been part of the national culture of Spain which had been translated into war songs.

The standard of the buildings which housed the children varied as much as the quality of care and understanding that each colony provided. In the lottery of dispersal from the North Stoneham reception camp to all parts of the country, some were decidedly luckier than others and those who went to the colony at Cambridge were among the most fortunate. In May 1937, even before the *Habana* had sailed, an appeal for funds had been made at a public meeting in the city's Guildhall, addressed by the Mayor and two university academics who were eventually to form the core of the local committee. It produced a flood of support from a wide variety of societies, organisations, laboratories, villages and individuals, each promising to 'adopt' a refugee child by underwriting the necessary ten shillings per week. House-to-house collections and money-raising fêtes were organised, and maintained throughout the two years of the colony's existence.[8] The initial public appeal also elicited an indispensable offer of premises – the vicarage in the village of Pampisford, five miles south of the city. Although somewhat dilapidated, it was potentially highly suitable. During the following month it was renovated and redecorated by groups of volunteers: students laboured during the day, and craftsmen offered their skills in the evenings. It provided a home for 29 children and three señoritas for the first six months; after that, the colony was transferred to a house in Cambridge loaned to the local committee by one of the colleges.

Before they were greeted by a crowd of several hundreds at Cambridge, station in the middle of June those 29 children were already a cohesive group. They, and one of their señoritas, had lived together in a hostel in Bilbao, established by the Spanish Socialist Party for children whose fathers had been killed at the beginning of the war; they had remained together at North Stoneham. This was not all they shared in common, for as Frida Stewart, one of the Committee members, commented: 'they had been brought up in a highly political atmosphere, and inherited their prejudices as a sacred trust'. A photograph of the President Aguirre, donated to the colony by a good-intentioned well-wisher, had to be removed from the wall of the dining-room at the children's insistence: they knew themselves as the sons and daughters of Spanish Socialists, and wanted nothing to do with Aguirre and his conservative Basque Nationalism.

Two years later, as the colony was being closed and the children dispersed, one of the older boys was encouraged to write his personal account of the experience. He was able to recall that first day:

> After tea we went in motors to Pampisford. We arrived and there I first saw the Señoritas waiting for us. We went in and it was a lovely house and they showed me where I was to sleep, and night came, and I slept.[9]

And, almost from the first morning, the days were full. There were lessons given by university staff in the loft above the stables which served as a classroom; in the afternoons it was painting and craftwork, or gardening, always supported by numerous voluntary helpers. Or there was writing and editing *Ayuda* (Help) the monthly magazine that the colony produced, or rehearsing plays or concerts, or practising football (like almost every other colony which contained boys, they fielded a football team to play against the locals). Each Thursday afternoon, Rosita Bal, once a student of Manuel de Falla, would arrive to take the music lesson. She was always greeted with enthusiasm and would always begin by playing the Republican hymn while the children stood silently to attention. Then, at weekends the

65

children were usually taken, in pairs or small groups, to spend the day with local families. Together, they frequently went to concerts or productions of the University's Spanish Society. During the summer of 1938 they all spent a month on the Norfolk coast at a mill owned by Professor Cornford, whose son had been killed in Spain, fighting with the International Brigade. The following summer the holiday was in another mill on the coast.

Here, those who worked with these children went beyond simply meeting their physical needs: they provided an environment and a range of activities which, as far as was possible in the circumstances, gave the days some sense of purpose. They understood the children's confusion and profound feelings of loss and their anxieties after the collapse of the Republican forces in the north of Spain. María Luisa was only six when she arrived in Cambridge but, she says, 'I have very happy memories of there':

> We were very fortunate in the people who were involved in looking after us. You know, I think a great deal of thanks has to go to them – Mrs Cornford, Mrs Stewart. They must have worked awfully hard to make sure we had what we had. And they gave their time unstintingly and tried to involve us in things.

Mrs Ryle, one of the organisers, also remembers the helpers who came to Pampisford:

> We had a group of quite exceptional people who gave much of their time and knowledge to teaching these children, and they were happily and fully occupied from the beginning, and very quickly the signs of strain disappeared.

An indication of that (and one which was remarked upon in other colonies) was to be seen in the children's paintings. At first they were a vivid reliving of the war – aeroplanes, and bombed and burning houses spouting fire. Later, even within a few weeks, these violent scenes began to give way to gentler, more familiar, images of villages and farms, and flowers. Even so, it was months before one of the boys was no longer terrifying other children by sleepwalking at night and crying out to them to look at the aeroplanes that only he could see on the moonlit lawn outside. Others needed sleeping draughts throughout the first year to protect them from their own recurring nightmares.

They were also fortunate in the three señoritas who accompanied them. Two of them already knew the children from their days in the Bilbao hostel and the matron had previously run two homes for refugee children in Madrid. Mrs Stewart described matron's way with the children:

> With a strong political sense herself, she knew how to cope with the revolutionary spirit of the older children with understanding and dramatic seriousness. She was wise, strong and loving.

Antonio, María Luisa's elder brother, remembered her as 'a matron who was one of the very best, but strict' and, like his sister, he speaks with affection for those who 'gave their time unstintingly'. After the colony closed he was destined never to go far from Cambridge and, thereafter, he always had an open invitation to use Mrs Stewart's tennis court whenever he wished.

If the Cambridge colony represented one extreme – 'a beautiful incident in these evil times', as one contemporary visitor commented – the opposite was found in Margate. Many seem to have passed through that colony at one time or another, and all who spent some part of their childhood there, however mercifully brief, vividly remember its horror. Even now their feeling is still palpable, just in that one word – 'Margate'. There, in a disused and dilapidated schoolhouse, the children went cold, and hungry. Life in the colony was devoid of order or purpose, bullying was rife, and the meagre staff, inadequate to the task, were unable even to establish minimal conditions of communal living. Herminio was an inmate during the brutally cold winter of 1939:

> Margate was dreadful. It really was shocking. Very little grown-up supervision. There was an English cook, but there was little if any food to cook. And who gave you clothes or shoes? As a youngster, you wore out clothes or grew out of them. Who gave them to you? In Margate, no one. Food? We used to steal from another big, nearby house, full of East European Jewish refugees. They were very well organised and provided for; in the air-raid shelter they had food stocks. Margate colony was really a dreadful place. And the cold and snow in that winter of 1939 – it was an appalling winter – made matters worse.

Mario, who was there at about the same time, recalls boys scouring the beach after winter storms, for drift wood: there was no other fuel for heating the colony, and the snow was blowing in under the doors and through broken windows.

Another who had good cause to remember Margate was the teacher, Laureana. When Redhill, the colony in which she had previously worked, was closed towards the end of 1939 she was transferred there:

> Margate – that dreadful place! You know, I remember the Christmas Day in '39. I did the cooking, because there wasn't anybody to do the cooking, and do you know what we gave those kids – some of them were fifteen, sixteen-year-old boys? A rissole, a piece of bread and a cup of cocoa. All day, Christmas Day. I'll never forget. And some of them were selling their clothes in second-hand shops to buy food. It was disgusting.

So disgusting, in fact, that she demanded to leave. The matron taunted her with being unpatriotic and threatened to report her to the priest who was responsible for all the Spanish teachers, but Laureana was not one to be intimidated:

> I said, 'So long as we are here they will keep this place open and the kids are starving. If we leave, they will have to close it down.'

And they did. Whether or not her rebellion was directly instrumental, the Margate colony was shut soon after. Ronald Thackrah, then Chairman of the Basque Children's Committee, remembers it:

> I went down there once and we closed it down as soon as we could, as soon as we got accommodation for them in other homes. It was a very bad home in Margate. I think the people who ran it were just incompetent; they didn't have a proper local committee.

The quality of the local committee, its ability to find suitable premises and to ensure that the requisite funds were available, was always what differentiated one colony from another. Thackrah's connection with the BCC had began when he had been invited to join the local committee which ran the Barnet colony:

> We had a very strong local committee in Barnet. We had a Lord who was the son of a General, the local doctor, Vincent Tewson who was Assistant General Secretary of the TUC, a lawyer who spoke excellent Spanish. And it was a well-run home.

The colony was housed in Rowley Lodge, a mansion set in three acres, which had been offered to the committee by three elderly sisters. Always renowned as one of the best colonies, it was almost the last to close. Pilar, who was to live in the colony until the end of 1942 (when the committee found a job and arranged lodgings for her), still remembers the day in 1937 when she arrived there:

Second of June and we came to Barnet. It was one of the happiest times of our lives. It was twenty boys and twenty girls. My youngest sister was the baby of the home and everybody made a fuss of her. It was a very, very happy time ... We were well-clothed and well-fed. It was one of the best-run colonies. Lady Tewson was the Secretary.

Years later she remembers how impressed the Scotland Yard officer was when her application for British nationality bore the supporting signature of Sir Vincent Tewson.

Yet, even in the better colonies, it was not easy for those *ad hoc* local committees to sustain their initial commitment to the children, when weeks turned into months and months turned into years. Charlie West used to organise the door-to-door collections which helped maintain the colony at Carshalton and recalls that only once did they have sufficient reserves for the coming month; generally they were living from week to week. Rafael, who lived in the Walsall colony from 1937 to 1939, has a clear sense of the stamina that the committees needed:

I believe our colony was sponsored by the Labour movement and the Cooperative movement. We were very fortunate in Walsall. I think we were fortunate because others went to some very uncertain places. Some of the children suffered a lot because people got tired of them very quickly. We were fashionable at the time, I believe. A lot of the kids weren't treated all that well, but we were; those of us who fell into the hands of the Labour movement – they were really concerned about us.

Labour Party and Trades Council members, most likely to be politically sympathetic to the Republican cause, were usually prominent on the local committees. But this was in marked contrast to the Labour movement's official policy of distancing itself from other Republican fund-raising bodies (such as Spanish Medical Aid) in which the Communist Party was known to be enthusiastically involved. Vincent Tewson, the Labour movement's representative on the Basque Children's Committee, consistently sought to impress upon Trade Union or Labour Party members the view that the Basque children required a broader base of support. He cited the case of his wife, who, as Secretary of the Barnet Basque Children's Committee, had drawn in some 40 organisations including 'three churches, each political party, the Odd Fellows, the British Legion and several others'.[10]

Certainly there were other organisations, without political affiliation, that displayed an equal concern for the exiled children and worked with the same determination. For over two years the Peace Pledge Union (PPU) maintained a colony for 60 children in a country mansion at Langham, outside Colchester; it was financed entirely from the donations of its members and sympathisers. Every week their paper, *Peace News*, carried a report from the colony headed 'Under the Oak Tree'. Here were the details of the routine of the colony and brief sketches of individual children. Often there was news of special events – an excursion to the sea, a football match against a team of Colchester boys, the opening of the tuck-shop – and always there was a gentle reminder of the continuing necessity for funds. In February 1938 the *Peace News* column spoke of the work of the committee's Secretary, liaising between Langham and those 'foster-parents and friends whose devoted efforts and often sheer personal sacrifice' had established, and maintained the colony:

> But now her work is not quite so happy, because many of the letters she has received lately have been in the following strain: 'I am sorry this is less than usual, but contributions have not been coming in so well.' 'I am afraid our support has become rather irregular.'[11]

And yet it was maintained even beyond the point when the colony closed in the autumn of 1939. Then, a number of the pacifist families, who had been supporters throughout the two years in Colchester, took the older children who could not be repatriated into their own homes. The younger children were transferred to another colony and the PPU continued to pay the required ten shillings per week for each of them.

There were also individuals who, almost single-handedly, succeeded in keeping a colony going. In August 1937, when the BCC was being pressed by the Eastleigh District Council to close the North Stoneham camp, Miss Poppy Vulliamy, who had been working there throughout the summer, volunteered to take responsibility for 50 of the older boys. The colony she set up was to become a migratory one: at first they lived in borrowed tents in the field of a Norfolk farmer – until they were flooded out after a violent autumn thunderstorm; then, after writing to the Bishop of Norwich, she was loaned an empty, run-down rectory on the marshes near Yarmouth.

Poppy Vulliamy's colony at Diss

There was no electricity in the rectory and we had to dig our own latrines. 'It was grim,' she says, 'but the staff were wonderful':

> None of them was paid, and my secretary became ill – she was not young – and I realised that we must find better accommodation. So I wrote to the Labour peer, Lord Faringdon, and told him that as a Socialist he should not be living alone in such a big house and suggested that he should let us all live there with him.

Lord Faringdon did not entirely agree to her suggestion but he did allow them to use two empty lodges on his estate, if she could arrange to have two temporary wooden buildings erected as extra dormitories. From an office

71

she set up in Oxford, Poppy Vulliamy distributed appeals for support, raising sufficient money to sponsor each boy in the colony and to build the additional huts. The new situation was a considerable improvement over the rectory, although the physical accommodation still remained somewhat primitive. Rodolfo, for example, has sharp memories of those huts:

> Rough? They were terrible: they were made from wood and asbestos, and they were very cold in winter, terribly cold, impossible to keep warm. They were meant for garages, weren't they?

In its final months the colony moved once more, to Shipton-under-Wychwood and a large house loaned by Alec Wainman. He was one of a number of wealthy sympathisers of the Republic, all of whom were to play an important part in the lives of the Basque children. At the outbreak of the Civil War he had previously left his job in the British Embassy in Moscow and gone to Spain, not to fight – he was a pacifist – but to sweep the floors of a military hospital in Barcelona. It was only when they reached Shipton-under-Wychwood that Poppy Vulliamy's colony of boys lived in any sort of comfort.

Poppy's sister, Chloe Vulliamy, also organised a colony – on the edge of the small Suffolk town of Wickham Market. There, an old Victorian workhouse had been standing empty for the previous year; for the next two years it became home to some 60 Basque children. José Mari was one of them:

> There were rats there, as big as cats, but the spirit was good because the people in charge were wonderful people.

There was also a girl among them who would sing on the staircase and the tune, as Miss Vulliamy described it, was 'strange and poignant, with long, sustained notes, swooping suddenly downwards, a tune to sing out in the lonely hills, and words fraught with tragedy now':

> If Vizcaya were burning
> I would quench the flames with my blood
> For Vizcaya comes first.

And yet, she wrote, there it was 'sung amid the sounds of children's laughter and the gaiety and chatter of activity'.[12] Mrs Benham, who still lives a few yards down the lane from the old workhouse, remembers that gaiety and laughter:

> The thing that always lives with me is the artistic side they had. They used to go up and down the road on roller skates, and they could do anything. Almost danced on them – so graceful, absolutely glorious. And when the snow came! Over the other side of the road there was, in those days, an orchard and in front of that was a big high bank, and the whole of the way along that bank were the most beautiful scrolls, and the most beautiful rhythmic patterns that they had carved in the snow.

Fenner Brockway, the Independent Labour Party MP, was another who helped establish a colony. In the early spring of 1937 he had conceived the idea of buying a ship, loading it with foodstuffs and, with a volunteer crew, running Franco's blockade of the northern Spanish ports. Despite the initial enthusiasm of the Basque Delegation in London the project eventually foundered. However, some of the finance that had been successfully raised was used to support a colony for Basque children. One of his most ardent supporters in the original scheme, Reginald Reynolds, enlisted the help of his cousin, Roger Clark. So it was that, for two years, Clarks Shoes, the Quaker shoemakers of Street, provided a fine mansion to accommodate the colony which, in deference to Brockway's political leaning, was reserved for the sons and daughters of Anarchists.[13]

There were a number of other large firms, often with an established tradition of philanthropy, that helped to support nearby colonies: Cadburys contributed substantially to the maintenance of several of the groups located in the West Midlands; Early, the blanket manufacturers in Witney, sponsored a colony in the town. In many of the colonies the children shivered during the winter, but they didn't in Witney. 'I cannot recall ever feeling cold there,' says Enriqueta:

> When we first went in, I remember there were only mattresses and they were covered with red blankets. All red. Everywhere, red blankets on the floor.

As so often, it is the specific detail – the red blankets – to which the fond memories became attached. She was the oldest girl in the Witney colony and Pili, the Señorita who was to become her lifelong friend, was not much

73

older; together, they organised much of the daily routine and were the last to leave when the colony finally closed in 1939. It was, she recalls, 'a very happy place with so much to do there'. At first they had been accompanied by a Spanish teacher, but she soon left:

> Untidy, miserable creature she was. We couldn't stomach her. Everything had to be done for her. So the only thing to do was to get rid of her by complaining to the committee.

Then, with the same resourcefulness that had once made her so useful to her father's battalion on the front line, south of Bilbao, Enriqueta took over teaching the younger children for a time, until the committee was able to place them in local English schools. At the weekends and many evenings Patrick Early would take groups of six or seven of the children out in his car and, once, Enriqueta persuaded him to allow her to drive as far as the gate. She smashed a wing against the gatepost:

> No, I don't think he did forgive me; he never let me drive it again. And then again, he took us to Oxford: we went punting, and I wanted to do it like he did it. I wasn't doing too badly either until one of the low branches caught in the pole and I left the pole right behind. We had to get it back again; he didn't like that much. He despaired of me, I think, poor old Patrick. I led him a dance – one way or another.

Many others speak of the happiness of their two years spent in the Basque children's colonies. 'They really were the happiest days of our childhood', some say, and they are talking about something beyond the basic necessities of food, accommodation and clothing. It is clear from their varied accounts that in some colonies the committee and staff, most of whom worked for minimal wages, provided a secure and loving environment. They understood the confusion of these displaced children and knew, intuitively, how to calm the fears they carried with them. Their stories speak of the dedication of committee members who called into the colony evening after evening. Indeed all those who devoted so much of their time to the children are still remembered with great affection.

Wherever there was a colony there was, almost invariably, a generous response from the local population and from nearby tradesmen – shoemenders and hairdressers who would refuse payment, and cinema managers who allowed the children in for free every Saturday morning. Sometimes the contributions were completely anonymous. Many years after his dreadful winter in the Margate colony, Herminio was playing football for the Working Men's College in Camden Town and one of the team, learning of his background, told him a story of how his older brother, an active trade unionist, had driven him to Margate in 1939. They had heard of a Spanish children's home where, as he put it, 'the children were virtually destitute: no fuel; no food to talk about'. Out of pity and out of his own pocket, his brother had ordered and paid for a lorry-load of coal to be delivered to the home. Without realising it, their paths had previously crossed.

Numerous people, in the same spirit, would visit the colonies with offers of help. They would take the children out, in twos and threes – Elvio lost count of the number of times he was taken to see the sights of London – or bring them into their own homes at weekends, and even occasionally take them on family summer holidays. Mario remembers, too, gestures of spontaneous generosity on the streets of East London after he and the other boys had absconded from the Salvation Army hostel:

> The East End people were working class; they were hard pressed; they had all the things that would make them sympathetic towards these children. If they found one of them in the street, they would take them by the hand, maybe take them to a shop and spend twopence on a bar of chocolate.

Similarly, throughout the time Rodolfo that lived in the colony on Lord Faringdon's estate, he was sponsored by the Oxford Women's Cooperative Society: they paid the requisite ten shillings per week:

> And they were so kind, those ladies; one of them would visit me two or three times a month. And they gave me a cricket bat! A cricket bat! I didn't know what a cricket bat was; I'd never seen cricket before.

Later, he was befriended by a lady from Chipping Norton who would invite him to stay for a week at a time, and he still speaks with relish about the feel of the 'lovely white towels, all wrapped round me, warm and wonderful' after she had given him a bath. Once, he suggested to some of the other boys in the colony that they walk the six miles to her house so they all might meet her:

> I said, 'You come and see my friend, the Lady; she'll look after us!' There were about ten of us and we all walked from Shipton to Chipping Norton. And I knocked on the door and she opened the

door – and all these kids. 'Come in, come in,' she said. Tea and cakes. And she said, 'Listen, you're not walking back. Here's some money and you can go on the bus.' She was wonderful. I mean – to arrive there with ten children.

Now, whenever he drives through Chipping Norton, he makes a point of going past the house where once, his friend, 'the Lady', lived:

Obviously she wouldn't be alive now but when I walked by and stood outside I thought, 'I wish I could see her now and say how appreciated was everything she did for us.' She was wonderful.

In some cases friendships were formed in these encounters which were to last for years. Alvaro, repatriated to Spain in 1939, returned to Britain eight years later on the basis of just such a friendship formed in the colony at Brechfa: he was given his first job in Carmarthen by a garage owner who had been a prominent member of the committee. Similarly, for many years, Mario remained in contact with a family in east London who had initially befriended his older brother over the wall of the Salvation Army hostel:

Somehow he climbed up there; he sat on the wall and he talked to them in their backyard. And they were terribly nice, charming and friendly, and they'd give you a cake or a sweet, or whatever. And we remained friends with them for many years after; I used to write to them. In fact I've got a photograph of them coming to visit me in Rowley Lodge – the Barnet colony – way back in 1941 and they had brought me a new pair of short trousers.

In Witney, Enriqueta met Cora, a modern languages undergraduate at Oxford, and they were destined to become lifelong friends. But for the Civil War, Cora would have spent a year in Spain; as it was, her tutor advised her to visit the nearby colony of Basque children, because that was the only way she would get to conversation with native speakers:

I arrived there one Saturday and Saturday night was bath night. There was a young, eighteen-year-old English boy who also came on Saturdays and he worked the pump outside to raise the water to the tank at the top of the house – it took twenty minutes to get a bathful. I helped to give each of the younger children a bath and, by the time we had finished, it was eleven o'clock, and I'd missed the last bus back to Oxford. I had to stay the night. I was very worried when I rang the Principal and had to see her next day, but she was wonderful: she said I could stay there every Saturday night, if the committee agreed, which they did. After that I was captured: I went back every weekend.

As with a number of volunteers, Cora's life was to become interwoven with the Basque children and be for ever affected by that connection. It was during one weekend in the colony that she met Luis Portillo. He was one of several exiled intellectuals who had been brought into the colonies by the Basque Children's Committee, after the end of the Civil War, and he was to become her husband.

Two sisters, Carito and Marina, continued to remain friendly with one man who used to visit them in the Colchester colony, and frequently took them out for the day. 'He often took us out for strawberries and cream teas', they recall, and, when the colony closed in 1939, he provided them with a home for several months. Many years later, when the two girls were completely independent and earning their own living as teachers, they were able to return this generosity, and invite him to live with them. By then he was dying from cancer and he was to spend his final months with them, their house his hospice during his last illness. 'He was that kind of friend', says Carito.

More often, though, these friendships were short lived, sometimes only fleeting attachments in the children's lives. They were significant none the less, for they are remembered still and recalled with great tenderness, often with the sad regret that, being so young at the time and speaking so little English, they perhaps failed to express the gratitude, and affection they now feel. 'It is a shame', says Eliseo, 'that we couldn't communicate better with them':

So many, so many did so much for us. And you couldn't say thank you to them. And afterwards you think – but then you leave it and leave it, and leave it. I mean there were so many people who were so good to us.

Their difficulty with English was, to some extent, the consequence of living in the Spanish-speaking environment of the colonies. But this was the policy the Basque Delegation in London had first urged upon the BCC: rather than dispersing the children individually into English families, it had argued that they be kept together, precisely so that they might retain their cultural identity. One practice which, in many colonies, certainly helped to reinforce that sense of collective identity was the formation of groups to perform traditional Basque songs and dances in 'homemade' costumes in the halls, and theatres throughout their locality. Many of Helvecia's most animated recollections of life in the colony are of those concerts and the rehearsals that preceded them:

> After a while we used to do concerts to raise money; we made the clothes and dressed up. We used to sing for the boys to dance the *Espatadantza* [a stick dance], until an English gentleman who could play the piano came round and he learnt the music gradually from us.

Some went on tour: a group from the colony in Cambridge, for instance, took their programme to the East Midlands, to schools in London and to a concert arranged for them at the Royal College of Music. There were also combined concerts – performers from half a dozen colonies – at London theatres in early 1938 to raise funds for the Basque Children's Committee. On one such occasion it was *Las Hilanderas*, a spinners' dance by the girls from Witney Home and the *Espatadantza*, by the boys from the Colchester group which most excited the critic from *The Times*; on another occasion he was most taken by the singing of the Cambridge children:

> The performances were marked by a complete lack of self-con-sciousness and a highly cultivated sense of rhythm. This was most conspicuous in the singing of a group of very small children from the Cambridge Home, whose performance of a group of folk-songs was the most musical thing in the programme.[14]

These concerts also had the more immediately practical benefit of supplementing the income of the local committee. A quarter of the funds needed to support the Carshalton colony in its first year was earned by the children: they sang for their supper. Similarly, some colonies produced magazines that were sold locally to generate additional income. The austerity under which they sometimes lived is hinted at in one edition of *The Grange*, a cyclostyled paper from the colony in Street: 'Buy our newspaper and help us through the winter.'[15]

Yet, beneath all the camaraderie engendered in the colonies, there was the constant apprehension over what was happening in Spain and, most especially, the fate of their parents: it could never be entirely removed from the children's lives. Even in the best of colonies there were times when those anxieties broke through into obstinate, wilful behaviour. Then, even the most patient staff had difficulty coping, not only with the child but with their own subsequent contrition. One of the weekly 'Under the Oak Tree' reports from the PPU's Colchester colony confesses:

> Loyalty and affection are the rule but occasionally, a child is betrayed by an unconscious current of thought into a position of rank perversity and ingratitude. In such a moment an exasperated member of staff was wrung to the exclamation, 'If you don't like your lot here, get out!' There were tears on the part of the child and remorse on the part of the adult.[16]

On that occasion the wound was healed, but Charlie West, one of the organisers of the Carshalton colony, remembers receiving one boy who was being transferred from another colony, after what had probably been a similar incident. The boy was described as being 'uncontrollable' but he never represented any problem in Carshalton:

> I got the distinct impression that there had been an attitude of 'you ought to be pleased with what we're doing for you'. If that was true, it's the kernel of the problem because you haven't got a relationship if you've got that attitude – that you're doing them a favour. They never had it at our place. Those kids – every time you came in – they were laughing, playing. They went to school every day in the colony; when lessons were over it was a laughing, happy family. It was a pleasure; it was not hard work.

Those colonies which did not convey the impression that they were living on charity were clearly the most rewarding for everybody involved and those children who were placed in such a colony, and remained there, were the luckiest. Others, however, had a quite different experience: some colonies were closed after only a few months because the organising committee could not sustain the financial liability and, later on, others were disbanded for the sake of economy after the process of repatriation had begun. So, while some of the children experienced two uninterrupted years in one home, for others life in the colonies meant constantly being shunted from one place to another, 'moved around like packages', as one remarked.

Luis, for example, was one of a select group of twelve of the oldest boys to transfer from North Stoneham to a castle at Hurstmonceaux. It was to be the first, and certainly the most luxurious, of the five colonies he was to encounter in the next two years:

> That summer, the owner – a very wealthy man, but he must have had a good heart – went to his country mansion in Yorkshire and left the castle to only twelve of us Basque boys and two teachers, whose only mission was to teach us English. And to teach us to be gentlemen, like playing tennis. They taught us bridge, and to keep us interested, there were always prizes – cigarettes mostly. We were dressed up like typical English boys of that sort. It didn't last long unfortunately – two months, actually. And so we had a very nice time there; the teachers had a very nice time there as well – swimming pool, butler serving us.

After that it was downhill. 'You couldn't go any lower, in every sense, than to that holiday camp at Dymchurch: it was below sea-level.' Its short life as a Basque children's colony ended abruptly during one high tide when some of the boys experimented with the sluice gates and flooded the camp. From there it was to Southampton and it was just as this colony was closing that he sought his brief, private exile in the New Forest to escape the repatriation boat. Thus he was sent to Margate and there, with the help of an ancient Hugo's dictionary he had brought with him from Spain, and his own tenacity, Luis laboriously translated *A Farewell to Arms*. In London, after the war, he was to supplement his income as a professional translator, but then, in Margate, the only profit was the linguistic confidence it gave him to write to the Basque Children's Committee. If he was not moved, he informed them, he would run away:

> Somehow – I don't know why – Leah Manning plucked me out to go to her colony in Theydon Bois, which I'd heard was one of the good ones.

It is not difficult to surmise why: the Basque Children's Committee was sensitive to any adverse publicity and, after his exploit in the New Forest, Luis was known to the Committee as a boy who did not make idle gestures.

The colony on the edge of Epping Forest, to which he was moved, was, indeed, one of the good ones. Supported by the London branch of the National Union of Teachers (of which Leah Manning was a senior official), it too was run by a committee whose intelligent interest in the children never waned. It was, in fact, the one committee which systematically arranged for all its children to attend local English schools. And, in that environment, Luis thrived:

> Practically all the children did well there. I was top in English at the end of the year. There was quite a to-do: in assembly the Head was to present me with a prize – a blazer and a school cap. Being a Spaniard, I got there late, and he presented them to me in his office, later on. I left the cap on the train the next day.

Deliberately? 'Of course.'

The consequence of being repeatedly transferred from one colony to another was repeated separation from friends. Older children could attempt to keep in touch by letter: a local journalist, who met some of the boys from Poppy Vulliamy's wandering colony in Yarmouth over the Christmas of 1937, wrote:

> I saw Bautista, after writing a letter to a friend [who had been moved to another colony], take three cigarettes and write on them the names of three boys and enclose them with the letter.[17]

But for younger children so many inexplicable moves could be both perplexing and distressing. Herminio was just seven years old when he arrived at Southampton and during the next two years, which he spent in five different colonies, he remembers being 'in a complete daze'. From North Stoneham he, and all the boys in his tent, first went to a colony in Swansea – a marvellous colony, as he recalls it, with the same freedom to roam the countryside that he had known in Spain. But after some unremembered length of time that colony was closed and, while most were transferred to Liverpool, he and five others found themselves in Tyneside. Here there was a very different atmosphere of 'early to bed and constant baths':

> Baths were something we had never been accustomed to – I mean, in Spain we didn't have water in the house. I certainly resented it bitterly and also the fact that I had been separated from all my friends from Swansea. And I was so unhappy. I remember standing on the beach on my own one evening, considering running away. That was the only time I considered running away. Somehow, I had found out that it took only three hours to get to Liverpool where my friends were.

81

He did not run away; instead, he was moved to a colony at Brampton, near Carlisle. When that too closed, he and a couple of others spent a few weeks living with one of the Spanish teachers who had married an Englishman. Then it was down to Margate for the winter of 1939! If all this capricious movement entailed grief at the constant fracturing of his friendships, there was also the occasional, unexpected joy at being reunited with them. It was the one compensation on his first morning in Margate:

> I went down to breakfast and there, in this dreadful, Dickensian place – it was quite, quite incredible – a vast dining-room, cold and unwelcoming, with long wooden trestle tables, and wooden benches; all these boys – we would use the term 'traperos', down and out kids; we had what you call a 'tanque' - an enamel bowl – for coffee, and two slices of thick white bread with margarine. That was our breakfast, you see. And I remember coming down and entering this vast dining-room, with all these boys, and the moment I entered the door, suddenly, from the other end, there was a shout: 'Herminio!' And, of course, there were some of my friends from Swansea.

Now, like most others, he speaks with great affection for those times in the colonies:

> I think that what made our life a real experience was, in fact, the colonies that we lived in. Some of them were awful places, but nevertheless you belonged to a group of people.

Despite the many hardships there were to be endured, or perhaps because of them, life in the colonies created a unique experience of the pleasures, the responsibilities, and the give-and-take of community life. The photographs which these exiles still harbour of their days there depict smiling, robust, but still occasionally serious-looking children. Faded and grainy as they are, these black-and-white set-piece snapshots somehow match the colourful descriptions they give of that life: there was gaiety and laughter for the colonies were fun, and yet, beneath that, invariably the echo of all the underlying sadness of separation, and anxiety when months passed by with no news from home. For many these were happy times and for some the attachments they formed became almost a substitute family which has survived a lifetime. Palmiro speaks today of the 'love' between them; Virgilio, who spent his time in the same colony, recognises that:

Oh yes. The ties are very strong, terribly strong. We have something in common which nobody else has.

Josefina perhaps speaks for many. She spent her first six months in England in the small village of Pampisford, where the Cambridge colony was originally set up. Today, when a stranger asks her where she comes from, she replies: 'I come from Pampisford. I come from Spain and I come from Pampisford.'

HELP THE BASQUE CHILDREN,

as the father of one of them says,

"TO LIFT LIFE UP AGAIN"

THE BASQUE CHILDREN'S COMMITTEE

TUC's fund-raising leaflet for BCC: 1937

4 THE GRINDING OF AXES

*...the high-pitched whirr of axe-grinding which has been the
accompaniment of the Basque children's career in this country has
drowned the still, small voice of truth.* (The Times, 20 August 1937)

One evening, in the second week of June, a fear that Bilbao had been
overrun by the advancing Nationalist army suddenly took hold of the 50
children who had recently arrived in the colony at Watermillock. Nobody
knew how the rumour began – the children, still under medical quarantine,
had not left the colony – but it spread rapidly amongst them. For all their
day-time cheerfulness, they were, according to the local doctor, 'still very
nervous': they had opted to spend their first night huddled together on the
extensive landings of this old rectory near Bolton, rather than confront
bedtime separation from friends and siblings. Whatever the rumour's
origin, the children were immediately and deeply affected by this premo-
nition, and the implications it carried for them. 'The matron and the other
helpers had a terrible night with the distressed children', reported the curate
in charge of the colony.[1] It was a minor incident, perhaps, and one that was
contained entirely within the colony, but it foretold what was to happen on
a far larger scale in the camp at North Stoneham on the night of Saturday
19 June.

Throughout the preceding week much of the non-combatant population
of Bilbao had fled from the city. Every night the main road westwards to
Santander had rumbled to a constant stream of piled-high lorries; a
swarming armada of fishing boats, some of which had been lying idle since
they had borne Republican refugees out of San Sebastián eight months
earlier, was pressed into similar service. By the evening of Friday 18 June,
the town of Bilbao was almost totally encircled – the only exit, a two
kilometre gap along the valley of the River Nervión. Since the Monday
night, when the evacuation had begun, Steer calculated that nearly 200,000
had left.[2]

Just after two o'clock on the morning of 19 June, the last bridges across
the Nervión were dynamited by the retiring militia, thereby severing the
main electricity cables: the lights went out all over the now silent city. At

daybreak the militia completed its withdrawal; at midday Nationalist tanks were making a tentative reconnaissance of the city centre; soon after five o'clock in the afternoon their flag was flying from the town hall. And far off, in North Stoneham, there was an urgently convened meeting of camp officials, and whoever of the Basque Children's Committee happened to be there at the time. Bilbao had fallen: that they knew. Sir John Reith, visiting the camp on behalf of the BBC, was able to confirm it. But were the children to be told – there were still nearly 3,000 remaining in the camp – and, if so, how, and when?

Some argued for not telling them at all; others pressed for a delay – one further night's respite before the news was broken – but neither of these were realistic options. The camp simply could not be insulated from the news, and anxiety had been growing amongst the children all that week. There had been no delivery of mail for several days, but they knew there was intensive fighting in their home town and that civilian evacuation was underway – that had already been announced over the camp loudspeakers. Visitors were besieged with questions and children were beginning to congregate in anxious little groups, pouring over newspapers they had picked up, the headlines and diagrammatic maps of which required no effort to translate. Rumours that Bilbao had already been captured were sporadically breaking out all over the camp. So the decision was taken: they were to be informed that evening; continued uncertainty was arguably worse than knowing the worst.[3]

At 7.45 p.m., after an early supper – a cause for suspicion in itself – nearly 3,000 children were instructed to assemble around the loudspeaker. There, the camp organiser, Henry Brinton, read the announcement which Captain Macnamara MP, one of the Committee's three honorary secretaries, had composed:

> We very much regret that enemy troops are now in the town of Bilbao. It is perhaps a small comfort to you to know that many of your friends and relations will by now be safe in Santander, and for those who remain in Bilbao there is, at least, not so much danger from bombs. We British people, who have taken on the care of you children whilst in this country, cannot express too strongly our sympathy with you all at this moment. We ask you all to remain calm, and carry on with your work and your play in the normal way. You can rely on us to care for you and to do our best for you in every way we can on behalf of your parents.

All this was greeted in silence. The microphone was then handed to one of the accompanying Basque priests to deliver the same message in Spanish. He did not get beyond the first sentence. That alone was enough to ignite the emotions of the previous week into a spontaneous, abandoned eruption of grief. At the word 'Bilbao', there was a fearful shriek followed by a keening wail. Stricken children hurled themselves to the ground or ran, wildly, in all directions. A small knot of boys, venting their frustrated anger upon the bearer of the news, hurled what sticks and stones were to hand at the loudspeaker van. To one camp official 'it seemed as if the whole camp had burst out crying and the noise of it froze me from head to foot'.[4]

Several hundred children broke free of the camp, many to cry alone in the adjoining woods, others to wander inconsolably in their distress – two girls were found almost at Winchester. On the road into Southampton, groups of distraught boys, bent on returning immediately to Spain, had headed in the direction of the docks. Virgilio was amongst them:

We were irrational then. First of all we didn't believe it; we thought it was propaganda especially because the priest told us and a lot of us didn't have much faith in priests anyway. And then we knew it was true. So we broke out, hoping the *Habana* was still in harbour, waiting for us or something like that. I remember that I walked nearly all the way to Southampton. Some got as far as the docks and into rowing boats.

At North Stoneham the sobbing and moaning continued for hours and camp officials, themselves deeply affected by the children's sorrow, moved among them for much of the night, offering, despite the barriers of language, whatever comfort they could. In the surrounding district, volunteers in cars, on bicycles or on foot searched for those who had gone missing. Until four o'clock in the morning forlorn children who had fled in tears were drifting back or being returned, some in ambulances or, as with Virgilio, in one of the many police cars urgently summoned to the area:

There were two of us, two boys, and we had our arms around each other, crying. Together like lost pals. And a woman opened her door and said, 'come here', and opened her arms out and we went in. And we cried and she cried, and we cried and she cried. Then they brought us some tea and biscuits, and then there was a police car at the door and they put us in the car which took us back up to the camp.

In the camp the following morning, the normal reveille – records of cheerful dance music played over the loudspeakers – was suspended and the children slept late. 'An air of deep affliction and great sobriety hung over the camp all that day', reported a camp official, Yvonne Cloud. During the course of the morning there were a few further escapes, but, generally, the turmoil had subsided.

In response to journalists' questions, Macnamara defended the Committee's decision to make the announcement:

It should be realised that it is impossible to keep news from the children. They are too keenly interested in events in Spain. Wild rumours were being circulated about the position in Bilbao, and so we decided to give a true and accurate statement. Unfortunately most of the children only heard the first sentence before breaking out into hysteria. They did not listen to the reassuring news of the exodus to Santander.[5]

88

It was, of course, impossible to isolate them from the knowledge of what had happened in Bilbao and, even with hindsight, it is not easy to see how the announcement might have been handled more delicately. Intense grief was inevitable once the truth these anxious children most dreaded had been confirmed. What was underestimated, perhaps, on that evening and certainly on later occasions, was the political awareness of many of them, and their loyalty to their parents' political affiliations. 'In our family we drank socialism with our mother's milk', says Helvecia. For the older ones, such as herself, the turbulent years of the Republic had been an intense political education, the lessons of which had been confirmed by a year of civil war. Their fiercely held political convictions were constantly to surprise warm-hearted English volunteers, anxious to help those they thought of simply as the 'innocent sufferers in their parents' war'. Many must also have been bewildered by the frequent newspaper photographs of groups of tousled-haired youngsters with their arms raised in a clenched-fist salute – the symbol of their sense of solidarity with the Republic.

There were no wild scenes in the colonies to which a few hundred of the children had by then been transferred, although the Duchess of Atholl was telephoned at her home one night by the Uxbridge police: they had picked up two little boys who had left the nearby colony at Southall intent on walking back to Spain.[6] In the more intimate atmosphere of the colonies, it was possible for the news of Bilbao's fall to be discharged with greater sensitivity, but never without it causing distress. In Cambridge, the señoritas quietly told the older children in the garden and allowed the news to filter down among the younger ones. Mrs Stewart from the local committee saw them 'one after another, crying silently, slip away into the house'. It was much the same in the Peace Pledge Union's colony in Colchester: the weekly column in *Peace News* reported the sorrow that the news had provoked:

> The older children realised to the full the implications of the fall and suffered the bitter frustration of being so many miles away from their unhappy parents; they suffered also from the knowledge that many of them would no longer have parents to return to. The younger children – who knows how much they understood? – we found weeping uncontrollably. Our staff worked unceasingly to bring the house safely through this crisis, and we owe much to their love and care.[7]

Valeriana was one of those younger children in the colony. She remembers the moment when the news was broken and, as so often, it is the minute, visual detail to which the memory attaches itself. Here was a day that was to have immeasurable significance for the remainder of her life and yet what has been retained most vividly is a picture of the dining-table:

> We all were having our lunch, and one of the Spanish teachers came to let us know that Bilbao had fallen. And I remember very clearly because we were all eating bananas and all the bananas were left on the table and everybody dashed away crying: we did not know what had happened, and were very worried about our parents and family. But the routine of the colony carried on.

The camp at North Stoneham also came through the crisis and its routine was soon to be re-established. Late on the Sunday morning a group of older children sought out Captain Macnamara. 'They came to us and apologised for all the trouble they had caused us last night', said a camp official:

> They promised solemnly that they realised now the English were their friends, and that such a thing as occurred on Saturday night would never happen again.[8]

What none of those responsible older children could have foreseen in that moment was that the circumstances under which they would continue to live in England had changed overnight. They had found refuge in a country whose government was the mainspring of the Non-Intervention Pact, but whose population was anything but neutral about the war. On the contrary, for many the Spanish Civil War was the paramount moral issue of their times. Transmuted into a myth which could mobilise their hopes and their dreads, its complexity and essential Spanishness was simplified into an ultimate clash between good, and evil. Some saw the Insurgents' cause as a crusade for Christian civilisation against the encroachment of atheistic Communism; others viewed the Republican resistance as an heroic popular struggle on behalf of democracy everywhere against the rising tide of European Fascism. Nothing which touched upon the war could completely escape being viewed through one ideological lens or another, not even the pity which had enabled a few thousand children to be plucked from its fire.

Until the evening of Saturday 19 June, these children were the innocent victims of Guernica; thereafter, Guernica appeared to have been forgotten and their continued presence on English soil was to render them the focus of intense political agitation. 'Unruly Mob of Basque Children', 'Mass

Hysteria Follows Night of Rioting', 'Basque Children Stampede' were among the Monday morning headlines in the right-wing press. Within a week of the Nationalists' capture of Bilbao, the BCC found it necessary to announce that, despite suggestions to the contrary, it did not intend to initiate the repatriation of any of the children immediately. As yet, it maintained, conditions in Bilbao were not sufficiently settled, but there was, it added, 'no question of hindering their return when the time comes.' But, for some, that time could not come soon enough.

With Bilbao now in Nationalist hands its civilian population would no longer be subject either to bombing or to the threat of starvation. In short, so the argument ran, the two reasons for the evacuation of the children had been removed: there was, therefore, no excuse for delaying the return of all the children to Spain. A letter to *The Times* on 28 June, nine days after the fall of Bilbao, characterised that view:

> Now that the entry of General Franco into Bilbao has removed the danger to that city, there is no further reason for the Basque children recently transported to England to remain here. Their return to their friends and relations in Bilbao will be welcomed and their presence will no doubt act as a surety against air raids by either President Aguirre or his friends in Catalonia.

During Question Time in the House of Commons, on that same day, the argument was pursued relentlessly until one Labour MP appealed to the Prime Minister 'to take some steps to discourage this campaign against these poor little children'. There were, in fact, few steps he could take and in the months to come, the Home Secretary was repeatedly badgered to use his office to enforce the children's prompt return to Spain. He made his personal position clear in a reply to the House on 4 November – 'the sooner the children go back to their families the better' – but he reminded the House, as he had done before and was to have cause to do several times more in the following year, the responsibility for the welfare of the Basque children, and for their ultimate repatriation, was not his, nor was it the Government's: it belonged to a voluntary body – the Basque Children's Committee.

At its meeting on 5 July the Basque Children's Committee determined that it would arrange the return of the children only as and when it received explicit written requests from the parents of each individual child; up to that date it had received only eight such requests, all from parents themselves now exiled in France.[9] A general repatriation of all the children, such as was being demanded, was unthinkable. So as to make this policy publicly known the Committee issued a press release:

> The Committee has already made it clear that it is acting as the temporary guardians of the refugee children on behalf of their parents and that the children will be reunited with them at as early a date as may prove possible. In the meantime the general position is being carefully watched. In view however of the uncertain conditions still existing in Spain, and generally, the Committee feels that the time has not yet arrived when detailed plans for the children's repatriation can be contemplated. The Committee would remind those interested in this country that the children were offered a haven here from war conditions. Until their parents are in a position to take them back under conditions of safety, the Committee feels it is their duty to continue to offer them refuge.

But those in England who saw the Nationalists' conquest of Bilbao (and subsequently the whole of the north of Spain) as a 'liberation' from the evils of Communism were unmoved by this. On the contrary, the BCC's clearly stated reluctance to return the children promptly, merely invited the allegation that these young refugees had only been brought to Britain, and were now only being retained, to fuel left-wing propaganda. In a House of Lords debate, on 8 July, Lord Newton could see no other obstacle to impede their immediate repatriation:

> It seems to be a perfectly simple business to send these refugees back to France and to ensure their being transported back to some portion of Spain where they will be safe. It does not seem to me that that is a very difficult task.

Difficult or otherwise, at the precise moment when few of the children had any secure knowledge of what had befallen their family, and many could only fear the worst, to have undertaken such a task would scarcely have been commensurate with responsible guardianship: it was to be a long time before some of those children learnt the fate of those they had left behind in Bilbao. Joseba, for instance, had begun writing home soon after his arrival in England:

> And no answer, no answer you see – nothing from father, nothing from mother, nothing from brothers or sisters. And – I shall never

forget it – in 1942 I got a letter from Spain. That was my father's letter, the first letter since 1937 ... Mother and father left Bilbao and got half-way to Santander. They went to live under a bridge in Ampuero. Under a bridge! Escaping from the Nationalist troops. And my father went into hiding for three months in a top flat, and he was looked after by a priest who used to take him a little bit of food. After three months, he came out of that hiding place and went to look for where my family was, and as soon as he got there he was arrested and taken to prison in Santander.

Of course, none of the politicians who were pressing for the children's immediate return had any direct contact with them. As for the children themselves, did they realise the extent to which their continued presence in Britain had become an issue and, moreover, one on which so many ideological axes were being sharpened? The younger ones probably not, although one scene that must have made an impression even on the most innocent is described by Glasser, then an Oxford student. He had been invited to a reception in Balliol College for a group of Basque children and there, while they sang one of their Basque songs to a benign audience of liberal academics, outside, a collection of undergraduates marched around the quadrangle, waving the Nationalist flag, and loudly chanting the Nationalist's slogan, 'Arriba España'.[10]

Even without such overt demonstrations, the older children, politically schooled as they were, almost certainly knew the symbolic significance that had become attached to their presence in England and, when Jesús speaks of it now, it is with a degree of undisguised bitterness:

Obviously when they were told that the war was over in Bilbao, everyone thought, 'Oh! It's alright for them to go back', without considering what's happened to our parents. My father was a prisoner of war for four years after the war finished; my mother was in France, scraping a living as best she could; we are here. Well, in that kind of situation what can we do? Go back? To whom? To what? Nobody. Our flat was gone, had been confiscated. And even if we had a flat, what on earth do I do at the age of fifteen or sixteen or whatever, without a father or mother?

They knew, also, of the growing hostility towards them in sections of the press, which contrasted with the warmth of their initial welcome into Britain. Virgilio, for instance, remembers how avidly any misdemeanours came to be reported and this was soon to become a persistent feature of the press campaign:

> The right-wing newspapers were totally against us. Anything we did wrong – they made it big. 'The little hooligans!' ... Now imagine all those children who left London and were evacuated during the war – at the beginning of the war. They also probably misbehaved quite a lot. Well, can you imagine 4,000 kids who didn't speak any English, and it's very difficult for them to get understood and not to be able to cry to anybody – you know, no parents? Well, anything can happen. And we were very good really!

The early escapes over the wall of the Salvation Army's hostel at Clapton, the first colony to have been set up, had received plenty of publicity. As the *North London Recorder* observed on 18 June, 'Their escapades, broadcast nation-wide, have given rise to several disturbing stories', but it was two later incidents that attracted the greatest attention.

The first took place in mid-July at the Scarborough colony. Here, some 40 boys, one of them brandishing a kitchen knife, chased the cook out of the camp and across several fields, until he sought refuge with a local farmer. It later transpired that the cook himself had accidently cut one of the boys with the same knife. But there was probably more to it than that: Wilfrid Roberts, sent to investigate the events on behalf of the Basque Children's Committee, no doubt touched upon the truth when he reported: 'the children were feeling that they were not now being treated as sympathetically as they had been'.[11]

The second and more serious incident occurred a fortnight later in the colony at Brechfa, a small village a few miles outside Carmarthen. Like Scarborough, it was a cold and inhospitable training camp on loan from the Ministry of Labour, and, like Scarborough, it was inadequately staffed. It also contained a number of older boys who had already proved difficult to handle in the transit camp at North Stoneham. Alvaro was an in that colony and, even today, in the kitchen of his home in Carmarthen, he speaks of the incident, in his pronounced Welsh accent, with apparent embarrassment:

> I wished you hadn't asked about that ... What happened was that four or five of the older boys had gone down to the village. And in those days there were not many cars and they saw this nice car and I suppose they were looking at it, and so on. And the farmer came out and thought they were doing damage to the car, and he gave one of the boys a boot in his bum. 'Go on, get out of it!' That sort of thing.

So the boys came back and some of the older boys said, 'We'll have
to take our revenge', sort of thing. So in the night they organised to
go down to the village and smash the windows.

Whatever was the spark (and explanations at the time naturally differed), a
group of boys broke free from the colony, armed themselves with sticks and
table knives taken from the canteen, and created a rowdy disturbance in the
village: a car was damaged, the windows of the hotel and of a cottage were
broken by stones, and a knife was thrown at a police car.

'Basque Children Must Go' declared the *Sunday Dispatch* headline and
its account of the event spoke of the boys 'terrorising the village'. The *Daily
Mail*, under its headline, 'Basque Boys Attack Police', reported the villag-
ers as saying they were living 'in bodily fear' and 'afraid to go to bed at
night'.[12] The local *Carmarthen Journal*, while expressing its sympathy for
the Basque children, was in no doubt where its priorities should lie – 'with
the people of Brechfa':

> In their own country – at Bilbao and elsewhere – they have had a
> close-up experience of the naked ferocity of a merciless civil war;
> with their fathers too busy fighting, and their homes possibly
> smashed up, it is not surprising if some of them have lost a sense of
> discipline in the wild anarchy of the times. Yet, taking all this into
> account, we would still say that extensive window smashing and
> such methods can only call for the strongest reprobation, and when
> it is done by foreign boys who happen to be enjoying this country's
> hospitality, then it is straining patience far beyond the limit.[13]

It was certainly straining the patience of some Conservative MPs. On 28
July, Sir Thomas Moore asked the Home Secretary whether, 'in view of the
repeated attacks made on British citizens by refugee Basque children', he
would not consider making arrangements for their early return. Vice-
Admiral Taylor demanded to know what action the Home Secretary
intended, 'in view of the riotous conduct of Basque refugee children'. In his
correct, measured reply, the Under Secretary, Geoffrey Lloyd, indicated
that these were but two isolated, local incidents, caused by a handful of
troublesome boys, amongst the 4,000 who had come to Britain. Furthermore,
he added, the Basque Children's Committee intended to return to Spain
those who had been identified as chiefly responsible for the Brechfa
incident. This, without doubt, was the 'strongest reprobation' that the
Carmarthen Journal had called for.

Within a few days eighteen boys had been sent back across the Channel, although not back to Spain, as was announced in Parliament and reported in the press, but to one of the many refugee camps in France. The decision was taken reluctantly, but the Committee was always acutely sensitive to the kind of adverse publicity that fastened on to such disturbances. In practical terms, the damage it did to the reputation of the Basque children was thought likely to reduce the level of donations for their support and certainly make the task of establishing additional colonies more difficult. There were still 800 in the transit camp at North Stoneham by the end of July, and the Eastleigh District Council was demanding to know when they would all finally be removed and the camp closed.

In August, Roberts contacted all the Secretaries of local committees, asking them to write to the press in an effort to counter what he identified as the 'hostile rumours being circulated about the children'. From the Cambridge committee, F. L. Lucas responded to the request:

> Picture 4,000 children from English towns, their nerves wrecked by months of war and air raids, many of them having lost, or lost sight of their parents, transported into the heart of Spain to a strange climate, strange surroundings, strange customs, strange faces, an unknown tongue – should we feel very tender towards charitable persons whose rush to play Recording Angel every time a window was broken or a temper lost? This is no matter for political prejudice; children's hearts ache in much the same way the world over, whatever the colour of their father's shirts ... We cannot foresee how long this war will last. It is not likely to be short. Many of the parents are dead; many are refugees. But few of us will envy the sort of person who from mere party feeling is in a hurry to make these children pass back through the fire to the moloch of Civil War.[14]

Señor Lizaso, a delegate of the Basque Government in London, issued a similar statement, critical of the efforts made by 'Franco's friends to vilify these helpless children and so to prove that they are unworthy of the succour afforded them'. The demand for the children's immediate return was, he insisted, another element of the same campaign, which the Basque Children's Committee was right to resist. By then, however, his was not the only Spanish voice to be heard in London. The Duke of Alba, the Nationalists' representative, began petitioning the Foreign Office for the return of all the children who had been evacuated. Their removal from Spain in the first place, he protested, had only been politically inspired – to brand Nationalist

Spain as a persecutor of children and to instil hatred in the minds of the children themselves.

The BCC continued to deny that its motives were anything other than humanitarian. The Committee insisted it had no desire to prolong the separation of the children from their parents but, in the overwhelming majority of cases, it had no conclusive knowledge of the whereabouts of the parents, let alone whether they were yet in a position to receive their children. Up to that moment there had been requests from only a handful of parents for their children's return and, even in these cases, the Committee was inclined to suspect they had been written under pressure from the Nationalist regime in Bilbao. In such circumstances it would not countenance the wholesale return of the children.

In an attempt at mediation, the Foreign Secretary, Anthony Eden, wrote to the Committee with two proposals: the first (which had originally been suggested by British Ambassador, Sir Henry Chilton) was that the Nationalist authorities in Bilbao be supplied with a list of the children and their co-operation in tracing the parents be invited; the second was that the BCC should send its own representative to Bilbao to interview parents, and satisfy itself that their requests for the children's return had been made and signed freely, without coercion.

With the exception of Canon Craven, the Roman Catholic representative, the members of the Committee rejected the first of these proposals.[15] To disclose to the Nationalists the names of those parents who had sent their children abroad would, they argued, be to expose them to very real danger of retribution. Eden's second proposal was, of course, acceptable to the BCC but, as events were soon to demonstrate, quite unacceptable to General Franco.

By the beginning of August, relations between the Catholic church, which was maintaining almost a third of the children, and the Basque Children's Committee were becoming increasingly strained over the repatriation issue. The Catholics church had taken no part at all in the original discussions about bringing the 4,000 children to England and had become involved only when the Home Secretary specifically appealed to Archbishop Hinsley. The Archbishop had acceded, but distanced himself somewhat from the venture in his request to all Catholics to lend their support to the children:

> Now is not the time to argue whether they should be evacuated or not, we have not had any say in their coming; the fact is they are coming and we must look after them.[16]

The Bishop of Hexham and Newcastle had been less guarded about his reservations: 'We did not bring them and many of us think they ought never to have been brought', he announced in his diocesan letter of appeal.[17] None the less, he had been equally emphatic that their Christian duty was to help the children. For all their suspicions, 1,200 children were being supported, out of parishioners' donations, in Catholic orphanages and convents.

Almost immediately after Bilbao had fallen to the Nationalists, the Catholic press had been vociferous in its demand: 'Bilbao Wants Its Children' ran the headline in *The Universe*, as early as 2 July above a report which spoke of the city 'swiftly being returned to normal' and its inhabitants 'rejoicing in their new-won freedom'. The *Catholic Herald* was even quicker off the mark: less than a week after the conquering tanks had made their first exploratory reconnoitre of the deserted streets, it invited Basque parents to reclaim their children.[18] In an extraordinarily presumptuous gesture, it announced that on receipt of such letters, the *Catholic Herald* itself would act as an intermediary, communicate with the centres where the children were living and endeavour to arrange for their rapid return.

Such cavalier and freelance moves to repatriate the children embarrassed, and were disowned by, the Catholic hierarchy. By the middle of August, however, the position was changing: Canon Craven was pressing the case within the Basque Children's Committee for rapid repatriation and Archbishop Hinsley was complaining to the Foreign Office about the delay. He had always opposed the evacuation, he maintained, believing it to have been inspired by purely political motives.[19] Throughout the summer, the Catholic press also steadfastly continued its demand for the return of all the children. 'There can be no excuse for retaining them in this country', stated *The Universe* and, on 20 August, under its headline 'Bilbao Safe For Children', it claimed, 'Every provision will be made for those children who have lost their parents in the war.'

Meanwhile, in its Basque Children's Report for the same month, the BCC was arguing:

> It is not conducive to peace of mind to explain to a child, whose parents have been killed fighting on one side, that now the other side has captured their home, all will be happy and quiet.

Then, at the end of August, the Vatican acknowledged the Nationalists as the lawful government of Spain and, within a week, Fr Henry Gabana, the representative of the Apostolic Delegate to Bilbao, arrived in London with petitions for the return of 855 children. To his intense irritation the

Basque Children's Committee, which up until that time had received applications for the return of only some 50 children, refused to accept the validity of his list. Apart from the fact that Fr Gabana's list included the names of children who had never been brought to England, there were, the Committee maintained, anomalies. Some, such as misspelt names, were quite trivial; others were more serious, as when only one child out of a family of five had been requested or when the request had been signed by both parents when the BCC had knowledge of one parent being in France.

All this was enough to excite the suspicions of the most influential members of the BCC that parents had made their applications only under the duress of Nationalist officials in Bilbao.[20] They were, in any case, aware that notices had appeared in the Spanish press demanding that parents request the return of their children; the Committee had also received several anxious letters from parents, exiled in France, warning of this. There were indications, in at least one of the Catholic colonies, that nuns were placing slips of paper in the children's letters home asking their parents to write and reclaim them; there were also letters from some of the señoritas, and indeed from some of the children themselves, speaking of the pressure their parents were being subjected to. Two brothers in the colony at Southall, for instance, wrote (in English) to the Committee:

Dear Sir: You will excuse us if we dare write to you on a personal affair, which lately became a common one. In several English Catholic Papers, as well as Spanish there appear long lists of Basque Refugees in this country claimed by their parents: and my brother was in the list. Believe me, Basque parents who have their children abroad evacuated from Bilbao have been forced to claim their children by the insurgents. We do not like to go back and be victims to the tyranny of Franco.[21]

If that was not enough, there was the person of Fr Gabana himself. He had, in fact, been in England earlier in the year, addressing public meetings organised in support of the Nationalist cause, until prohibited by the Home Secretary. On his return to London in August, with his list of reclamation letters, he had reinforced the suspicions of the Basque Children's Committee with his quite ingenuous admission that half of the parents' letters – he did not know which half – had been filed in the Bilbao office of the Falange, the Spanish fascist party. He was also frank in his assertion that the adults who had accompanied the children – the teachers, señoritas and priests – were regarded as having committed treason, and would be decidedly unwelcome back in Nationalist Spain. Throughout the month of September, while he was kept waiting by the Committee, he wrote a series of increasingly angry and threatening letters, first to Wilfrid Roberts, and finally to the Duchess of Atholl:

> As things are so much delayed by your Committee I want to inform you that people are getting impatient and the parents are more and more bitter every day against your Committee. Last Saturday night I heard a broadcasting station reporting these feelings and I am told the Spanish press is full of the same idea. They cannot understand why you want to keep the children here against the will of their parents ... You must all realise that in Spain there is the impression that those children were only sent to England for political purposes and the more the repatriation is delayed the more this impression will prevail.[22]

Needless to say, the Spanish press was divided: from Nationalist-controlled Bilbao, the *Gaceta del Norte* was demanding the children's return and, with increasing urgency, ordering parents to sign their reclamations.[23] Conversely, the Basque newspaper *Euzkadi*, published then in Barcelona, was urging parents to write to inform the Basque Children's Committee in London that they wished their children to remain there. In England, the Catholic press gave weekly prominence to Fr Gabana's frustrations: 'Fr Gabana Fighting for the Basque Children' ran a typical headline in the *Catholic Herald*.[24] To the repatriation effort was then added a new voice, that of the 'Spanish Children's Repatriation Committee', which had been formed at the behest of Archbishop Hinsley. Chaired by the Duke of Westminster, its avowedly partisan membership included several prominent apologists for the Nationalist cause, notably Sir Nairne Stewart-Sandeman MP, who had most frequently complained to the Commons about the children's presence in England, and Sir Arnold Wilson MP who, even at this stage, was still insisting that the fire-storm which had engulfed Guernica had been an act of self-immolation by Republican arsonists. Also on the committee was Douglas Jerrold: he had piloted General Franco from the Canary Islands to Spain on the flight which was to instigate the army's rebellion against the Republic.

In an effort to prevent the Basque Children's Committee from fracturing under all these strains, Captain Macnamara twice wrote to Roberts urging him to use his conciliatory influence with the Duchess of Atholl so as to persuade the Committee to 'pay a little more attention to the views of the

Roman Catholic church,' which had, he argued, 'borne the biggest burden of all':

> In my opinion unless the committee show a more reasonable attitude over repatriation soon and are less suspicious automatically of everything the new authorities of that part of Spain do or propose, the Roman Catholics will start repatriation on their own ... I very much hope that even now there may be a possibility of the committee working to the end without a split.[25]

But the opposing views amongst those English men and women as to which course of action was in the best interests of the Spanish children proved to be no more amenable to amicable reconciliation than those that had given rise to the Civil War in Spain itself. They were, at heart, the same irreconcilable conflicts. Both sides insisted theirs was the purely humanitarian interest and both sides were deeply suspicious of the political motives of the other. In the end it was the very attempt at compromise which broke the unity of the Basque Children's Committee.

On 1 October, Fr Gabana at last met the full Basque Children's Committee: he left the meeting furious, stating in an angry letter to the Duchess of Atholl that he had simply been brought there to be cross-examined. Only later was he informed of the Committee's decision, which was to submit his list of names to the arbitration of three neutral English lawyers. For the English Catholic hierarchy this was the final indignity – that the Committee appeared to prefer the judgement of three lawyers with no first-hand knowledge of Bilbao, rather than the word of the Apostolic Delegate whose representative had just come from the city. On instructions from Archbishop Hinsley, Canon Craven resigned from the Basque Children's Committee. 'I do not think you can possibly realise quite how insulting your attitude to the Delegate appears to us', he wrote to Roberts.[26] Whether or not other members of the Committee realised, Roberts probably did. At least, when he wrote privately to the editor of *The Tablet*, a few days later, regretting Canon Craven's resignation, it was with the admission that 'our committee may or may not have been wise in the past'.[27]

By then, however, the die was cast and the tribunal of lawyers was examining the authenticity of each one of Fr Gabana's 855 names. Before the end of the month, they pronounced that '500 or more' of these applications were genuine, and that these children should be embarked at the earliest possible date. At a specially convened meeting of the BCC on 28 October, one of its members, Miss Rathbone, expressed her deep regret at the tribunal's judgement, but, having set it up, she observed, they had little alternative but to comply with its findings. What was important now, she insisted, was to secure 'guarantees from the Nationalist authorities for the Committee's representatives to stay in Bilbao and to be given every facility for investigating the authenticity of applications for repatriation'.[28] There was never the slightest likelihood of such a guarantee being forthcoming.

On the morning of 12 November, the first contingent of 160 children were assembled on Victoria Station to begin the journey back to Bilbao and so, nearly six months after the *Habana* had arrived in Southampton, the process of repatriation had begun. It was to continue for the next two and a half years. Month after month, until May 1940, groups of Spanish children were to follow the same route: London to Newhaven, ferry to Dieppe and then down the length of France to the border crossing at Hendaye where they were escorted over the international bridge, and taken to Bilbao. But the repatriation process was to prove slow: in February 1938 there were still some 2,500 children distributed among the colonies in Britain. The difficulty, as the BCC explained to the Foreign Office, was this: those remaining fell into three categories of roughly equal numbers: those whose parents were known to be in Bilbao, but had not reclaimed them; those whose parents had requested them to remain in Britain for the time being since they themselves were now refugees; and those children whose parents could not be traced, their fate unknown.[29]

Typical of those in the first category were Amelia and her sister, Josefina, then living in Cambridge:

Mother could not have supported us. There was great hardship in Spain. There was no widow's pension for those whose husbands had fought on the Republican side.

Eliseo was in the second category: his mother and sister were in Gerona, having escaped from Bilbao, first to Santander, then by boat to France from where they had returned to eastern Spain. What had befallen his father, nobody knew, at this stage:

The night Franco's troops were entering Bilbao and Baracaldo, my father was working out of town, at a place called El Regato. And one of my uncles – he was a big political man from Bilbao, Deputy Minister of the Diputación de Vizcaya – and he said to the family, 'You've got to get out. They're on their way. They'll be in Bilbao any time, any hour now.' So he managed to get a car to Santurce and he arranged for a fishing boat to take them to Santander – he managed that. My mother said to my uncle, 'Well, you know, Timoteo's in El Regato.' 'Well,' he said, 'you leave him behind, because otherwise they're going to be here.' And my mother being what she was, always mixed up in politics, he said to her, 'You know, they're going to come looking for you. As soon as they come here they're looking for you. And me, both of us.' So he says, 'You've got to go, now.' So she went. My father got home next morning – the troops were there, and my mother and sister had gone. They never saw him again.

Amador, was in the third category and, like many others, he was to wait years before receiving word from his father:

I got my last letter from my father around Christmas 1937. It was many years later, 1946, before I heard from him again, from Venezuela. He had been in hiding till 1942, when he was able to get a boat to Venezuela. I had no idea whether he was alive or dead.

Faced with a multitude of such difficulties, the Basque Children's Committee was far from sanguine about the prospect of soon being in a position to repatriate all the children. 'They've Not All Gone Home', declared the headline in its bulletin for March 1938. 'We expect to have most of them with us for some time to come', it predicted.[30] But to the members of the Spanish Children's Repatriation Committee, these difficulties, together with their continuing financial implications, were simply of the BCC's own making. The state of affairs in Bilbao was 'completely normal', as far as the children were concerned, Sir Arnold Wilson had claimed in a letter to *The Times* on 1 February 1938. He had nothing but praise, moreover, for the authorities' arrangements for 'caring for orphans regardless of politics'. Therefore, all of the children, he concluded, except those whose parents specifically requested otherwise, should be returned to Spain, rather than remaining in England where they would continue to be, as he put it, 'a burden upon the charitable'.

Such action was unthinkable to the Basque Children's Committee, as the Duchess of Atholl replied in a letter to *The Times*, the following week:

It would be a dishonourable breach of trust if they were returned to Bilbao where, in the absence of their parents, they would almost

certainly be put into reformatories or other institutions, there to be
– in the insurgent authorities' own phrase – 're-educated', ie brought
up to believe that the cause for which their parents are fighting and
suffering is not merely misguided but wicked.[31]

And as for the financial burden of their remaining in England – to which,
she pointed out, the Repatriation Committee had contributed nothing – that
ought to serve as the best guarantee that 'we shall pursue energetically the
task of reuniting them with their parents as rapidly as is possible and safe'.
This was a slice of economic realism which was to become effective far
sooner than the Duchess, in all probability, anticipated.

Until that time, the BCC had been punctilious about returning only those
children whose parents had specifically requested them, but this policy was
very soon to be relaxed. The Committee began to anticipate parental
requests and to organise the return of children whose parents were known
to be living in Bilbao, and were thought able to receive them. The names of
these children and instructions for their repatriation would be sent to the
local committees, and for some of the older and politically conscious
children, especially those whose parents had advised them not to return if
they could avoid it, this was the start of some anxious times. It was just such
a time for Rafael in the Walsall colony:

I remember Councillor John Whiston, who was in charge of the
colony, reading the list at breakfast time and my stomach would turn
over ... I was very determined not to go back to Spain.

Inevitably, these lists sent out from the London office of the Basque
Children's Committee also presented the local committees and their staff
with painful decisions. It was, after all, they who knew the children most
intimately and cared for them day by day in the colonies. On one occasion,
angered by the BCC's instructions as to which children should be repatriated, the chairman of the Kingston Hill colony wrote to the Committee
accusing them of 'doing Franco's work for him'. Similarly, after receiving
from the BCC the names of fifteen children who were to be sent back from
her colony in Wickham Market, Chloe Vulliamy protested:

At its last meeting my committee expressed its dissatisfaction with
the present list, and its hope that the children who had not heard
recently from their parents might be retained until further enquiries
could be made. I would ask that in future there should be far more

opportunity for co-operation in the preparation of lists, and that time should be given for letters to be sent to parents notifying them that their children are to be repatriated, and asking them to communicate with us at once so that we may be certain that the addresses we have are still correct.[32]

The fathers of three of the boys, she argued, were believed to be in prison; the parents of two of the children constantly urged them not to go back to Bilbao; the mother of another of the girls wrote often, but never spoke of her father; yet another had received no news for more than three months. In view of all this the local committee asked for a further delay before these particular children were returned. The request was rejected: Victor Tewson, replying for the BCC, pointed out that the names of these children had previously been sent to the local committee and its comments invited, but it was now believed they could be safely repatriated. Each case, he insisted, was always thoroughly examined:

> In all those cases where there is reason to believe that there is grave danger in the children returning owing to their parents not being in Bilbao or one or both of them not being free, I know of no case where the children's return has been insisted upon ... Out of the 1,200 children returned there are only two cases of doubt and these are subject to special enquiry.[33]

Tewson, as well as being the TUC's representative on the national Basque Children's Committee, was closely associated with the Barnet colony (of which his wife was secretary). Despite his undoubted personal concern for the children there was surely an element of wishful thinking in this confident assertion regarding the precision of the Committee's selection procedures. The Nationalist authorities had always refused the BCC any opportunity to place a representative in Bilbao who could personally interview the parents; thus, its knowledge must have been too scanty to have enabled a thorough examination of every case. It would be surprising, therefore, if there had not been a number of errors of judgement: certainly most of those who were destined to remain in England speak of knowing children who ended up in a convent or orphanage in Bilbao, or who returned to a family manifestly unable to support them. This was probably the fate which Rodolfo narrowly avoided:

> When we were in Faringdon, they were supposed to have had a letter

from my parents reclaiming me – my mother and father wanted me back. Now my mother and father had been separated for years! So my brother went to the Basque Committee and said no way was I going back.

Clearly there were also numerous anomalies. The Basque Children's Committee was dependent for its information on the willingness of local committees to disclose their knowledge of the parental situation of each child. Some local committees were prepared to thwart the return of older children while others complied more readily with the instructions received from the BCC. Thus, one girl describes how she came to be sent back to Spain while her brother remained in the colony:

My brother was three years older and he wasn't just a brother to me, but father and mother too. So I don't want to speak about how I felt on the day they told me that I had to return to Spain and he was staying. They told me that it was only so that I could visit my parents and that afterwards I would be able to come back to England. Unhappily for me, I believed it.

In fact, her brother was also sent back, a year and a half later, and in neither case did their parents know of their children's impending return, but this, too, was not uncommon. Children often arrived back in Bilbao without their parents' prior knowledge and were retained by the authorities until they could be contacted. One boy spent three weeks in a convent until his parents were informed that he was now in Bilbao. He had travelled with a small group who were being escorted by the BCC's representative to Barcelona to be reunited with their parents who had fled there after the collapse in the north. At Limoges the train divided and he had continued alone to Hendaye. He can still recall the border guard's gesture of utter astonishment as he, a fourteen-year-old boy, made his solitary way across the International Bridge back into Spain.

But, for the Basque Children's Committee, caution and concern for the welfare of those who were being returned had to be set against hard economic realism. At the end of the previous June, little more than a month after the children had arrived in England, the BCC had received donations amounting to £27,000 with a further £5,000 promised from the TUC.[34] Most of that, however, was to be absorbed in running the camp at North Stoneham. By March 1938, although the camp had long been disbanded, the central Committee still required £750 per week to sustain itself and subsidise those children who were not fully supported by local committees.[35] If it was to continue being able to maintain those who simply could not be sent back to Spain, it was necessary to return all those who could. This was the point Tewson emphasised in his reply to Miss Vulliamy:

> The financial position is very grave. Everyone who has come into contact with the children would like to keep them here until Spain is again in a peaceful state, but we have to be practical in our outlook, particularly in regard to those children who must still remain here.[36]

Despite a number of general public appeals and the TUC-sponsored 'Save the Basque Children Fund', the Committee's financial resources had become increasingly precarious ever since Bilbao had fallen. A major reason for this, they claimed, was the campaign against the children conducted in the press and the persistent efforts of the Spanish Children's Repatriation Committee to nullify the BCC's fund-raising activities: 'Don't pay a penny towards the upkeep of these Basques ...They are a pretty expensive cup of tea', Sir Nairne Stewart-Sandeman was quoted as saying at one of the many public meetings organised by the 'Friends of Nationalist Spain' that he addressed.[37] But, even without that counter-propaganda, the BCC would probably have faced increasing financial difficulty after that first generous flush of public philanthropy. 'Charity begins at home' was a theme in a number of letters to newspapers and, at home, unemployment made for no shortage of British children living in deprived circumstances – a point that was made in the pro-Republican *Daily Herald*, even as the Basque children were disembarking from the *Habana*.[38] Furthermore, of course, the longer the Spanish war dragged on, the more remote in the memory were the horrors of Guernica which had first placed these young refugees at the mercy of English charity.

By July 1938, 2,000 still remained in England; in March of the following year, this number had been reduced to 1,642. By then the war in Spain had ground to its weary end, and Britain and France had unconditionally recognised the Nationalist administration as the legitimate government. 'I think we ought to be able to establish excellent relations with Franco, who seems "well disposed towards us",' Prime Minister Chamberlain wrote in his diary.[39] A few days later his announcement of official recognition provoked the last of the many passionate exchanges about Spain that had taken place in the House of Commons throughout the previous three years.

It did not, however, mark the end of parliamentary questions about the remaining Basque children. Sir Nairne Stewart-Sandeman persisted in nagging the Home Office; in response to his question on 18 May 1939, the Home Secretary informed the House of Commons that, as of that date, 2,500 children had been repatriated and another 400 were due to leave for Spain later in the month. Nor did British recognition of Franco's government presage any lessening of demands from Spain for the children's return. On the contrary, the Duke of Alba, by now the Spanish Ambassador in London, continued to petition the Foreign Office for their repatriation. On 6 May, for example, he protested vehemently against, as he put it, 'their continued detention', and insisted they be 'released and sent back to their own country', and that he be provided with the names of all those children still living in Britain. Orphans, and those whose parents could not be located, would, he declared, be well cared for by the Auxilio Social.[40]

The Basque Children's Committee was utterly sceptical of those assurances and with good reason. One of the girls who was sent back has vivid memories of the return journey:

> It was fine through France but arriving in Spain – my God, what a difference! They put us in what seemed like cattle trucks and the ladies, if you could call them that, who were in charge of us, treated us abominably. Accustomed, as we were, to the affectionate and generous treatment we had received from those we had known in England, it gave us a feeling of fear and hatred at the time.

Yet the BCC was beginning to come under considerable pressure from the Foreign Office to comply with the Spanish Government's request. With the Civil War concluded British foreign policy was immediately driven by the imperative to distance Spain from the Axis powers and secure its neutrality in the likely event of a wider European war; any delay in returning the children was seen as an increasingly irritating obstacle to that aim. Twenty children in the PPU's colony in Colchester were among those due to be repatriated with the May expedition and the weekly column in *Peace News* explained why:

> The decision to return them has been adopted very reluctantly. It was originally pressed upon us by the National Joint Committee for Spanish Relief, who warned us that if we did not send back every child who had any kind of chance in Spain our Home Office would in the event of this country being involved in war, take the matter out of our hands and send back all the children, without discrimination, including those who would have no chance at all. Whether this

argument is true or not, it has had the effect of breaking down our resolve to hold a number of these children any longer, and Sunday's [21 May 1939] expedition is the result.[41]

In the following month, Lord Halifax, who had succeeded as Foreign Secretary after Eden's resignation, decided that greater pressure should be applied to the Basque Children's Committee to accelerate the process of repatriation. One strategy, proposed within the Foreign Office, suggested that the Home Secretary should revoke the permits which allowed the children to remain in Britain. For whatever reason this idea was never acted upon but, on 10 July, R. A. Butler, the Under-Secretary at the Foreign Office, wrote to Roberts:

> May I enlist your good office in helping us to solve a technical difficulty in which we find that we are placed as a result of the reiterated requests we have been receiving from the Spanish Ambassador for a list of the Basque children who are still being supported in the UK?[42]

The 'technical difficulty' was that to provide a foreign government with a list of its nationals who were political refugees in the United Kingdom would have been a quite unprecedented act. However, these were only children, Butler argued, and it had always been the intention that their stay in Britain would only be temporary. He wondered, therefore, if Roberts could see his way to furnishing the Duke of Alba with this list. It was, in the circumstances, a remarkably conciliatory letter and Roberts agreed to put the request to the Basque Children's Committee.

The Committee refused, just as it had refused Eden, two years earlier, when he had made the same proposal. Disclosing the names to the Nationalist authorities, it again argued, might lead to the discovery of those parents who could well be in hiding and, inevitably, to their punishment. Although now confronting greater governmental pressure than in 1937, the BCC insisted upon holding to the same principle. The next time Butler asked the Committee to comply with the Spanish Ambassador's demand for the names of the remaining Basque children, his tone was far more insistent. But that was in September and, by then, Britain herself was at war. The principle of appeasing the dictators of Europe had run its inevitable course. An integral component of appeasement was the non-intervention agreement – but only in Britain was this shamelessly disingenuous pact interpreted as demanding the prohibition of all public assistance to a handful of refugee children.

These children had been brought to Britain to spare them the perils of aerial bombing but, with Britain now at war, it could be argued there was a prima-facie case for their return to Spain in order to remove them from identical risks. There can be no doubt, however, that the Government's resolve to see their departure was driven primarily by its concern to secure Spain's non-intervention in the Second World War. Butler indicated the urgency to the Basque Children's Committee and, on 28 September, Roberts presented him with a detailed analysis of the 1,054 children still living in England, and what was known of their parents' circumstances.

The total number was divided into two groups: the first group consisted of 477 children who could be repatriated, subject to individual investigation and with the proviso that those over the age of fourteen be given the option to remain; the second group comprised 577 children who should, in the Committee's view, remain in Britain. The official minutes of the meeting between Butler and Roberts give a clear indication of the Government's determination:

> The position had been changed by the outbreak of war. It was not only a question of relations with the Spanish government. It was not in the national interest that foreign children should remain in this country without any strong reason, nor was it easy to justify their exposure to risk in the United Kingdom. He [Butler] made it clear that the Foreign Office would press very strongly for the return of the greatest number of children.[43]

All the children in the first group, Butler argued, should be returned. Even 'borderline cases, where the Committee were in doubt', should, in the prevailing circumstances, be sent back to Spain. Any exceptions the Committee wished to make would have to be submitted, with a sufficiently convincing justification, to the Foreign Office. With regard to those in the second group, the minutes record that Butler 'fully appreciated the scruples of the Committee' in not wishing to return to Spain children whose parents were in prison or exiled in France. There were, however, 76 children in that group whose parents' fate was unknown and these, Butler suggested, could be included among those to be returned. When Roberts indicated the BCC's fear that their parents, if still alive, might eventually be discovered in France or in a Spanish gaol, Butler again proposed that a list of their names be sent to the Spanish Government so that a search might be made for them. Once more the Committee refused to comply.

Butler was to repeat the suggestion at their next meeting on 16 November.

He 'would not wish to press the Committee unduly on this point', the minutes reported, 'but he requested them to give the matter some further consideration'.[44] Only later, when Roberts was able to point out that some of the missing parents, contrary to Franco's instructions to all Spanish nationals, may well have joined the French forces to fight against Nazi Germany and would hardly take kindly to the names of their children being revealed to the Spanish Government did Butler finally concede the point. The Committee did agree to the names of all the children being sent to the Foreign Office, but, to the very end, it resisted the proposal that they be submitted to the Spanish Ambassador.

Outside of these meetings, the Foreign Office continually harried the Committee to accelerate the process of repatriation: 'The question has become more pressing and the utmost importance is attached to getting this matter settled with the minimum of further delay', the Committee was informed at the end of October. They were in frequent, sometimes weekly communication, as more up-to-date lists of additional names for repatriation were prepared and hurriedly dispatched to the Foreign Office. While, in November, Butler congratulated the Committee on the number of children they proposed to return to Spain, he reserved the right to question any individual case which the Committee was unwilling to return if the reason offered appeared inadequate to the Foreign Office. There is little doubt that the destiny of individual children was haggled over; one boy, whose return to Spain was probably a consequence of that bargaining, recalls:

> My sister and I were included in the group of children that returned to Spain in December 1939, although with the closing of the colony we had already been assigned to a new home, that of an English family. But the night before the departure, when everybody was in bed, we were informed that at the last minute we too would form part of the group that was going back.

Not surprisingly he speaks of the anxiety this created, for at no time had they received any notification of their reclamation either from their parents or from the BCC. Nor had another boy who returned with him, but who might so easily have remained:

> My parents never reclaimed me and in fact my father had written to tell me never to return to Spain but to become a naturalised Englishman. I never received that letter because my mother read it

and destroyed it, fearing that she would never see me again. I am certain my father never found out what she had done.

There were moments of anguish for the staff who worked in the colonies too. For them it was more than a matter of statistics, deeming some to be – in the Foreign Office's phrase – 'returnable'; inevitably, throughout the previous two years they had developed particular affections for the children. It was at this time that John Whiston offered a home in Walsall to Rafael; it was at this time, too, that Revd. Balmer placed himself in the doorway of the bus that would have begun the return journey, from Keighley to Spain, for Mario and his brother. It was then, also, that the fate of José and his younger brother, Luis, was decided when Charlie West visited the colony in Carshalton one evening:

> I wasn't too sure about the position we were in: war starts, call ups, no money, food rationing. Where would the money come from? I realised all these things. We're alright now, but the future's a bit bleak. José's dad had said, 'Come home, if Charlie says so; it's up to him.' And I thought to myself, with all these problems, and the bombing, they'd be safer at home. 'Write to your father,' I told José and say, 'thinking all things over, I think you'd be safer at home.'

The memory of that decision in the autumn of 1939 is, perhaps, made more painful because, years later, after the war, Charlie met the brothers again – José in Paris, shortly before his death from tuberculosis, and Luis in San Sebastián. But Luis, too, was soon to die of cancer. 'I still get a card from his wife, Christmas time', he adds.

From December 1939, until the fall of France in May 1940, batches of children, each one clutching the gas mask distributed by the Committee, were regularly assembled at Victoria Station for the return journey to whatever fate awaited them. The Foreign Office had suggested the use of a Spanish merchant ship, but this had been rejected by the BCC on the grounds of wartime danger even to neutral shipping. So, a total of almost 600 children followed the now-traditional route: blacked-out ferry bound for Dieppe and train down the length of France. Amador, who was destined to remain in England – with his mother dead and his father's whereabouts then unknown – remembers seeing one group leave:

> Because I was working in London in December 1939, I went to see them off at Victoria; they came from all over. Those who were going

were not looking forward to it at all. Well, very few.

At the same time, reports from the Basque country, which came into the BCC's office, indicated just how miserable were the conditions to which many of the repatriated children had been returned. On Butler's invitation, one particularly detailed eye-witness account was copied to him, with Robert's request that the Under-Secretary read it himself:

> ... and I think you will understand the reluctance of my Committee in the whole question. It seems hard that individual Basque children should have to pay as heavy a price as some of them well may, for the sake of British foreign policy.[45]

Whatever might have passed privately between them, the official minutes of their next meeting, later in November, contained no reference to this report.

The cost of returning the children was entirely the responsibility of the BCC. This had been understood from the start; indeed it had been one of the Government's stipulations when granting the children entry into Britain: the entire financial liability – not only for their welfare, but also for their eventual repatriation – had to be accepted by the Committee. Although this was often resented, it had always given the Committee a considerable measure of independence from ministerial intervention, as well as protection against questions in the Commons; but the outbreak of war had created the quite unforeseen circumstances of irresistible governmental pressure to repatriate large numbers at very short notice, with funds that were now severely depleted. Should the time ever come when the Committee was forced to appeal for financial help from the Government, it would forfeit its independence and the bargaining rights which this had always conferred. In November, Roberts wrote to Señor Lizaso of the Basque Delegation in London to explain the political and financial strains on the BCC and the dilemma this created, as well as his own personal anxieties:

> I am apprehensive about the position because if our funds are exhausted we have to appeal to the British Government for assistance. They have already indicated that this would alter the position about retaining any children in this country ... For myself, it has been a pleasure to do what I could for the Basque children, and I am very concerned at the possibility of the work ending in a rather unpleasant collapse.[46]

Roberts had, in fact, written to Butler somewhat earlier to enquire about the possibility of governmental assistance, but had received scant comfort from the Under-Secretary's reply:

> His Majesty's Government can accept no financial responsibility for the children's return so that in the event of the Committee refusing to accept such responsibility it will fall to be borne by the Spanish Government. In that event the Spanish authorities will be in a position to demand greater control over the numbers of children who are to be returned than they otherwise could have done.[47]

This, of course, was precisely the eventuality the Committee had sought so long to avoid. With its funds close to exhaustion, the BCC issued an urgent appeal to the 22,000 individuals who had supported its efforts at various times in the previous two years: this temporarily safeguarded its position. Local committees had to do the same: the Kingston Hill committee, for instance, distributed a final letter of appeal to those who had helped in the past. The colony, it explained, had been expected to close in October, but delays to the travel arrangements of those being repatriated had obliged it to remain open:

> We are now faced with at least another month of existence without any financial reserves and a weekly expenditure of £25 which will only be half covered by our income. A sum of £50 has to be raised immediately, and we are sure that if all our friends send what they can, we shall be able to get it. For most of our children who have refugee parents in France and who cannot go back, we have been able to find private homes; can you help us to support, for these few weeks more, those who are soon to go back?[48]

It was such letters that prevented the collapse which Roberts so anxiously feared.

The repatriation of the adults who had accompanied the children was an altogether different problem. At their November meeting Roberts reported to Butler that there were currently 59 señoritas, some of whom had children of their own, who wished to go back to Spain. Butler agreed to discuss the matter with the Spanish Ambassador and anticipated no difficulty. The BCC, however, was already fully acquainted with the difficulties. Two years earlier, in October 1937, it had been advised by Fr Gabana that none of the adults should attempt to return to Nationalist Spain. There they were regarded as having committed treason, he informed the Committee, and they would assuredly be imprisoned. More recently, one of the teachers had herself received a similar warning from her daughter in San Sebastián, which she then passed to the BCC. Unlike the heavily coded letter which had persuaded Señorita María to remain in England, this one was quite explicit:

> Prisons are full of prisoners and people are killed daily. If you come back you will be in danger of going to prison because you are accused of being a children's ravisher. If you have to return then come through France and do not say that you have been a teacher in a Colony … My opinion is that if you can remain in England then do not come back.[49]

Furthermore, soon after Franco's victory, the British Embassy had confirmed the BCC's fears that there was no chance of obtaining any assurance from the new Spanish authorities that señoritas who went back to Spain would not be prosecuted; to return safely, the women would require written guarantees of their Nationalist sympathies from two personal acquaintances of standing in Spain. 'Those who could not obtain such statements would be well advised not to attempt to return at present', the Foreign Office lawyer had informed the Committee.[50] Thus, a number of the señoritas, due to return with the contingent of children in May, had remained in England and when Roberts informed Butler, in November, that there were 59 señoritas wishing to return, he also reported that even in cases where the necessary guarantees had been acquired, the Spanish authorities made difficulties. Perhaps the young Spanish teacher in the Catholic colony of Nazareth House, Carlisle, was one of those cases: Sister Ignacious, living in the convent at the time, remembers her being unable to return to Spain:

> The teacher was not allowed to go back to Spain. She was very disappointed and very, very hurt that she was not allowed back to Spain. It was very sad. She said she came for the sake of the children, but it was held that those who had come with the children were 'communistic' in their views. She went to America.

Meeting Franco's demand for the repatriation of the children was seen as essential to Anglo–Spanish relations, but securing the safe return of the señoritas served no such important interest of state.

Nor did the return of the priests who had left Bilbao with the children:

British foreign policy exacted a similarly high price from them. The Basque Country was the one area of Spain in which the Church had not sided with the Generals' rebellion, but, instead, had declared its support for the Republic; the Bishop of Vitoria was one of only two who was not a signatory to a *Joint Letter of the Spanish Bishops* which embraced the Nationalist cause, portraying it as a Christian crusade against atheistic Communism. Only in the Basque provinces, ironically, widely regarded as the most Catholic region in Spain, did priests flee before Franco's advance; sixteen were executed and more than 250 others subsequently suffered deprivation, imprisonment, or deportation.[51] Ten of the fifteen who had accompanied the children aboard the *Habana* remained in England. They had, in any case, already come under the scrutiny of the Vatican in 1937, during the dispute over the repatriation of the children, and been accused of trying to prevent their return and of conveying anti-Nationalist propaganda. Archbishop Hinsley had instructed them to be warned that 'the Holy See is aware of their attitude and disapproves'.[52] One of those priests was well known to Luis, for he officiated at his marriage to Marí in London during the war:

> The Basque priest who married us could not go back; there was a death sentence on him. He had been sentenced to death *in absentia*. He returned only after Franco's death.

In Britain there was also one notable casualty among the thousands who had made the fortunes of these refugee children their concern: the Duchess of Atholl. Even before the Spanish Civil War she had begun to irritate many of her Conservative parliamentary colleagues with her outspoken objection to the Fascist regimes in Europe, her repeated warnings of their expansionist aspirations and her criticism of her own Government's accommodating policy towards them. But it was her espousal of the Spanish Republican cause that brought about the rift between her and her party. She chaired both the National Joint Committee for Spanish Relief and the Basque Children's Committee; she constantly condemned the Non-Intervention Pact, and tirelessly campaigned for Republican Spain, all of which infuriated Conservative Central Office, and earned her the absurd epithet 'the Red Duchess'. The most influential members of her Scottish constituency association also fiercely resented her actions. Finally, in April 1938, the whip was withdrawn from her and, a month later, the local Conservative association resolved not to adopt her at the next general election.

In October 1938, shortly after the signing of the Munich agreement, the Duchess resigned her seat, thereby forcing a by-election. Standing as an

Independent she narrowly lost to the Conservative candidate, and it signalled the end of her parliamentary career.[53] Her defeat was greeted by a triumphant telegram from one prominent Conservative, with large landholdings within her Scottish constituency, and a home in Suffolk:

> Am delighted you are out. Hope my Rannock people voted against you. Now you may find time to remove your Basque children from Suffolk.[54]

Nothing could illustrate more succinctly how the Basque children, whose presence was never to cost the tax payer a penny, were used to vent the political venom that was aroused in Britain by the Civil War in Spain.

Just eighteen months later, when the perspicacity of all Her Grace's foreboding was beyond any dispute, the final exodus of Basque children took place. By then, July 1940, it was no longer feasible to travel across France and so this last group of 26 children sailed from Manchester aboard a Spanish vessel. In England, they left behind some 470 out of the original 4,000 children, now stranded in a country at war with those whose bombs had once rained upon them in Bilbao.

5 OUT TO WORK

It can never be easy to be a refugee. And when the country in which you have found refuge is at war the difficulties both for children and for men and women are even greater. (National Joint Committee for Spanish Relief, 1940)

The Basque Children's Committee had accepted full responsibility for the 4,000 young evacuees in 1937, imagining this would be a relatively short-term duty. Three months was the Committee's belief, just as it had been the parents' expectation. Even Leah Manning, who had supervised the evacuation in Bilbao and who was later to state publicly that the children were likely to remain in England 'until after Franco has been defeated', could scarcely have foreseen how circumstances were to prolong the responsibility far beyond their initial, optimistic calculation.

By the middle of 1939 it was clear to the Committee that many of the children would not be returning immediately to Spain: their families were scattered or their parents were themselves in exile following the Republic's defeat. Furthermore, with war in Europe looking increasingly probable, it might be some years before their repatriation would be possible. That realisation, coupled with the never-ending financial implications of maintaining the children in the colonies, persuaded the Committee, for the first time, to look beyond its day-to-day concerns towards the longer-term future. In the case of the older children that meant helping them to secure a job. In May of that year the Committee formed the Basque Boys' Training Committee, its purpose outlined in a circular sent to local Trades Councils:

> There are some one hundred and fifty boys between the ages of fourteen and eighteen, whose parents are dead or missing, in prison or in the concentration camps, or being subjected to political victimisation. For each of these boys, with the co-operation of the Trade Union Movement, we aim to provide a training in agriculture or industry that will enable him eventually to support himself, whether he emigrates or whether he becomes a naturalised British subject.[1]

The Committee had obtained the Home Office's approval for these boys to be employed, on the understanding that they did not displace any British workers, and provided they were given the same wage and terms of employment that would be afforded a comparable British worker. The Basque Boys' Training Committee sought help from trade unions to secure openings for these older boys, as apprentices or trainees. As always, of course, it also appealed to union branch committees to 'adopt' a boy by supplementing his earnings for a period of time and by helping him find suitable lodgings: 'Their life tomorrow depends on today's help. Please help us to make it a good life': thus spoke one national circular in 1939.

Similarly, the National Joint Committee for Spanish Relief continued to issue letters of appeal to those who had contributed previously. It also asked local committees to help in securing work, both for the older Basque children and for those adult Republican refugees who were arriving in Britain in the aftermath of the Civil War:

> We are making a very great effort to make the Spaniards in this country independent. We want your help to find work. The Committee must be something more than a mere dispenser of allowances – and very small ones at that. Could your Committee not undertake to find and settle at least one Spaniard in work in your district?[2]

That letter, distributed in the middle of 1940, pointed out that of the many voluntary organisations concerned with refugees from various parts of Europe the National Joint Committee for Spanish Relief was the only one which was receiving no governmental assistance. Despite this, however, it was able to announce that more than 100 of the Basque boys were, by then, apprenticed in skilled trades. This figure was something of a misrepresentation: it is true that many of the older boys were to become skilled engineers, draughtsmen or toolmakers, over the course of time, but certainly not always through formal apprenticeships. Many, in fact, travelled a longer and more uncertain route, beginning as trainees or unskilled operatives in the first job to which they had been directed by the Basque Boys' Training Committee, and eventually working their way up.

Often it was the local committee which placed its older boys in jobs and settled them in nearby lodgings. Sometimes it was the final and farewell gesture of support, having maintained them for two years in the colony. The outbreak of war had brought immense pressure to repatriate the Basque children, but with it came one immediate compensation: for those remaining in England there were numerous job opportunities – albeit often unskilled jobs in factories and on the land.

Fifteen-year-old Antonio and his brother, José, then just sixteen, were sent to work on the land. It was to prove a very different life to the one they had known in the colony in Cambridge. 'The old man', says Antonio, 'still thought that a farm labourer was equivalent to what he was in the 1800s.' They found themselves tied to the unremitting routine of 'seven days a week, in winter and summer, Sundays and all' for five shillings per week. It was early to bed and early to rise, with no time off for themselves. Just once did they venture out to the cinema and arrived back at nine o'clock in the evening:

> He kicked up merry hell, he did. He says, 'You can't go to bed at that time and then expect to get up in the morning.'

Perhaps he had a point because their morning began at a quarter to six; at least, as Antonio explains, it did for his brother:

> We used both to sleep in the double bed, my brother and me. I was lucky because the only name he seemed to pick up was Joe – José, you see. And at a quarter to six every morning, he used to rattle the wall from his room to ours and say, 'Joe! Joe!' So I'd say, 'Go on, Joe. He's calling you.' So he says, 'Well you get up first, this time.' 'No', I says. 'No, there's no sense in that. He's calling you!'

That position was to change, however, when José was promoted to driving the tractor and Antonio was given the job of bringing in the herd of 52 cows for milking, first thing every morning:

> The regular cowman was knocked over by the bull and all the old man says to me was, 'Right. You be in charge of the cows.' So I had to get up at half past four in the morning ... I had to go and fetch these cows because they spent all night out and, I mean, I was nervous. I was frightened. Not of the cows – I used to be frightened of the dark! I mean, I used to have to go across three or four fields.

Agricultural work, such as they were doing, was defined as essential war work and, once engaged in it, they were not at liberty to change to a different occupation. They could, however, move to a different agricultural job and when one of the other farm-hands, with whom he had become friendly, told Antonio that he could lodge with him and his wife, he didn't hesitate:

And straight away I changed my job to another farm: I went to pest control, which was a little bit more exciting. We used to go spraying all over the country, in a caravan, like gypsies. All around East Anglia.

Once there, he managed to secure a similar job for José. The work was more varied and better paid; it also gave them both sufficient time to play football. Before the end of the war both boys were playing for Cambridge Town F.C., in the premier amateur league, and had thus become well known in the town. Many years later, when Antonio's son, was applying for his first job, the immediate question in his interview was, 'Who was your father – the goal keeper or the outside left?'

Palmiro was another who was put to work on the land. Not yet fourteen years old, he was judged to be well suited; even while in the colony on Lord Faringdon's estate he had volunteered to work on the farm and then to tend the gardens of the house in Shipton-under-Wychwood where the colony was later relocated. But isolated on a farm in Devon, he was easy prey for exploitation:

I said, 'Right, I'll go.' So I went and, needless to say, they used me. It was from dawn to dusk, you know, seven days a week. I was living on the farm and, actually, in fairness, it was the best bed I'd had since I'd been in England, and it was the best food. But they took advantage of me, really, because they never gave me any money for buying the clothes that I required for the jobs that I was doing.

At first he worked for nothing but his keep – only after six months was he paid a wage of five shillings a week – and it was a lonely, friendless period. Shut in upon himself because he spoke very little English and cut off from any other Spaniards for ten months, he bitterly concluded that the Basque Children's Committee had forgotten about him. 'They didn't know if I was dead or alive,' he thought. He couldn't even write to his brother because he had no idea where he'd been sent.

In fact, as he was soon to discover, the Committee was aware of his situation: they asked George Cadbury, who was visiting the area in the summer of 1940, to look him up. He arrived with the three Basque children he'd adopted – Helvecia, who was then in a secretarial college in Birmingham, and her younger brother and sister who were still in boarding school. And so it was that working in the field one morning, Palmiro heard Spanish voices from the other side of the hedge:

121

I was working there on the farm, like a horse, and nobody came to see me, and I didn't care about anybody, and that was it! But, out of the blue one day, they all turned up – Mr Cadbury with all the three children. What a relief, to be able to speak my own language; I was so excited, so elated … Oh, good Lord, fancy that. He took a liking to me, Mr Cadbury, and he said, 'Would you like to come over for tea next Sunday?'

Palmiro went to tea the following Sunday, and on subsequent Sundays during that summer, but it incurred the displeasure of the farmer and his wife:

I was not able to milk the cows on a Sunday afternoon, you see. They had to stay, instead of going to chapel. Then they began to pick holes in me. 'Well,' they said, 'You're not doing your work as you should do,' and that sort of thing.

It was the beginning of the end of Palmiro's life as a farm labourer. His brother, he learned, was working in Birmingham and lodging in the home of a Mrs Gibbons and when he wrote, inviting him to visit, Palmiro decided he deserved a fortnight's holiday:

And I had a wonderful two weeks. I came to Birmingham and I stayed at Mrs Gibbons and it was wonderful. I thought, 'What a life this is.' You know, to be along with my friends and everything.

There, he met George Cadbury again and he offered him the opportunity to move. The Cadbury Trust was prepared to provide him with an engineering apprenticeship if that was what he wanted. Palmiro accepted, and tried factory work, but found that he loathed it; within a short time he knew he would always prefer a life in the open air. What he really wanted, he said, was to go to sea. As an alien he was debarred from the Merchant Navy, but Cadbury was a director of the Gloucester Steamship Company and able to secure him a berth on one of their coasters, working the Bristol Channel as far as Swansea. Aboard ship there were as many hardships and as much danger as ever there had been during the worst moments in Bilbao, but, he says, 'It taught me a lot – washing my own clothes and, with only four of us, taking my turn doing the cooking.'

Unlike the other Basque boys who worked in factories or on the land, he had no lodgings: he lived permanently aboard the vessel. When they tied up at the docks in Gloucester, the rest of the crew would depart to their homes, leaving Palmiro aboard. So, as often as he could, he would return to Birmingham where the Gibbons family kept open house for the Basque boys. These he remembers as 'the most enjoyable moments of all'.

From the outset Mrs Gibbons had been deeply involved in supporting the efforts of the local Basque Children's committees, as had her daughter, Peggy, who had worked in a number of different colonies. Also living there at the time was Peggy's fiancé, Walter Leonard. A refugee himself from Nazi Germany, he had been in charge of Poppy Vulliamy's colony at Faringdon and then at Shipton-under-Wychwood. After its closure in 1939 the BCC had invited him to look after the welfare of the Basque boys who were working in the wartime factories throughout the Midlands. In the early years of the war the Gibbons's large house in the suburbs of Birmingham provided a regular meeting place for these boys.

Jesús was one who often went there. Like many, he'd been sent to one of the Midlands factories that had responded to the appeal of the Basque Boys' Training Committee. His working life had begun in May 1939, as a pattern-moulder's apprentice:

I was simply told: 'You go to Leamington; we've got a job for you.' I didn't even ask what it was; I was just presented with this job. I liked it. Probably I was lucky; some other people probably didn't like the jobs they were chosen for.

He was the only one from the Theydon Bois colony in that particular factory, but starting there on the same Monday morning were Ignacio, who was to become a lifelong friend, and three other Basque boys. They were met at the gates by Miss Marjorie Main; she had been involved in various ways with the Basque Children's Committee and, living in Leamington, she had been asked to keep an eye on the boys being transferred there. It was a morning that Jesús remembers well:

I remember we met her there in this foundry works where the manager, a Scotsman, came out and greeted us. And she introduced everyone in turn. When she said my name – Jesús – the manager said, 'My God. We can't call him Jesus. We'll have to call him – Jim.' I've been Jim ever since.

He was soon to have need of Miss Main's help again. Within a fortnight he was anxious to change his accommodation. Living in lodgings was difficult for many of the boys and often a cause of acute loneliness. Even with a kindly and sympathetic landlady, there was no escaping the contrast with the previous two years of cheerful camaraderie in the colony. For Jesús, the problem was more immediate than that: his landlady barely fed him:

> She'd buy a bone for the weekend and from that bone we'd have soup for the rest of the week. So I was taken to Mrs Young's, and that was as different as chalk from cheese. Mrs Young lived very near the factory where I was working. She fed me properly; she fussed over me, her 'Jimmy'.

Now, with good lodgings and enjoying a job, and working closely with Ignacio, he might have remained longer, but the firm was taken over, and with that his apprenticeship was abruptly ended. He soon became bored with the humdrum routine of the new task to which he was assigned – riveting ammunition boxes. Like Antonio, like Palmiro, indeed like almost all of the boys, he had taken the first job that he'd been offered; their position as young refugees, sometimes with no more than rudimentary English, gave them little option other than the implied, and sometimes explicitly stated, one of returning to Spain. With little or no advice, or guidance, some were to remain in those jobs, which often did not reflect their capabilities; others, however, did begin to develop the self-assurance to seek alternative work and, on their own initiative, to effect a change in their lives. Invariably, it meant utilising whatever local friendships they had managed to strike up or personal contacts they had formed: Antonio accepted the offer of accommodation from a fellow farm-hand; Palmiro was befriended by George Cadbury. And so it was with Jesús: he spoke to Ignacio's landlord:

> Somehow I said, 'I'm so fed up with this job. I would like to be able to do something a little bit more constructive, requiring a bit more intelligence.' They managed to get me a job as a machine operator.

He remained a machine operator until 1943, when he learned news of a trust – the Juan Luis Vives Trust – which had been set up to provide educational scholarships for the Basque children and older Spanish exiles in Britain. The Basque Children's Committee had persuaded Negrín, the exiled last Republican Prime Minister, to use some of the funds he had removed from Spain to establish the trust. Between 1942 and 1947, a total of 83 Basque children, and eight of the señoritas who had accompanied them, received grants to enable them to undertake various kinds of educational courses – from university degrees to day-release and night-school classes.[3] Jesús was one of the first to apply, and was offered a three-year grant to take a Higher Diploma in Building and Construction at the Regent Street Polytechnic in central London.

In the polytechnic, at the same time, was Amador, although his route to London had been rather more circuitous. He had begun to put his native language to use, even in the colony in Huddersfield, by working most afternoons in one of the town's export firms. There he had also learned to type and, at the outbreak of war, he moved to London:

> I was put to work in an office, for next to nothing. Then it closed and I was sent to a clothing factory making uniforms for the army. I was working there for two years and, when the factory was bombed, it was moved to Lancaster.

Amador went with them. He was not to remain in Lancaster for long, however: 'Somebody got me transferred', he explains – again the fortuitousness of a chance connection. The 'somebody' who had befriended him was the director of an under cover agency that was engaged in sending propaganda to South America. Amador, as a native Spanish speaker, was employed translating Churchill's speeches. And, back in London, he began going to the polytechnic, in the evenings, to take his matriculation. Equipped with that, he won a scholarship from the Juan Luis Vives Trust to study full-time for a diploma in architecture. The scholarship was just about sufficient to live on, he says, at least 'for someone with a Basque, frugal sort of mind'. And, when it wasn't, he supplemented it by giving private Spanish lessons.

At the same time as establishing the educational trust, Negrín had agreed that the lease should be paid on a large house in the Bayswater area of London. Number 22 Inverness Terrace was 'el Hogar Español' (the Spanish Home) and it became a convenient and convivial meeting place, not simply for the Basque children, but for all the many older exiles who had arrived in England after the Civil War. Through the range of cultural, social, sporting and political activities it sustained, the Hogar was the focal point for the expatriate Republican community which had formed, close by, in west London. Its choir, conducted by Manuel Lazareno, once a junior arts minister in Negrín's government, often performed for BBC Radio and Jesús, drawn back to London to study in the Polytechnic, decided to join. Once more, therefore, he found himself living, as he puts it now, 'all the time in Spanish company':

We lived in various furnished rooms; we were all in odd furnished rooms – somebody would get a basement somewhere, or up in the attic somewhere. That's one thing that was current in those days – 'You Spanish? Oh, you must be in the roof-tops.' It was always some furnished room that would cost us, maybe, fifteen bob a week.

London was becoming a magnet for many other boys, too. Rafael, for example, had been in the colony in Walsall and, after it closed in 1939, had remained there with the family of John Whiston, who had been the mainstay of the local Basque Children's committee:

I was part of the family, really. I started to work with one of the sons, who had a small garage. We bought second-hand cars, repaired them and sold them. Then he had to join the forces, and his father and I ran the garage ... I could have stayed there. I could have stayed there quite easily. I'd started going to evening classes in draughtsmanship and I was very attached to them.

But, at the same time, he was finding himself increasingly drawn by a more fundamental attachment:

I used to come weekends to London, and go back very, sort of, sad, you know. We'd go to the Hogar Español, stay with somebody – somebody would always offer us a bed. And there were special fiesta weekends: there'd be a dance and the choir would sing, and the *paso doble* would be going! And that was it. I remember walking along the street with Mr Whiston and I said I'd like to go to London to live. And he said, 'Raf, no problem. You want to go, you go.'

The response was an instinctive acknowledgement that however close their attachment had become, it was necessarily temporary. In its immediacy lies the generosity of all those who gave not only their time, but who opened up their homes and their hearts to the Basque children long after they had ceased to excite the interest even of local newspapers. 'He had three sons, and he treated me just like one of them', says Rafael, but, in 1941, with John Whiston's blessing, he set out for London to resurrect his Spanish connections and memories.

This was eventually to become a well-trodden route: many quit that first job which the Basque Boys' Training Committee had negotiated for them and said goodbye to their landlady, or their foster family in the Midlands.

The labour shortage in London's wartime factories meant they were able to find their own means of making a livelihood. It was, of course, the aspiration of the Basque Children's Committee that they should become independent, but there must have been many occasions when they left behind considerable heartache. Caireles, who made the same journey, senses that now:

> It must have been very painful for them to let me go. In those days, I didn't give it any thought. If I had been grown up enough, I think maybe I wouldn't have come down. Because they were wonderful people.

In Dudley he had been working for, and living in the home of, a master decorator and sign-writer. Without any formal training, simply putting his natural artistic talent to use, he had found himself practising every skill of that trade and helping to keep the business going after all the apprentices had been called up into the armed forces. Coming down to London, however, meant the chance of going to the Croydon Art School.

Despite the appeal of the growing community of Spaniards in London, a few, miserable in their lodgings and bored by the jobs to which they had been assigned, left the city for good. Virgilio, for example, had begun working in a Spanish bookshop in London, but that had closed at the outbreak of war. Jobless, he had gone to the Basque Children's Committee and been sent to sew army uniforms in a firm of East End tailors where the Committee had negotiated jobs for several Basque boys:

> I used to do the waistband and the flies, and you were paid according to the amount – piece-work, you see. There were about four or five Spaniards, and I was getting very good money, actually, because I was getting good at my job. But I didn't like it; I was depressed. Also the lodgings we were living in!

As was so often the case, it was the personal contact with somebody who had befriended the Basque children that effected the change: he wrote to Marjorie Main, whom he already knew, having once stayed with her in Leamington :

> She had an Austin 7, a little thing, and if you weren't well, she would take you to Leamington and keep you there for a fortnight, feed you, build you up, and then take you back again.

She collected him, drove him to Leamington and found a job for him, pasteurising milk in the local Hygienic Dairies.

Joseba, who had been addressing envelopes in the London office of the Basque Children's Committee, was another who left. He and his friend, José Mari, spending the Christmas of 1939 at the home of the Gibbons in Birmingham, were invited to work on the farm owned by Mrs Gibbons's son, in St Neots in Cambridgeshire. Joseba found he enjoyed the open-air life; the work was good and the lodgings excellent: he decided to stay:

> I used to go to London regularly to see the boys and, of course, because I looked so strong and healthy, they used to say, 'Where you come from, Joe?' I said, 'I work on the land.' I worked on the land twenty-one years for Mr Gibbons. Twenty-one years I was on the land. I enjoyed it.

José Mari, however, did not stay long. He yearned to return to London and to work of a very different kind: above all, he wanted to be an engineer. Previously, he had been with Amador and Virgilio, sewing uniforms in the same East End tailoring factory, and how he came to be there is indicative of the difficulties these older boys faced at the outset of their working lives:

> The Basque Children's Committee said, 'What do you want to do?' And, at the time, I didn't know how to explain myself. I wanted to say, 'I want to be an engineer.' So I said, 'I want to work with machines.' So they sent me to a machine factory – sewing machines!

Eventually, he did get his wish. By dint of his own inquiries and effort, he learnt of a government training scheme which would enable him to become an engineer. It had been a long journey, beginning with the job that the Basque Boy's Training Committee had been able to obtain for him.

However unrelated that first job happened to be to their abilities, or inappropriate to their aspirations, hardly any felt themselves able to refuse it or to attempt to negotiate something different. They were young; they were exiled; their education had been severly disrupted; the country offering them refuge was itself at war and, in many cases, their own horizons were clouded by the expectation that their stay was still merely temporary: when the war was over, so most of them assumed, they would be returning to resume their lives in Spain. One of the few who was sufficiently strong-minded to resist the demands of the moment was Luis. He and one other boy had been taken by Molly Garrett, the Secretary of the

Basque Boys' Training Committee, to a factory in Birmingham. At the end
of their first day, the manager spoke to them:

> The manager was very nice, and asked us, 'Do you think you are
> going to be happy here?' The other boy said, 'Yes', and I said, 'No.'
> So I was sent back to London in disgrace. Molly Garrett was very
> cross with me.

Even now, Luis cannot say why he refused to stay. A factory was not an
unknown environment to him: his father had worked in a foundry for
making ships' propellers, which, during the Civil War, had been converted
into a munitions factory. For months he had gone there to take his father his
lunch, 'fascinated', he says, 'at how they were now making shells for guns'.

> I had been brought up in that – it was not that it was something new
> to me – but I said, 'No.' So I was sent back to London and it was the
> best thing they did for me.

The 'best thing', Luis says, because back in London he moved into a flat in
South Kensington which was occupied by a group of intellectual Republican refugees, all of them somewhat older than himself. The flat was rented
for them by Alec Wainman, who had previously provided Poppy Vulliamy's wandering Basque children's colony with its final, and most
comfortable, home in Shipton-under-Wychwood. Wainman, himself an
academic linguist, had been instrumental in securing the release of a
number of Spanish intellectuals from the concentration camps on the
French beaches, where they had been held after the Civil War, and
subsequently helping them to settle in Britain. That was the new milieu in
which Luis found himself:

> To a provincial boy like me, falling in with such a group was a whole
> new world. Most of them were really intelligent; most of them were
> very kind and very nice to me.

There, he was encouraged to enroll at Birbeck College. At first he paid for
himself, from his earnings in a lowly job he had been given in the Argentine
embassy; later, a scholarship from the Juan Luis Vives Trust enabled him
to complete his degree.

Many other Basque children were fortunate to have close contact with
these educated and cultured Spaniards who had joined them in exile in

Britain. They were among the new generation of liberal progressive thinkers and artists whose talents had been encouraged, and allowed to flower under the Republic. The cultural renaissance of which they had been a part had been abruptly terminated by the Nationalist victory – indeed, it was always to be Franco's boast that he had rid Spain of every vestige of post-Enlightenment influence – but Spain's loss was to be Britain's gain. Among this group was Luis Portillo, a lecturer from the University of Salamanca, whom Rodolfo had met in the colony at Shipton:

> Señor Portillo taught us at the colony and I had nice feelings for him. I knew him – as a young kid to a grown-up man – but I knew him well because he used to give us lessons: he used to teach us the history of Spain.

Amador, too, when he was studying architecture in the Polytechnic in London, remembers how much he learnt about Spain and Spanish literature from his numerous encounters in the Hogar Español with those who were willing to take the Basque children under their wing:

> I took the opportunity of trying to get knowledge from these people and they were good at giving it.

Initial problems with work permits or simply with their lack of English, often meant these older exiles were obliged to take menial jobs, or else be dependent upon the goodwill of Republican sympathisers. While there were still colonies left open, the Basque Children's Committee was able to provide them with a number of opportunities. Thus, Luis Portillo taught at Shipton-under-Wychwood and, later, in the colony at Witney. But when both these were closed he was reduced to peeling potatoes in a café and then labouring on an emergency wartime aerodrome, before he knew enough English to find a job in Reuters newsagency. The Carshalton colony remained open throughout the war and, for much of this time, was run by Pepe Estruch, another of these exiled intellectuals. He was later to have a distinguished theatrical career, first in Uruguay and then, after Franco's death, in Spain itself. In 1991, he was awarded the 'National Prize in recognition of his services to the Spanish theatre', but it was with the handful of Basque children still living in Carshalton that all that work began. Together they produced plays from the Spanish Golden Age repertoire and performed them before Republican audiences in the Hogar Español, and the nearby Twentieth Century Theatre in west London.

As often as not, the help that these older men and women provided to the increasing number of Basque children drawn towards London was more immediate and practical – finding them accommodation, for example. And Jesús, living as he then was 'in the roof-tops', and struggling to make ends meet on his scholarship from the Juan Luis Vives Trust, remembers how often he would be given a meal when the grant was exhausted:

> I got two pounds, ten shillings a week from the Trust. I got it on Friday and by Wednesday it was over. And Ganivet and his wife, this lovely woman from Burgos, would say, 'Ven a comer con nosotros.' ['Come and eat with us.']

On other occasions it would be Manuel Lazareno, the Hogar's choirmaster, or Chano, the trainer of their football teams, who would feed him.

El Hogar Español was where they met and it is difficult to overstate its importance. Living in exile, in foreign lodgings, was frequently a lonely experience for many, but throughout all those years, until the lease expired, the Hogar provided some kind of buttress against that isolation: their association with it was to play a vital part in ensuring a continuity of identity among all the Republican exiles. Teaching the young Basque children was one means by which a number of the older generation were able to maintain their own sense of Spanishness as well as preserving the values they had struggled for; and for the children themselves, the Hogar brought them under the moral influence of those 'father-figures', as Jesús calls them:

> If we hadn't had the Hogar Español, what would we have done? Go to the pub or stand around street corners?

Although those who lived in London benefited most, El Hogar was also the natural place for those in the provinces to come and meet up with friends and siblings – Joseba, for instance, travelling regularly from the farm in St Neots to London 'to see the boys'. So it was with Enriqueta: when the last of the Basque children from the Witney colony had drifted away from the town, and only she was left, often she would journey to London to see her sister. 'That was invariably where we ended up,' she says, 'in the Hogar.'

In the Midlands, away from London and el Hogar Español, the only equivalent was the meeting of Basque children that took place on the first Sunday of each month at the home of the Gibbons. Helvecia, perhaps because she had taken a secretarial course, or more likely because she was the only girl among all those boys, was made the secretary of the club they formed: her job was to organise the meetings and inform all the boys. Later, to improve the facilities, she obtained permission from her guardian, George Cadbury, for them to use the football ground and pavilion at the Cadbury factory. She speaks with a nostalgic affection for those gatherings of exiled Spanish boys, scattered across the Midlands, on wartime Sunday afternoons:

> We tried to get as many of them to come as we could, but not everybody came – the boys working in Stafford at General Electric or in Wolverhampton were a long way away and in winter it was difficult. We used to make sandwiches and have a nice tea there, and the boys played football. And we had a gramophone and played music, and we danced or sang.

Eventually Helvecia herself followed the route taken by many of the boys. In 1944 she was invited to work for the Secretary of the Juan Luis Vives Trust and moved to London. It was a job for which her bilingual secretarial training and her continued acquaintance with many of the children in England equipped her well. And, in that respect, she was fortunate because the older girls proved to be more difficult to place in occupations than the boys.

In a report to the Basque Children's Committee in June 1941, Miss Picken (then its secretary) outlined the problems: the girls appeared to be more hindered by their broken education and lack of formal qualifications, and wartime conditions further reduced their training opportunities in technical schools. Five of the 18-year-old girls were then training to be nurses, but, in general, she commented, 'for girls between the ages of fourteen and sixteen, there is a limited choice of work':

> It has been necessary, therefore, to place them in domestic work, and wherever possible encourage them to attend classes in such subjects as will enable them to move on to other work in a year or two.[4]

In fact, of the 88 girls who were beyond the then-statutory school leaving age of fourteen, 29 were in domestic work and a further 21 were, in Miss Picken's phrase, 'living as daughters of the home'. There was no equivalent, for the girls, of the Basque Boys' Training Committee, which may well have been a reflection of prevailing attitudes towards the social position of women – an ironic reflection, if so, given the extent to which the fortunes of all the children had been so profoundly affected by the determination of a number of publicly prominent women. Almost invariably, therefore, the girls depended on the local committees for their first jobs. Thus, Salomé, and three other girls from the Cambridge colony, were all found domestic service jobs by the Cambridge Committee – first as cleaners in the university's women's colleges, and later in private homes. It was not work of their choosing. 'But what could you do?' says Salomé. 'You had to do it, to earn your living at least.'

Similarly, when Enriqueta's colony in Witney closed, she was sent to sew military uniforms in one of the many textile factories in the town:

> We all had to do war work and sewing was ours. Some went into engineering and some women were put sewing. I was pretty good with a sewing machine anyway – I already had been instructed in Spain before I came away – so it was automatic that I would go and do some work in that factory. And I loathed every minute of it, but, it was bringing me money, and I was very good at managing my money.

And, in Barnet, Pilar remembers there was one particular member of the committee who was adept at placing the girls in employment:

> There was a lady on the committee who was very good at finding us jobs. She took me to North Finchley and I said 'I think I would like to work in this big store.' So we went in and she got me a job as a junior in the underwear department.

She remained in that store, eventually in charge of that same department, throughout her working life.

Like the older boys, the girls saw no alternative but to accept the first job that was obtained for them, and only later were they able to change to something more congenial. In the case of Salomé and her friends, it was not to be some new talent, acquired in evening classes, but reliance upon an older, traditional skill, learnt from home, that eventually enabled them to move on. The four of them had each been given the day off to attend a reunion of the Basque children in the Hogar Español which was to be addressed by Negrín:

> And then talking to the other boys and girls in the Hogar, they said, 'Oh, domestic work? Come here and you can do sewing.' Because we all knew how to sew; in Spain your mother taught you how to

sew. 'You come here and earn your living, and two of you can go into one room, you know, and you can sort your life out.' So that's what we did.

They shared rented rooms and Salomé became a seamstress in a department store, a stone's throw from the Hogar Español.

Amelia first worked as a personal secretary to the veteran suffragette, Mrs Sylvia Pankhurst – a job obtained for her by a member of the local committee. When that ended, she acquired for herself a succession of secretarial jobs in which her native Spanish was her prime asset. 'I didn't want to lose my language', is how she explains it, but her facility with her own language was obviously a marketable talent. She worked first in a City import/export firm, then at the newly formed Instituto Español and finally in the Argentine embassy. The ambassador at the time was a member of the International Commission for Refugees and especially sympathetic towards the Basque children: a number of them were provided with work in the embassy.

The older girls proved to be less inclined than the boys to apply for scholarships from the Juan Luis Vives Trust and the trustees – conscious of the severe shortage of nurses in Britain – encouraged some of them to train for that profession. Few completed their training, however. It was not surprising, the Trustees' Report in 1947 conceded, that 'without the moral and material support of their family', they should have become discouraged by the difficulty and length of the course, and the poor salary it offered. On the other hand, the Report noted, the scholarships had been more effective with seven girls who were training to become nursery nurses where the course was shorter and easier.[5]

Two of the girls, encouraged by Dr Margarita Camps, successfully trained to become teachers. Dr Camps, once a lecturer at the University of Barcelona, was another of those exiled Spanish intellectuals who was to play a significant part in the lives of some of the children. Speaking excellent English, she had begun working for the Basque Childrens' Committee soon after her arrival in Britain, and it was in the PPU's colony at Colchester, in the early part of 1939, that she had first met Carito, and her younger sister, Marina. Two years later, by which time she was teaching in the progressive, independent school at Dartington Hall, Dr Camps wrote to the girls and proposed that they themselves should go to Dartington. With scholarships from the Juan Luis Vives Trust, they obtained their 'London Matriculation' at the school and then transferred into its teacher-training department. 'We didn't even have to be interviewed by anyone from the

Vives Trust,' Carito recalls. 'Dr Camps' word was considered to be good enough.'

One of the señoritas was also offered a scholarship from the Trust and qualified as a teacher, but, like the older girls, many of the young women who had accompanied the children from Bilbao went into domestic service when the colonies were closed. Señorita María was one of them. For eight months, she says, she was worked 'like a slave', supposedly for ten shillings a week, although throughout that time she recalls being paid for only four weeks. Eventually, in despair, María decided to return to Spain and face the very consequences she had previously been warned against. She took the train to Cardiff, on the off-chance of getting aboard a vessel bound for Spain:

> In Cardiff I went to the police station and I told them exactly what I felt. So P.C. Jones – he was a big, fat man, poor chap – he said, 'Can we do something for you?' I said, 'Yes, you could do plenty but nobody wants to do anything. I'm fed up with it.' My God – ten shillings a week and they were not even paying that! So he said to me, 'What about the Spanish Consulate?' 'Oh no,' I said, 'I don't want to know anything about the Spanish Government.' He said, 'Well, he's a good man. He doesn't look like an ordinary Spaniard; I'm going to phone him.' He phoned and, very luckily for me, the consul was of Basque origin. He came to see me at the police station.

And, in the Cardiff police station, the Consul interviewed her about her schooling, and qualifications. Was she prepared to learn to type? If so, he would offer her a job and a wage of five pounds a week: 'Better than ten shillings and never getting paid!' she thought. So she enrolled immediately in a typing class and began working in the consulate. In all probability she would have remained there longer, but this sympathetic Basque consul was recalled and replaced with somebody far less predisposed to help anyone who had been involved in the evacuation. So Señorita María returned to London. The colony at Barnet was still functioning and for a time she worked there. Then came a job in the Chilean embassy and a proposal:

> The Chilean ambassador was very kind to refugees. So he said to me, 'In the diplomatic corps, we have a lot of people of Basque origin, and they could help you. Why don't you start a Basque club? We'll help you; we'll come for meals every day.'

135

So began 'Basque House' in South Kensington. Members of the Basque Delegation voluntarily helped to furnish and decorate it, and, true to his word, the ambassador ensured that it was well supported by members of the South American diplomatic community. María would scour Soho every week for food that could be obtained without food rationing coupons, and generally she would succeed in providing a menu with four or five dishes. With its bar, restaurant, room for dancing and lectures, and basement workshop where English volunteers taught carpentry and mechanics lessons to Basque boys, it provided another meeting place for those exiled in London. For the twenty-six-year-old señorita, it was a new life.

One person who regularly visited Basque House was the teacher, Laureana. Having played her part in bringing about the closure of the colony in Margate in February 1940, she was sent to Nazareth House, the convent in Hammersmith, to teach the few remaining Basque children who were still living there. But they were soon old enough to go out to work and, with little then to do, Laureana resolved that she too should earn her keep. That incurred a disagreement with the Mother Superior:

> I said to this woman, 'I think I should be doing some work, working in a factory or something. It's awful to think I'm only doing some sewing and embroidery for you.' She said, 'Your English is not good enough.' I said, 'I can make anything; you don't need any English – just use your hands.'

With that, she set off for the local labour exchange, but they would not hear of her just using her hands:

> They said to me, 'And you were a teacher? Oh, no. We can't have you in a factory. The offices are sending all the girls to the land army; you could go and relieve some of them.' I said, 'But my English is not good enough.' 'Oh, never mind,' they said. 'You go there.'

So Laureana became a relief wages clerk, taking the wages to the cashiers of the firm's various branches all over the City. 'I got to know London so well', she says. Whatever she thought of it at the time, she laughs now, incredulous at the idea of her being let loose to carry her bags of money, by bus, from one end of London to the other. But no doubt her manager knew what he was doing; he knew enough to ask her to take responsibility for the nightly fire-watching duties of the entire staff – determining the rota, and ensuring that everybody in the office had their blanket and gas mask at the oppropriate time. 'I suppose he thought I was an organiser', she says, with the same note of astonishment.

Fire-watching during the Blitz was also a duty undertaken by a number of the older Basque children. It carried the bonus of allowing a special permit to be attached to their Alien's Registration Book so that for one night a week they were excused curfew restrictions. Throughout the war all the Basque children over the age of sixteen, and all the adults, were required to carry such a book, into which every change of address had to be recorded at the local police station. Even a brief holiday required them to report their departures and arrivals. They were debarred from certain parts of the country that were deemed to be militarily sensitive and, fire-watching apart, subject to a 10 p.m. curfew.

Antonio was one of the few to be exempted from those regulations, but only after his brother, José, had been arrested. For a couple of months Antonio had been crop spraying around Hunstanton in Norfolk, without ever bothering to report his presence, but when José was sent to spray in a part of Essex which, like the North Norfolk coast, was classified as a restricted area, he did the proper thing:

> The first thing he does is go up to the policeman's house. Knocks at the door. 'My name is José Gallego; I'm reporting that ...' 'I'm sorry, my son. You're in a restricted area,' says the policeman. 'I must put you under arrest.'

José was not convicted, however. In court, the firm's director admitted that the boy had been in the forbidden area only on his instructions and clearly he had no ill intentions because he had, quite correctly, reported immediately to the police. Afterwards, he wrote to the Home Office and obtained, for both boys, permits which freed them from all alien restrictions.

If these regulations were an occasional nuisance to employers, they were more than irksome to the Basque children themselves. They seemed to imply that they were unwelcome visitors, for all that they were doing essential war work, and enduring the same hazards and privations as every other member of the civilian population. In some cases the dangers were vividly real, as for Palmiro aboard his coaster in the Bristol Channel:

> You never knew when you were going to be blown up. We were collecting a load of steel one particular night, at Cardiff, you know. And, good Lord, we thought that the Germans threw every plane into Cardiff that particular night. They lit everything like daylight with

flares, you know. And I was helping the troops that were there in the harbour; I was helping them to put out the incendiary bombs and that. Fifteen men killed in a boiler house ... And a bomb was so close that when I heard it come down, I hung on to one of the cranes, you know, and the impact nearly blew me away, it was so close. So you never knew. Many ships were sunk in the Bristol Channel there.

Yet the Basque children were only marooned in wartime Britain because their fathers had already fought their own war against Fascism and, occasionally, despite the authority's suspicions, the restrictions were interpreted with generous leniency by the police – tiny gestures of human solidarity which have lived long in the heart. Late one Sunday night, for example, Helvecia arrived back in Birmingham an hour after curfew. In some distress, she approached a policeman to confess that she was an alien, only to be escorted to the head of the taxi queue where the policeman instructed the first taxi-driver to take her home. At much the same time, Eliseo was playing his clarinet in a Leamington dance band three or four nights a week and, each time, he was required to take his alien's registration book to the local police station. There, the 'aliens' Sergeant' was required to sign the authorisation for him to be out beyond ten o'clock: Sergeant Gibbs and Eliseo came to see a lot of each other:

He was that fed up with me. I used to go and knock on the little window. 'Oh, can I see Sergeant Gibbs?' And he'd pick up the phone: 'Er, Mr Ochoa is ... ' 'Not him again.' And he says, 'Alright, go up.' And he used to open the side door, and I used to go up because I knew where Sergeant Gibbs was, and knock on the door. 'Come in!' I used to go in. 'Not you bugger again! Christ, give us a rest.' And one time the Chief Constable was coming down and he says, 'Everything alright, Sergeant Gibbs? Oh, it's you again is it?' he says to me. 'What are you up to now?' I said, 'Oh, just a permit for tomorrow night.' So he says to Sergeant Gibbs, 'Look. Why waste your damn time?' he says. 'Give him a permanent permit. He's going to be bothering you every week. Give him a permanent permit so he doesn't have to bother you again.'

Not only did Eliseo receive a permanent permit, but also one that gave him permission to ride a bicycle, albeit only 'within the Royal Borough of Leamington Spa' – a further relaxation of alien's restrictions. In London, however, Luis found that he did not need a permit for his bicycle:

During the War, when I was working for the Argentine embassy, the First Secretary had given me a bicycle to get to and from work, and in those days, foreigners were supposed to declare their form of transport. And I had a bicycle. So I went to the police and said, 'I've got a bicycle.' And he said, 'Oh yes, and who are you?' I said, 'A Spaniard.' 'Ah yes,' he said. 'You're not..? Are you one of the Basque boys?' I said, 'Yes', and he said, 'Oh you're not a foreigner. Go away.'

By contrast, 50 years later, Virgilio, still bearing his Spanish passport, is sometimes stopped and interrogated, as he passes through British passport control:

They say, 'Do you live here?' So I say, 'Yes.' 'Oh yes, how long have you lived here?' I say, 'Fifty odd years. Do you want me to prove it?'

And, on those occasions when he is required to prove his identity, he takes some pleasure in informing the immigration official that he spent four years of the war in the Royal Air Force – one of a handful of Basque boys who served in the British armed forces. He had eventually grown to be lonely in the Hygienic Dairies – the job Marjorie Main had found for him in Leamington – when, one by one, all the other young people had been conscripted, so he applied to join the RAF. His first application was refused: 'We don't take foreigners', he was told. So he wrote again to the Air Ministry, explaining why he wanted to enlist, and was invited to Birmingham to be interviewed by a Squadron Leader. There he was given reading and writing tests, and a medical examination, and, a fortnight later, told to report to the RAF base at Cardington:

There they gave me an intelligence test, which I passed. Then they gave me a number and they gave me a uniform. Then they made me take the Oath of Allegiance, which I refused. So, panic. Why? Why? Impossible. If you are a volunteer you have to take it. But, you see, it said in it you had to defend King and Country, in peace and war, from foreign or domestic interference. And I said, 'No.' For the period of world war, yes, for the duration – but no more. So they said, 'It can't be done.' So I said, 'Well, I'm very sorry, but you alter it or I don't take the oath.' So my entry went and I was left behind, and I was left behind there for about a week. And then a bloke from the

Air Ministry came with a document, and he says to read this. And I read it. 'You agree to that?' I says, 'Yes, I agree to that.' 'Well, sign here.' And I signed there. I was signing that I was willing to serve in the British forces and obey all orders and commands and all the other things, during the duration of the War. Only! Only for the duration. Also, if there was going to be a war against Spain, I refuse!

In its wording, it must have been a unique oath, and probably not quite what the National Joint Committee for Spanish Relief had in mind when it declared its aspiration that those Spaniards who had been stranded in England by the tides of war should come to be 'independent'.

Uprooted and exiled, and with their education truncated, these older children did become independent – able to support themselves and make their way with growing assurance around a foreign land. They endured the dead-end jobs to which many of them were assigned and the moments of acute loneliness in their lodgings. There were tears to be shed and Antonio is not ashamed to admit it:

I was a very lonely person at times, especially when I was in lodgings. I don't mind saying it, when I was seventeen or eighteen, I'd be in lodgings, I'd be in my bedroom, and I'd cry my eyes out – through a desire to see my mother and that. I wouldn't wish that on anybody.

Throughout all of this they were helped of course – sometimes in gestures of unstinting generosity, often in tiny moments of kindliness – but increasingly what mattered was the help they and that slightly older generation of Republicans provided each other, in the community they fashioned out of their common fate.

They gave voice to that fate in *Amistad* (Friendship) – a bilingual, cyclostyled newsletter written by the Basque children and edited, first in the London office of the Basque Children's Committee, and later in their own room at el Hogar Español. Its first edition appeared in 1940, and it was produced, and distributed to the children in England, every two or three months, until 1944. The pages of *Amistad* continued to remember the Spain they had lost and to speak longingly of the Spain to which they might return, for, at that time, few imagined their residence in Britain would be permanent. That future was still obscure; mostly they were like Virgilio – in Britain only for the duration.

El Hogar Español: 22 Inverness Terrace

6   ADOPTION

But ... they took me in, didn't they?

Despite the mass repatriation in the early months of the war, there remained a substantial number of younger children – too young to go out to work or contribute to their own upkeep – who were obviously going to remain dependent upon adult care and supervision for some considerable time to come. Even two years later, in June 1941, 148 children were still under the age of fourteen.[1]

One answer was to retain a handful of colonies, principally for them, although this was certain to put a considerable financial burden upon the local committees involved, as well as upon the national Basque Children's Committee. Public interest in this last remnant of the evacuation had inevitably been overtaken by more pressing concerns, not least the evacuation of British children from cities that were likely targets of German bombs. The committee responsible for the colony at Carshalton reported their income had fallen by 40 per cent after the outbreak of war and, by November 1939, their reserves were almost exhausted.

Nor was fund-raising the only problem: several of the buildings housing the colonies were deemed necessary for wartime purposes and had been requisitioned. Thus the old sanatorium, home to the Keighley colony, once more became a military hospital; the Shipton-under-Wychwood colony closed when the house was acquired by the Army; in Colchester, the Peace Pledge Union's efforts to maintain a home for half a dozen of the youngest Basque children were thwarted when the smaller house into which they intended to move was taken over for English children who had been evacuated from London.

Despite all these difficulties, the Basque Children's Committee persuaded six local committees to keep their colony open; Carshalton was one of them, as its newsletter later commented:

We had three children remaining in January, 1940, but very soon came requests from the joint committee to take children who could not be sent back to Spain, and who had been left stranded when the colonies they were in were closed. We agreed, and the committee took on a new lease of life, for we realised that while there yet remained Basque children in the country, our work could not be called finished, and to this view we still adhere.[2]

Another colony to survive was at Plymouth, where twelve children from the original 40 remained. A letter from its local committee to the TUC, towards the end of 1940, makes for sad reading:

We have maintained in Plymouth for over three and a half years a hostel for forty Spanish children, the necessary funds being raised by the children themselves in concert work (£400 in this way), and by voluntary contributions and donations from individuals and organisations in Devon and Cornwall. Had the war not broken out we could have carried on our work without anxiety about finance but during recent months our supplies have been much depleted. We are therefore asking you to consider the possibility of giving Trade Union assistance.[3]

Characteristically, the plea ended with a poignant reminder of their frugality:

The work of carrying on the hostel is done by voluntary helpers and overhead charges are at a minimum.

It was in these colonies, the last survivors of the 70 or so that had been operating at one time or another in 1937, that some of the youngest children were looked after during the war. One by one, they too were to close: there were six in 1940, three by 1943 and only two by 1944. Soon after the end of the war, all that remained was the vestige of the Barnet colony, reduced to a hostel in Finchley for a few of the older boys and girls who were then working in London, and the colony at Carshalton, which had been relocated to 'The Culvers' because of bomb damage to its original home, 'The Oaks'.

An alternative policy for ensuring the welfare of the youngest children was to arrange for an English family to take individuals into their home. Ever since their arrival at Southampton, the BCC had sought to avoid separating the children in this way. It had always been the Committee's express intention to keep them together, so that they might preserve their sense of Spanish identity, but, by 1939, financial stringency had rendered this ideal an impossibility.

143

In fact, however, despite the Committee's publicly stated aversion to individual separation, a few children were being taken out of the colonies to live with English families as early as 1938. Often this had developed spontaneously from the sponsorship scheme, whereby a person guarantied the necessary ten shillings a week to maintain a particular Spanish child in a colony. This was how Helvecia, and her younger brother and sister came to be adopted. Responding to one of the numerous appeals for sponsors that were placed in newspapers sympathetic to the Republican cause, George Cadbury agreed to be responsible for the upkeep of one of the youngest children in Carshalton. He had been allocated Helvecia's younger sister. Only later did it transpire that there was another in the family, after he had sent the little girl a dress and Helvecia had written to thank him:

> I wrote back a letter, with the aid of a dictionary, saying, 'Thank you very much. My sister looks lovely. It's a bit long but I will shorten it.' And they wrote back and said, 'Oh, we didn't know she had a sister. Could we both go out one Sunday?' They would come and fetch us, and take us for dinner.

Then, on that Sunday, the Cadburys learned of Elvio, the brother, who was also in the colony. Some months later the Cadburys proposed to take the three of them out of Carshalton and send them to a Quaker boarding school. Helvecia agreed, but with the proviso that they should spend all their school holidays in the colony with the other children.

Similarly, after just one year in the Peace Pledge Union's colony in Colchester, Valeriana was taken away to go and live in South London with a PPU family who were helping to fund the colony. How that came about, she has no idea, nor any recollection of being consulted about the decision. She was sent first to a private school and later to Stretham Girls High School; during the blitz, the High School was evacuated to Chichester, where the girls lodged with local families and had their lessons in the Deanery of Chichester Cathedral. It was seven years before she next saw any of the other Basque children.

Rodolfo might also have been adopted at about the same time, albeit into a very different kind of family. Among those who regularly visited the colony was one young man who frequently invited groups of the boys to his parents' home at weekends. Rodolfo was one of them and they obviously took a particular liking to him. He stayed for a couple of months during the summer holidays and, had he not been so apprehensive at the thought of attending an English school, he would have remained there:

144

'If he stays here, he's got to go to school', they said, and I was a bit frightened. I hadn't been in England all that long then and I didn't speak much English. I said, 'Oh no. I have to go back.' But I wish I had stayed there because they were wonderful to me. They were rough, real rough people. I remember they had quite a few sons who used to get into fights, but they were a wonderful family. I was very happy there.

Young though he was – just ten years old at the time – Rodolfo had some choice in the matter. One year later, when so many of the children were being hurriedly dispatched back to Spain and most of the surviving colonies were being wound up, he had no choice. He was sent to an English family in Eastleigh and, like it or not, he did find himself attending an English school. In the frantic haste at the end of 1939, there were few options for any of the younger children.

The Basque Children's Committee, in its search for possible homes for the children, wrote to all the local Secretaries of Spanish Aid Committees, and contacted anybody whom they might recommend. This letter, to one such prospective host family, barely disguises their desperation at that time:

The Secretary of the Lancashire & Cheshire Spanish Aid Committee, when writing to us a few days ago in reply to a letter of ours asking for hospitality for several of our Basque children, gave us your name, telling us that you might be able to offer hospitality to one of our younger boys. There are several for whom we are anxious to find happy homes, and would be most grateful for the help which we need so badly just now. We should be pleased to send the boy for a trial period of, say three months, to see if he fitted in. We think that this would be the best way as it is not always easy to know just which boy would be suitable.[4]

No doubt the irony of a trial period of 'three months' was unintentional, but clearly the boy fitted in: to this day he still lives in that part of Lancashire.

Sometimes, it was the local committees themselves that sought homes for their own children, as often as not from among those who had supported their efforts in maintaining the colony over the previous two and a half years. The weekly dispatch in *Peace News* from the PPU's colony in Colchester reported this process:

Our numbers are dwindling by ones and twos. Teresita went the other day. Her going is a loss for us and an acquisition for the friends who have taken her ... Teresita was snapped up by friends of the Acton group by return of post on their receiving notice of our intended dispersal. She was a little stunned when she learned that in a week's time she was to leave for good the big old house which had been her home for more than two years, and said she wished she could take the small children of her dormitory with her ... 'She doesn't speak much English,' we told the guard of the train in whose charge we sent her to London. 'Better put her in here, then.' So we last saw her, a little scared but smiling, on the guard's seat in the luggage van.[5]

By contrast, Leno made his own arrangements when the colony in Street was closed. It had been housed in The Grange, a large comfortable house belonging to the the local firm of Clarks Shoes and substantially supported by them:

> Just before the break up of the colony, the Clothier family, who were related to the Clarks, gave a tea party for the children, which a lot of people were doing. I said to Mrs Clothier, without thinking as I gobbled down those lovely cream cakes, 'I would love to come and live here'. Just off the cuff ... And so I stayed with them for the next four years – the only Spanish child left in Street.

That was somewhat unusual. Herminio's experience was much more typical. When the BCC eventually closed the Margate colony, at the beginning of 1940, he had been transferred to Carshalton, but then, with scarcely any warning, he was told that he would be moving yet again:

> One day, out of the blue, I was told: 'Herminio, you're leaving this afternoon.' I was told to get washed and to gather my few belongings – my gas mask, which was, I think, all I could say was my own. I was introduced to this little man and I found myself walking down through the park to the main road, my new guardian trying very hard to communicate with me and get through to me that he was Charles Green. And he took me to Leicester.

His 'uncle' and 'aunt', as he was to call them, had read, in a Methodist journal, of the Basque Children's Committee's search for suitable homes for the younger children. Having a daughter of their own, they had written, offering to take a little girl, and been put in touch with Carshalton:

> He had gone there, hoping to take away with him a little girl. Well,
> there were no little girls: I think they had already been issued out! So,
> he was told there were a number of young boys, and – something that
> I really think was lovely – he never asked to see me or any of the
> others. He just said, 'Yes.' This was lovely and generous. Conse-
> quently, I finished up in Leicester ... and there, of course, I
> encountered English life for the first time.

He also encountered some stability in his turbulent life since, over the
previous three years, he had been shunted from one colony to another.

It might have been the same for Javier: he, too, had passed through
several colonies before being sent to live with an English family in
Coventry, but he was only to remain with them for six months. In 1940,
following the ferocious bombing of Coventry, he was sent back to the
colony in Barnet – an ironic decision, as it turned out, because the colony
itself was later hit by a land-mine. Those six months in Coventry were to
have a permanent influence: Javier was introduced to rambling, which was
to become an important feature of his adult life:

> They were ramblers, actually, which is where it all started. And they
> were a nice couple, socialists, Labour people, and interested in the
> Spanish children. They didn't have any children themselves – I think
> that is why they took me. He used to come and visit me in Barnet,
> and I kept in touch with them till they died.

For others, however, the sequence was reversed and the closing of the
colonies marked the end of anything resembling a settled life. María Luisa
had lived in the Cambridge colony with four older siblings since her arrival
in England. 'I was very lucky,' she remarks, 'since being the youngest in the
family I always felt well looked after.' Then, when the colony closed, the
family was scattered and her life became a series of stays of varying
duration in various private homes. First she was taken to Southport, together
with one of the señoritas and two other children. Why Southport? Perhaps
it was a university connection which took her there, for she found herself
in the home of a Manchester University lecturer:

> I have no idea how long I was there. Then I went to Liverpool
> because one of my older sisters was living in Liverpool with a family

there and I went to friends of theirs – a couple who had two grown-up, married children of their own, and they took me in, you know, as their own. Then, when the bombing got bad in Liverpool during the war, they sent me back to Cambridge. I went back to Cambridge and I think I had three stops there. Isn't it awful – like a rolling stone, aren't I?

It was the same for Ascensión: when the colony in Street closed, she was abruptly isolated from her older brothers who had previously taken such care of her. Eight years old at the time, she has little recollection now of the first home to which she was sent, beyond a lingering sense of the unhappiness of separation:

Apparently, I used to keep running away, trying to get back to Oscar or Leno. I couldn't tell you how long I was there. I suppose it must have been about twelve months or so, but she couldn't cope with me as well as having a family, so she got rid of me. She put me on a train by myself, with my little case and a card on me saying, 'I am Spanish; I can't speak English.' And I went from Wales to Walsall and a dear old lady had me. She was a single lady and she was getting on in years, but she was a lovely person.

Invariably, they speak of their confusion at that time, of 'living in a daze', of not knowing what was happening to them and, still less, why. If explanations were offered to these children they appear not to have been meaningful to them. But meanings are embodied in relationships and these were so often severed by the dissolution of the colonies. The loss was not simply of friendships or ties of kinship: their sudden, seemingly capricious, transposition into the isolated privacy of English homes attenuated their connections with the past, with Spain, and with their own language. All of this had been richly maintained throughout their time in the colonies but, once on their own, the very youngest had too few memories with which to sustain, and take into the future, these pictures of their past. So they lived, as María Luisa puts it, 'from day to day':

I had no say at all in the decisions that were being made about my life. None whatsoever. I suppose I must have accepted the fact that I was living here, until I was taken back or sent somewhere else. I just went on living where I was, for the moment – either months or years or whatever it was – from day to day.

The nature of that existence, living for the moment, could alter quite unpredictably. In Liverpool, her days had been happy, cared for by a kindly, elderly married couple who behaved towards her, she says, as if she were 'their own daughter'. Then came the return to Cambridge and into a cold, patriarchal household ruled over by a strict disciplinarian, whose wife she remembers as 'working extremely hard for no thanks at all'. In this harsher climate the days were very different. Rather as the older children were rarely able to think of their 'digs' as anything but a temporary lodging, this was not a house that María Luisa could think of as 'home':

> You never had the liberty of asking people round to your home. I never felt I had the freedom to say, 'Come with me.' You always had to wait to be asked.

A scholarship from the Juan Luis Vives Trust took her to the Perse School in Cambridge but only exacerbated her difficulties, as well as bringing her sharply up against the English class system:

> No I didn't fit in; I felt quite out of place. My 'guardian' felt I had no right to be going to the Perse really. I think that also made me feel out of place: it was drummed into me. Two girls at the Perse kept their ponies in his field; he used to call them 'Miss' and things like that. I know it's a long time ago, but I remember it clearly. He thought I was going to address them in the same way he did.

She didn't, of course, although in the large houses near by, where many of her fellow pupils lived, she used to earn some pocket money by washing up in the evenings after finishing her homework. Her memories of the time spent with that family are far from joyful. 'But', she adds, as if those childhood resentments need redressing with appropriate gratitude, 'they took me in, didn't they?'

Others might have found that humility more difficult to express. Certainly there were a few who knew a far more unkind environment: Fausto, for instance: when the Brampton colony closed he was transferred briefly to Montrose for the final few weeks of that colony. Then, somehow, he found himself living in a house in the mining village of Consett, the only Spanish boy for miles around. As was so often the case, he has no idea how or why that came about:

> It was a bad house, very poor food. They used to take in lodgers. It

was nothing for me to have to get up at five in the morning, clean the
grate and light the fire for breakfast. I was often hungry. I used to go
picking up carrots and turnips from allotments, and eating them raw.

Similarly, Juanita: until 1942 she and her sister were still in the Manchester
convent where, seemingly, they had been abandoned ever since their
arrival:

There were a lot of tears. We cried an awful lot because we thought
we had been forgotten ... I always remember the injustice of it all.
There was no one there who understood you. There was nobody who
wanted you. We were always told that by the nuns – we were there
because we were unwanted, or we were forgotten. It was not a very
nice experience.

The one compensation was that they were given an education, 'a very
intense English education', as Juanita puts it: 'It was there that I was made
to appreciate good music and reading.'
  Most of the younger children, however, were far luckier. The three years
spent in Leicester, in the home of the Methodist pacifist family, were to
prove a joyous experience for Herminio:

I was suddenly thrown from my background of roughing it and
toughing it in the colonies to this home. How my aunt and uncle
tamed me, I don't know. How I adapted to that sort of life, I don't
know. Physically I was very, very active; I was tough and of course
I couldn't keep still; from the moment I left the house I would tear
down the road, jumping over all the garage entrances. I went to
junior school. Oh, in no time at all, I had no end of friends. I think
I adapted to that way of life incredibly well.

Adapting to that way of life entailed learning English and this he also did
'in no time at all'. Indeed most of the younger children appeared to learn
English rapidly after they had been abruptly removed from the Spanish-
speaking environment of the colony. 'It's a hard way to learn a language,
but, by Jove, do you learn it!' says Juanita, now with barely a trace of
Spanish intonation beneath her London accent. The nuns in the convent had
made no concessions, and she and her sister had been forbidden to speak
Spanish from the moment the señorita, and all the other girls returned to
Spain.

Adapting to an English way of life also meant going to school. In 1941 the Basque Children's Committee was able to report that of the 148 children in its care who were still under 14 years of age, a dozen were in convent schools, 14 were at private schools and all of the remainder were attending local state schools.[6] For most, this was their first experience of English schooling, and for the very youngest it was the first experience of any kind of formal education because, in Bilbao, the schools had been shut with the onset of the Civil War.

Today, when older exiles suggest – as many of them do – that the youngest are the ones who have been best able to adapt to their lifetime in England, they are mainly referring to the fact that they all experienced some kind of English education. Many of them, too, received a scholarship from the Juan Luis Vives Trust enabling them to continue in school to complete their matriculation. They were young enough to take full advantage of their scholarships and, unlike the older children, they had not had their education interrupted at so crucial a stage in their intellectual development, as the report from the Trustees pointed out:

> As was to be expected, the successes in this category of scholarships have been, in general, excellent. These students had the language, had the experience of English schools and have been able to adapt more easily to a more advanced level of instruction.[7]

The brightest and fondest memories that they still carry of whatever kind of English schooling they encountered are almost invariably associated with a particular teacher, someone who took a special interest in them. In the secondary school in Leicester where Herminio spent two years, it was the headteacher:

> The secondary school was also excellent. The Head was a Frenchman who, in a sense, took me under his wing. He seemed to know and understand my background, and I was very happy. I had an urge, a zest for education. I liked school. If I was ill and couldn't go – which was very, very seldom – I was as miserable as sin because I loved school.

Leno also speaks of being 'taken under the wing of the headteacher' at Millfield School. This was, in fact, his second encounter with English education. For reasons that are no more obvious to him now than they were then, he had previously decided that he wanted to join the merchant navy and had been sent, by the Clothiers, to the nautical school in Parkstone. There he excelled, coming top in his year in navigation and seamanship. He also earned the whole school a half-day holiday by winning an English essay competition on the subject of birds. Perhaps this was significant, because natural history was to remain an abiding interest in his life, while navigation and seamanship were to prove more transient concerns. He only ever went to sea once and, on that single trans atlantic trip aboard a Norwegian vessel, one of the lifeboats was carried away at the height of a February gale, and all hands were called to the deck:

> We were there for quite a long time, wet through, and the ship was like a cork, going up and down. I must have been pretty exhausted. Near the windlass – that's where they found me, hours after. That's when things started to go bad.

Going bad meant acute pleurisy and, immediately his ship docked in Glasgow, he was transferred to hospital, weighing less than six stones. Mrs Clothier can vividly recall the letter she received from the Scottish consultant, informing her that nothing could be done to save the life of this young Spanish boy, and her anger at his suggestion that she need not bother going to see him:

> I was furious. He suggested that there was no point in me wasting my money going all the way up to Glasgow because he only had 48 hours to live. He asked me what I wanted to have done with the body!

But she did make the journey, from Street to Glasgow, and Leno did survive, to spend the next year recuperating on a bed made up in a downstairs room of the Clothiers' house. Eventually, uncertain as to where his future might lie, they sent him to Millfield school and there he had a wonderful time:

> I mean who wouldn't, going to a school like that? And although we were taught in Nissen huts it was such a difference from the life, the experiences I had had prior to that … The Head took me under his wing because of my sporting contribution, although I should not have been playing any sport for five years.

Mario was another who was to be given a second educational opportunity. During his final days in the Barnet colony he had gone to a local secondary school and, although he was there for only a short time, it was a 'happy experience'. He remembers it particularly for one sympathetic teacher who took a liking to him and would give him extra lessons in English while the others were out at play. But later, he was to get another chance, by virtue of the Juan Luis Vives Trust:

> I was interviewed by the Duchess of Atholl, and I think it was through Ronald Thackrah – he must have said, 'Well, try Mario.' And she came and said, 'What do you know? Do you know any French?' And I said, 'No.' And, 'Do you know any algebra?' 'No. But I'm very good at arithmetic, geography, history.' Well, history – the little history one knew from Spain, but nothing about the kings and queens of England. All I remember was that she said, 'It's very poor, isn't it?' And my heart sank. But, anyhow, subsequently I heard that I had been given a scholarship for one year to study towards matric.

With this promise of a scholarship, he and another Basque boy were taken by the Secretary of the Trust first to a conventional boarding school, but there they were rejected. 'They more or less said, "We can't take them: they're too far behind"'. And so they finished up at the Beltane School, one of those progressive, coeducational schools, established between the wars, and patronised by a certain liberal, intellectual, artistic section of the English middle class. With the outbreak of World War II the school had been evacuated from South London into the Wiltshire countryside. 'It was superb,' says Mario, and the teachers – mostly conscientious objectors – were 'dedicated, terribly tolerant, helpful and enormously friendly'.

He was given private tuition where he was made to discard the ungrammatical English he'd previously picked up. And it wasn't simply his command of the language that was relearned: two years spent in such a very particular English boarding school meant assimilating far more:

> When we first went there we thought they were mad – they were young children, they were juveniles, they were trite, you know. And little by little we saw how they were much more than that: they were beginning to be cultured. And we were less cultured, although in another sense much more grown up and probably more experienced in a much rougher way. And the culture rubbed off on you: you began to accept that, yes, you could read more books and, yes, you could listen to music ... You began to take a more active part in the life of the school.

In a quite different, but no less powerful way, living in an English family home and attending a local state secondary school, also constituted the inevitable process of Anglicisation which the Basque Children's Committee, in the far-off days of 1937, had sought to avoid. Herminio recalls that influence:

> I joined what was really a typical English way of life: I went to the cubs, I went to Sunday school, went to English school. I really loved school. I threw myself into it: I used to play rugby – like a madman – for the school; I used to play cricket for the school.

A few were legally adopted, although with Herminio the question never arose. His guardians, like most who were looking after these younger children, felt an obligation to his background and his parents, such that they insisted that he wrote to them regularly. But, in spite of that, during the time he spent with them he became very Anglicised and began to lose the command of his own language.

Perhaps in an effort to minimise those predictable consequences, the Basque Children's Committee produced a set of written Spanish exercises and asked the guardians of some of the isolated children to ensure that they practised regularly. It is difficult, nonetheless, to believe that this did much to arrest the process; that required direct contact with other Spaniards. When María Luisa returned to Cambridge, mid-way through the war, she and a few others from the colony who were still living in the town, used to gather at the home of one of the señoritas. It was only once a week, usually on a Sunday afternoon, but it was, she says, 'the one way of keeping our Spanish up'.

There were others who were equally anxious to maintain their Spanish contacts: Mario, for instance, despite being willingly drawn into the Englishness of the Beltane School. Several times he was invited to spend the holidays in the homes of English children in the school, but he declined. Once, he did go back to Yorkshire, to stay with an elderly couple who had befriended him during his days in the colony in Keighley, but most often the pull was towards the other Basque children:

> We always wanted to be with the other Spaniards. If we could go back to Rowley Lodge in Barnet, we did. The colony became smaller and smaller; it dwindled until it became a little detached house in Finchley, and there was room there for about 30 people – you slept six to a room. We felt very much at home there, although

we were – well not ostracised, but treated slightly differently because we were away at school.

For those who were isolated from even the most sporadic contact, the process of 'becoming English' was inexorably rapid. Ascensión, arriving in Walsall at the age of ten, with a placard pinned to her chest announcing she was Spanish and spoke no English, went to school for the first time in her life. She learnt English very quickly, so she has since been told, but on the way, lost her Spanish. Yet, she remembers that Spanish was the language of her dreams:

> I was able to speak Spanish in my sleep, which seems a strange thing. Yes, I was regularly talking it in my sleep and yet I couldn't speak it in the day. I was so confused as a child; I suppose that's how it affected me.

It must have been much the same for Elvio. Supported by the Cadbury Trust, he spent four years in a Quaker boarding school and he has an even more precise recollection – of the first occasion he dreamt in English:

> I was at school then, at boarding school and I woke up one morning and there was something different. I had actually dreamt in English, as opposed to Spanish, and, from then on, that was it – it was a turning point.

By then all his friends were English and the pattern of his life was set. 'You grow into it,' he says, 'but you become, to a certain extent, reliant upon yourself.'

The self-reliance he speaks of was a quality that the younger children had to discover within themselves as soon as they reached school-leaving age. The older children had been found employment and accommodation at the outbreak of war, either by the Basque Boys' Training Committee, or by local people who had previously helped maintain them in the colony. The jobs had often been undemanding of their talents and 'digs' could be lonely, depressing places, but many found themselves working together in the same factory, and this offered some comfort and the opportunity to sustain each other. A few years later, however, when the younger children were leaving school, and in search of work, that local structure had largely vanished: it disappeared with the closing of the colonies, and the dissolution of the local committees. The fortune of each of these children was very much a matter of chance: some were lucky, and had good career advice and continued material support from their English family; others had to fend for themselves. Either way, working within a wholly English environment could amplify the process of Anglicisation they had first experienced by living with an English family and attending an English school.

Rodolfo had to seek his own work from the moment he left school and, because of a mistake on his original registration card, he left school at thirteen: in the haste and anxiety just before the *Habana's* departure from Bilbao, his date of birth had been incorrectly entered on his card. He was not the only one to find himself the victim of that kind of clerical error: Javier could never understand why he stood head and shoulders above the English children in the primary school he attended when he was in Barnet, or why he was the only boy to have started shaving! His registration card had indicated him to be two years younger than his real age, a blunder that was still pursuing him, more than fifty years later, when he went to collect his state pension. But in Rodolfo's case the error had exaggerated his age, so his already brief acquaintance with English schooling was reduced by a further year and his working life initiated that much earlier. At thirteen, therefore, he found himself a temporary job in a factory in Eastleigh and when that came to an end he became a labourer on a nearby building site:

And they were amongst the happiest days of my working life. I was a navvy, but it was wonderful. There was a ganger and a manager, and they were – they both were – so kind to me, you know. The ganger was a real rough-house, a big man. He had a lot of Irishmen working for him and he was very rough with them, swore a lot. But me? I couldn't do anything wrong. It was incredible. Obviously I worked hard, but I enjoyed it. We did a lot of pick-and-shovel work, barrowing, stuff like that, but I enjoyed it. And in the summer it was wonderful and he must have taken a liking to me.

By then, he confesses, he had forgotten most of his Spanish. So too had Juanita and her older sister, María Angeles, when they finally emerged from the convent in Manchester where they had been living ever since their arrival in England. For a few months, they stayed with the doctor who had secured their release, but while María Angeles began working in his laboratory, Juanita could see no ready-made future there; she would have to make it for herself. The doctor contacted the Basque Children's Committee and arranged for her to go down to the hostel in Finchley, where all but two of those living there were, by then, working:

In the hostel in Finchley everyone was chatting in Spanish and I thought, 'My God, I seem to be neither one thing nor the other.' When I started speaking Spanish, I had such an English accent. So, of course, they used to roll on the floor, laughing at me. And I'd gone from a convent – girls only – and the hostel was mixed. Sixteen years old – I mean, I used to blush at the slightest hint of anything. It's a terrible thing to say, but I was glad to leave there.

She stayed barely six months before moving to a residential training nursery in Bethnall Green to train to become a nursery nurse. So began another period of separation from any other Basque children – only this time by choice – and another lonely existence. The weekends, she can remember, would be spent walking through the bombed streets of east London and down to the river just to gaze at the blitz damage. For a while she became friendly with an older girl from Yorkshire who used to take her dancing at the Lyceum. Clearly it was an important friendship and all these years later Juanita still remembers that more sophisticated young Englishwoman with affection. Yet, even then, it was an attachment that was always touched by the prescience of its inevitable loss:

It was a very good friendship, but I knew nothing could come of it because she was going to go back to Yorkshire, and lead a very different life. And it's a long way away – Yorkshire.

Even those upon whom fortune had smiled much more kindly were thrown back upon their own devices when they left school. Mario had a suitcase, and three pounds and fifteen shillings in his pocket when he left the Beltane School. 'So, what are you going to do with yourself?' the headmaster asked, but, in truth, he had no idea what he wanted to do or how he might earn a living. He had gained his matriculation, but, by then, there were insufficient funds left in the Juan Luis Vives Trust to hold out the possibility of continuing his education. At the headteacher's suggestion he remained throughout the final summer holiday, painting the school buildings. Then, very much at a loose end, he met up with a school friend who had joined the Friends' Ambulance Unit: 'Why not me too?' Mario thought – he knew of the relief work of the Quakers – and the next three years were spent in that organisation for voluntary community service. It was to be several more years before he was finally able to give his life a clear sense of direction.

Leno, by contrast, might have continued his education after leaving Millfield School, but he rejected the place he had been offered at

Loughborough College. Much later in life he was to regret that decision, but at the time it offered him the independence he had longed for: although he was to remain closely attached to the Clothier family, who had supported him ever since the colony in Street was on the point of closing, he would no longer be dependent upon their good will:

> I felt that I was independent, paying my way, and not living off charity. The desire for independence, and not charity, is what dictated ... Charity. Yes, I would give to charity now, but when you're growing up and emotionally mixed up with the upheavals, the last thing you want is charity.

His natural athletic talent, which had so endeared him to the headmaster and which could have taken him to Loughborough, was still to shape his life during the next few years. It brought him into Somerset county's rugby XV, and thereby helped to complete the process of Anglicisation that had started with that childlike remark – 'I would love to come and live here'. Leno was the only Spanish boy left behind in the town and, although he could not have realised it fully by then, at the age of twelve virtually all his connections with Spain had been permanently severed:

> I said goodbye to the whole thing. This is one of the sadnesses of life
> ... I often wondered: why did I keep contact with the Clothiers when I broke contact with my own mother?

And, yet, that complete absorption into English life, begun after the colonies had closed and the young exiles had been sent on their separate ways, did not always prove irrevocable. Many were to re-establish their connections with each other and, in so doing, to rediscover, and come to cherish their Spanish origins. Sometimes it required a conscious effort, born out of loneliness. Thus, when the building contract finished, at the end of 1945, Rodolfo refused the foreman's offer for him to stay with the gang and move with them to their next job. For all that he enjoyed the work, he was finally tired of living in lodgings and he had also lost Angel, his one Spanish friend in Eastleigh:

> Angel went to visit his parents in France with permission to stay for two weeks. But he overstayed and they wouldn't let him back in to England. I was amazed because he was training to be a cook with the Co-op; I'm sure if the Co-op had said he was an apprentice, they

would have got him permission to get back in. He was broken-hearted because he was happy in Eastleigh. They had it rough in France.

So he wrote to his brother, Virgilio, who helped him move to the Midlands, where a number of the Basque boys were still living, and get a job there. And his Spanish returned: 'Oh, the words come back.'

For Valeriana the desire to rebuild those bonds was to involve a greater struggle, in which all the dilemmas eventually reduced to a stark choice. By the time she was eighteen years old she had been given a thoroughly upper-middle-class English upbringing; it had ostracised her completely from any other Spaniards ever since she had been taken out of the Colchester colony six years earlier. Then, when she could write to her mother only in English, her guardian sought to arrange for her legal adoption. But her mother, visited at her home in Portugalete by a representative of the Basque Children's Committee, refused permission for the adoption. Instead, she sent Valeriana's address to a couple of boys who had also originated from Portugalete, asking them to call on her and introduce her to others among the Basque children then living in London. 'And then,' says Valeriana, 'the whole situation changed':

> I was becoming more and more unhappy. I wanted more to be with Spanish people. I think the family resented this. I think they resented the fact that after all they'd done for me – that's what they told me – educating me and so on, that I should feel like this. But I didn't want to reject them really. The thing is, they wanted to keep me under their own conditions.

Unable to retain her undivided affection, her 'guardian' finally decided that Valeriana would have to leave their house and wrote informing the BCC. Miss Picken was able to find a household of Spaniards who were willing to accept one more under their roof and thus Valeriana was drawn into that vibrant community of Spanish Republicans in west London.

With others, however, it was not so much a consciously determined action, but more a chance intervention that enabled them to rediscover and reaffirm their Spanish attachments. When Fausto, the only Spanish boy in Consett, reached school-leaving age, his destiny was the local coal mine. 'I was a Spanish Bevan boy', he laughs. In all probability he would have remained there but for one afternoon when Mrs Badsey who, years before, had been his matron in the Tynemouth colony, called to see him:

She arrived just as I was coming into the house, black, covered in coal dust from the mine. She was in tears; she was so upset to see me like that and living in that place. 'You can't stay here', she said, and she wrote to the Basque Children's Committee.

As a result Fausto was sent to Oxford and apprenticed to a Spanish shoe repairer. From there it was easy to visit his brother who was living in the last of the Basque hostels in London. This was the link that brought him into contact with the Spanish émigrés. As with Valeriana, as indeed with many others, it was to provide him with a lifeline in the years immediately after the war.

A similar stroke of fate brought Juanita back into that orbit after eighteen months of self-imposed exile in Bethnall Green. Suddenly, another Basque girl arrived at the nursery:

When Rosita turned up, she and I became the best of friends, and we left the nursery job and we went to live with the Basque children again, in Holland Park. We had a room in the flat that belonged to her brother. The whole house was occupied by Spaniards.

Thus her Spanish attachments were re-established. In fact, she says, 'they took over', even though she had to relearn her native language. For several years more she remained nervous whenever she was speaking it, 'always afraid people were going to laugh at me'.

Herminio, too, had to relearn his language, for after three years of living his 'thoroughly English way of life', he was returned to the last surviving colony in Carshalton because of the economic hardships his pacifist guardians in Leicester were undergoing. Not only was his command of Spanish 'awfully rusty' by then, but, in many other ways, he recalls having to 'pick up the pieces again'. But the Carshalton colony was then at its zenith, run in its final years by Chloe Vulliamy, who had previously organised the colony at Wickham Market and who was to remain a member of the Basque Children's Committee until it was formally disolved in 1951, and the exiled Republican, Pepe Estruch:

Whilst I think I was very lucky to have spent those three years with my aunt and uncle in Leicester, I think really that – looking back – it was a period in my life that I value but I'm glad didn't continue, because I was losing my Spanish background. I was losing my language. Going back to the colony at that particular time meant returning to an environment which brought out the best of Spanish culture. Pepe and Chloe and all the others did marvellous work with, and for, the children.

7 THE BRIDGE AT HENDAYE

It wasn't feasible for us to go back. If you ask anybody in that town, they said there was no way we could have gone back there, to Rentería.

Some came early to the realisation that their exile was to be permanent. Just six months after arriving in England, Enriqueta received her first letter from Spain. The fact that it was written by her mother, rather than her father, was worrying since he had always been the one to write letters; the fact that it contained no news of him made it doubly so. She replied at once and the second letter from her mother confirmed her worst suspicions: her father was dead:

I read that letter once, and it took me about twenty years before I found the courage to read it a second time: it was so heart-breaking.

With their three girls safe – two in England and one in France – her parents had joined the Republican retreat from Bilbao, first to Santander, and then westwards into Asturias. Outside Gijón, her father had been killed when a bomb fell directly on to his lorry. After the final surrender in the north, her widowed mother had escaped by boat to France and from there had made her way back into Republican-held Spain. For the next twelve months she wrote regularly to Enriqueta from Barcelona, but then, abruptly, the letters ceased:

The last letter I had from her was to say she was going to try and make her way to France to meet with my sister. She never got there. What happened to her we just do not know. They were machine-gunned; they were bombed as they made their way.

When no more letters arrived she knew the perpetual silence could only mean that her mother had been among those who had died anonymously as that despairing column of half a million of the defeated, trudged through snow and rain in their dreadful retreat towards the French frontier in February 1939. Once she had reached that conclusion she realised her future was in England: there was no home awaiting her in Spain and nobody to whom she might return. Two years later, at the age of nineteen, she was married to an Englishman in Witney:

> Had Mamá been alive, I would have gone back; my life would have been completely different. But she wasn't there and I had to make a life for myself here. And I did the best I could.

Javier was another who quite soon relinquished any thoughts of a return to Spain. 'I didn't have anybody there', he explains. Not until after the war, when the Red Cross contacted the Basque Children's Committee, did he learn that his parents were still alive and living in a refugee camp in France. He visited them for the first time in 1948, hitch-hiking down from Paris to Dax:

> I went to see my father and mother, and – oh, how they lived! In an army hut – it was leaking – on a camp, down by the river in Dax. They never got anything in France; they were just evacuees from the Civil War. They died poor.

In fact, he was to visit often; cycling all the way to Southern France in the early years and, later, taking time out from his expeditions to the Pyrenees with the Ramblers. Over the years he was also to help them financially, but that first trip, in 1948, confirmed, if confirmation was needed, that his future was assuredly in Britain.

However, most of the Basque children who remained in Britain came more gradually to acknowledge that their exile was likely to be permanent, for, in the immediate post-war years, many felt certain that their return to Spain was imminent. Their optimism was buoyantly sustained by the anticipation that Franco must surely be removed by the international effort of the victorious Allied nations. The fact that he had acquired power through the intervention of Hitler and Mussolini, had overtly sympathised with the Axis nations throughout the war, and made no secret of his aspiration to be part of a triumphant fascist world order, provoked an enmity that was by no means confined to the political Left. There was widespread international hostility towards his regime which encouraged the hope that, however belatedly, the western democracies would finally come to the Republic's aid. In Britain, 'the betrayal of the Spanish Republic' was one of the campaign slogans by which the Labour Party had successfully fought the general election of 1945. For a while it seemed such a plausible hope. Helvecia remembers that period of optimism:

> We were all hoping to go back to Spain and help Spain to reform again. At the back of our minds we were only here for a temporary period and we wanted to educate ourselves as much as possible, to be a good citizen when we went back, and perhaps take part in the reformation of … Oh, but that was a vague thought.

The passage of the years may have rendered it vague, but it was clear and urgent at the time. Like Helvecia, Rafael can recall the vibrant political meetings at the Hogar Español and their regular anti-Franco demonstrations in London:

> Oh, we were getting ready. We thought we were going to go back with flags flying. Once you got involved in the Hogar Español and all the activity that was going on there, the idea seemed to be first it would be when the big war ended. Then it was when something else would happen – you know, the Labour Party came to power. Well, any time now. Then there was the constant argument of the boycott of Franco's Spain.

Jesús remembers those heady days too:

> At the Hogar, we kept our thing for Spain, for the Republican cause, alive. We kept our illusions alive.

And they were to prove cruel illusions. In Britain the Labour government's foreign policy never matched its pre-election rhetoric, while the exigencies of the Cold War, coupled with Franco's fervent anti-communism, dissipated whatever initial resolve the Allied nations might have had to intervene in Spanish affairs. So, for many thousands of Republicans, exiled in various parts of the western world, that once-bright vision of concerted international action which would rid Spain of the Franco regime eventually faded, and with it withered the expectations the Basque children held dear – that they would soon be returning to a new Spain. Some, José Mari for instance, never entirely abandoned that hope – he would return one day, for sure, even if not in the foreseeable future:

> I never lost hope. Never. Sometimes you were more interested than

at other times. Sometimes you almost had your suitcase already made ... But it never evaporated.

It was the spirit of retribution which forever characterised Franco's regime that blighted the prospect of their return. They were, in so many cases, the sons and daughters of Republicans, and it was upon those who had declared themselves for the Republic that Franco's vengeance turned. Legitimated by his Law of Political Responsibilities, which decreed opposition to the Nationalists to have been a crime, the execution of captured Republicans continued for decades after the end of the war; hundreds of thousands were incarcerated, at one time or another, in appalling gaols, or despatched into forced labour camps. The regime's rhetoric spoke of a reunited Spain; the reality was a nation that continued to be harrowed by the abiding memory of its Civil War. Indeed, it was the dictatorship's policy not to cauterise those wounds but to keep them constantly festering, to intimidate the vanquished and to reward the victors. The scrolls of honour for the dead, carved on to public buildings, honoured only those who had fallen for the Nationalist cause; only their widows received a war pension.[1] Safe in England, the Basque children were warned by friends or relatives that they should not return for fear that the sins of their defeated fathers should be visited upon them too.

Some parents in Spain, perhaps fearful of their personal letters being opened, or simply to emphasise their urgency, called on the British Consulate in Bilbao to communicate their warnings. One mother, for instance, after learning that her sons were contemplating returning to Bilbao, went immediately to the Consul, who wrote to the Basque Children's Committee:

> She has asked me to inform you that, while she greatly appreciates their concern for her welfare, which has doubtless inspired their request to be allowed to return, she would much prefer for their own sakes, that they should remain in England at least until there is a change in the present Spanish régime. She fears that, if they are repatriated now, they may – by reason of the political convictions which were the original cause of their evacuation – be subjected to persecution, if only to the extent of being debarred from seeking employment.[2]

Her fear was not exaggerated, for obtaining a job in Spain at that time required certificates or letters of commendation to affirm one's political, and religious reliability. This was consistent with the regime's policy of exacting continued revenge upon those who had fought for the Republic; those defeated Republicans, or their sons, who could find no employment, faced the real possibility of starvation. The mother's anxieties were passed on to her children by Miss Mary Picken who, during the post-war years, was to establish particularly close relationships with successive Consuls in Bilbao.

There were others who were to make use of this channel of communication with their exiled children. When, in 1948, an anxious mother called at the Consulate to report that she had been forced to divulge the English addresses of her two sons, the Consul informed Miss Picken:

> [She] is very much afraid that some pressure may be brought to bear on her sons by the Spanish authorities in order to persuade them to return to Spain, and she would wish it to be made clear to them that it is their parents' wish that they should at all costs avoid doing so. On the contrary, it is desired that they should remain in England and take out British nationality as soon as possible.

Alternatively, relatives wrote directly to the children in England, advising them not to return in the prevailing circumstances. Beside political persecution, there was extreme poverty in the decade after the end of the war: wages had been forcibly reduced to barely half their 1936 levels and infectious disease was rife. Joseba, still working on the farm in St Neots in 1946, wrote to his father to let him know that he was thinking of coming back:

> But my brother in Bilbao got to know and he wrote, and said, 'Joseba, don't you ever come here. Even if you have to sweep the streets of St Neots, don't you come here. The situation is ever so bad here. Not bad, very bad.'

Leno was another who was deterred by a letter from an older brother in Spain:

> I remember when I was arguing the toss about whether I should go back, he wrote and said, 'Don't you dare even contemplate coming back. All they'll do is just snap you up and put you in the army, and that's that.'

That was a prospect hanging over the heads of all the boys still in England and was enough to dissuade most of them. 'Three years in Franco's army? That was out of the question', was Herminio's blunt assessment, for the army – more like a foreign army of occupation, was a major instrument for the suppression of dissent in Spain. In fact, since they had not made themselves available for national military service, the boys were now officially regarded as *profugos* – deserters or, more accurately, those who had fled before their call-up. They faced the threat of immediate arrest if they set foot in Spain; even a brief excursion across the border was potentially hazardous. Some, therefore, sought to make their first reunions with relatives, after ten years or more, on the French side of the frontier, and even this caution could prove a painful confirmation of the wisdom of remaining in England. Virgilio, not wishing to take the risk of entering Spanish territory had gone with his brother, Rodolfo, to the frontier town of Hendaye in 1947, with the intention of seeing their mother. She was still living in Irún, as she had been when they last saw her in 1936:

> The first time we went we waited the whole fortnight for her to be allowed to cross for an hour. They were only allowing so many people to cross, and everybody was very nasty: the French were terrible; the Spaniards were as bad. So it was quite a harassing affair, really. On the Spanish side they said they would only allow 100 a day because the commander thought it was a good number. Nobody told him to say 100; he just didn't want to be bothered. So he says, 'a hundred and that's all'.

Throughout the fortnight they waited in vain: their mother was never among that arbitrarily selected few who were permitted across the bridge at Hendaye. But they went back, the following year, having told their mother to get herself a frontier pass which would allow her to leave Spain more easily and this time they were able to see her. She would cross the bridge into France in the morning, with food for a picnic, stay with her boys for the day and return to Irún in the evening. As an insurance against illegal immigration, the French authorities operated the policy of retaining one of the boy's passports until their mother had recrossed the bridge into Spain, and of prohibiting them from entering the town of Hendaye itself. All of the countless, sad family reunions, which must have taken place during those years, were restricted to the immediate frontier zone beside the bridge – virtually in no man's land. Once, however, Rodolfo remembers they did make the mistake of venturing into the town:

Virgilio asked a French policeman if we could go and he said, 'Yes, alright.' And, then, when we go back to collect the passports, the man that held the passports said, 'Oh, you shouldn't have gone. You had no right, you had no permission. I am going to hold your passport and make sure you never come back into France again, and I will make sure your mother doesn't cross the frontier again.' And he swore in Spanish and he swore in French.

It was on this occasion that Rodolfo first began to believe that he would never return to his native Spain. Perhaps it was the same for Virgilio, although he can look back and find one compensation: he met his wife at the frontier. She had wanted to visit her aunt in Biarritz, but had been prevented from crossing the border:

> She had a parcel for her auntie and she gave me the parcel, for me to deliver. I wrote to her. And, in the end, she came to England and eventually we got married. So, actually, the frontier served for something.

If there was no safe way over the bridge for the Basque boys, Luis found an alternative: he went under the bridge! Carrying his one-year-old son, he was at last reunited with his ailing father, on a sand bank, midway across the tidal estuary of the river that forms the international frontier at Hendaye:

In 1949 we wanted to take ourselves and the son to Spain, for the grandparents to see the child. Well I couldn't go, so I got as far as Hendaye, the frontier. Marí was able to cross and her father had 'bought' the Guardia Civil in Irún. They hired a boat on the Spanish side and when the boat sailed, the Guardia Civil turned their backs to the boat. I hired a row boat on the French side. I couldn't row but somebody else rowed us, and we met on a small sandy island between France and Spain – it's a sandy island at low tide. And that's what we did; we were there for two or three hours.

Not long after the reunion on the sand bank, Luis might have finally returned to Spain: he was offered an attractive job with the country's largest ship-building company. Its director was confident he could guarantee him freedom from arrest, but, just to be certain, he took the precaution of checking with the Spanish Ambassador in Britain:

> The Ambassador told the director, 'Oh yes, indeed, I can give him a passport to get through. But what happens if he gets to Irún and there is a bastard of a Guardia Civil there who wants to do him some damage? He has more authority at the frontier post than the Spanish Ambassador at the Court of St James.

So Luis declined the job, sadly, but probably wisely because one of his friends, tempted back on a similar promise of a job, was arrested immediately after crossing into Spain. Another boy who successfully took the chance of entering Spain on a Spanish passport was Mario, but he presumes he was simply lucky. The frontier guards produced a huge tally book and searched in vain for his name among their records.

The girls, although not liable for military service, could also find themselves subject to lengthy and intimidating interrogation at the border post. Amelia, on a brief excursion to visit relatives in 1954, was held for several hours and accused of being a 'political extremist' for not having returned. Frightened and fearful that her passport was going to be confiscated, she was continually asked, 'Why didn't you return?' And yet, such is the arbitrariness of repressive regimes, it was another border guard who rescued her from the ordeal. During a break in the questioning, he hurried her away to a waiting train, bought her a ticket and promised to delete her name from the record book.

'Some of them were very awkward; some of them were more human,' says José Mari. He encountered the awkward sort at the frontier on his first journey back in 1957, even though, by then, he had received his *indulto* – the amnesty document that released him from any obligations of military service:

> When I went through the customs office, the first question they asked was, 'What side of the Civil War did you fight on?' So I told him. I said, 'Look, can you see? I wasn't twelve when I left Spain, so I didn't fight.' So he says, 'Yes, but what side did you fight on?' 'I'm telling you, I wasn't twelve years old.' So he repeated the question three times and then I said, 'Right, put it there – I left from Bilbao. Bilbao was on the Republican side, wasn't it?' He said, 'Yes.' 'So put that I fought with the Republicans.' He let me through, then, but he just had to be awkward.

Eliseo was witness to a similar event, travelling back into Spain in 1951 with his mother, who had been living in France ever since the fall of Bilbao:

> Good God, I never felt sorrier. As soon as we got to the frontier there, we were wanted. They took her round into a back room and they kept hold of her for about two hours. 'What are you doing here? Where are you going? Why are you coming back?' And I was outside waiting, wondering what the hell was going on. They told her that as soon as she got to her home town, Baracaldo, she had to report to the police station.

Eliseo himself, travelling on a British passport, was not questioned and it was specifically to obviate these risks at the frontier that a number of children began to apply for British nationality. Helvecia was one. She had married a Catalan who had ignored Franco's wartime injunction and had fought with the British forces. After the war his family were imploring them to visit his ailing mother in Spain, but they had heard of others who had returned and been imprisoned as a consequence:

> Therefore we thought, 'Oh well, we've got nothing to lose and it looks as though we've settled here.' To have the guarantee of a British passport – we thought that if something did happen, at least we could ask the help of the British authorities.

The possession of a British passport was not, in fact, a cast-iron guarantee of immunity from arrest. Palmiro discovered this when he decided to take his English wife and their two children to Spain, to visit his mother in 1951. He planned to go via Paris because living there was an older brother, one of many young Spaniards who had escaped into France following the clandestine trail over the Pyrenees:

> We got as far as Paris and my brother said to me, 'You don't go to Spain!' 'Why is that?' I said. It was the first time I'd seen my brother, too, for fourteen years. And he said, 'They'll put you inside straight away, as soon as you get there.' My other brothers were still in prison – they served years, years after the Spanish Civil War, you know, for no reason at all, only because of their political views.

Surely, Palmiro argued, there could be no danger for him after all these years? He had come to England when he was only a boy. True, he had not returned for military service, but now he was a naturalised British subject, married, with a family of his own. How could he conceivably be arrested? But his brother was adamant. So they compromised by seeking the opinion of the British Consul in Paris:

> 'We would advise you not to go,' he said. 'The British passport can give you protection anywhere in the world except in your own country of origin. We cannot protect you there; as far as they are concerned, that's only a bit of paper. You were born there and they've got their records that you were born there. And you've got a wife and two children. It's a risky thing to do because we cannot protect you once you go over the border.'

That same evening Palmiro telephoned his mother with the news that it would be too risky for him to enter Spain. 'Oh, she sobbed her heart out,' he recalls. So, the following year, he arranged for her to come to England and he has no words to describe that first emotional encounter on Victoria Station. She stayed with them for six months; it was a further ten years before Palmiro himself ventured to set foot in Spain and even then he was held at the border for three hours:

> They allowed everybody else to go; they scrutinised my passport, and there were some real sour looks for me, that I had left Spain. The people who were returning from abroad, they were still regarded as politically dangerous. I explained: I said I was only a boy.

171

Tony, though he too was carrying a British passport, was similarly interrogated at the frontier, and ordered to report his arrival and departure to the police in Bilbao. He had finally been persuaded to seek British nationality because of the frustration he had experienced applying for a visa to enter Spain. For a year he had been continually calling at the Consulate in London:

As far as they were concerned, I was a *profugo*, so the first thing I had to do was ask for a pardon. And this takes time: the new papers come in so they never get to the bottom paper. That was first. And the second: I had to ask for a guarantee that while I was there, they would not call me up. Then they said I wasn't married. 'So you've got to get married.' 'But I am married.' 'No, no, you're not married. You must go to the Catholic church in Barnet. Go there and get married again.'

Neither registry office nor Anglican marriages were recognised by the Spanish authorities and so, without a Catholic wedding, Tony would have been eligible only for a single person's passport. He recalls how his wife, Pilar, greeted the Consul's proposal: 'Get married again?' she said to the Consul. 'To him? You must be joking!' She might have been, but the Consul certainly was not and it was this legal stipulation which finally prompted their decision to apply for British nationality.

This was also the turning point for others who had similar experiences in the Consulate: Eliseo met the same interminable delays and bureaucratic obstructions when he sought to obtain his *indulto*; Rodolfo was confronted with the same denial of the legality of his marriage; and Laureana, one of the teachers who had accompanied the children, was simply refused an entry visa on her stateless passport. The adults who had journeyed with the children had always been viewed with greater enmity by the Spanish authorities:

They told me they wouldn't give me a visa to go in. We were – what did they call us, when we didn't return? They called us 'traitors to the State', or something like that. And they wouldn't let my mother out of Spain either.

Naturalisation was the recognition that they were destined to remain in England for ever and some could not reconcile themselves sufficiently to that probability to apply for British citizenship. For them, the vision of their eventual return to Spain was never lost. Rafael and his wife, Valeriana, refused to accept that their exile would be permanent: 'We fed ourselves on hope and that never died.' And what fed hope, they insist, was the determination not to be beaten by Franco:

> We were always going to go back; we were certain of that. We wouldn't be beaten. We had to see that man out.

Marina was another who held on to the same resolve that made it impossible to relinquish Spanish nationality:

> Franco never allowed that terrible wound to heal, not even scar: he was so unforgiving that you could never overcome the sense of injustice ... And the only promise I made myself was to die after Franco, to survive him.

But many did lose hope of returning, 'particularly,' Helvecia explains, 'when we began getting married and settling down; oh, yes, it died then'. Marriage, even between Basque children, does seem to have been a watershed; at least, they speak of it now as the point when many began to accept the inevitability of living the remainder of their lives exiled in Britain. Pilar recalls travelling with Tony to visit his family, themselves exiled in France, long before their confrontation at the Spanish Consulate:

> When we went to see Tony's family, a year before we got married, in '47, we had made our life in England. Then we knew we were going to get married in England and we were going to stay in England. It was clear to us.

Perhaps, though, it is only in retrospect that such clarity has emerged. Others admit that, even after marriage, it took years before they truly felt their journey had become irreversible. For Jesús, it was not until his English wife and children had gone to Spain, 'with the express intention of spying the land out', that he finally began to accept the permanency of his life in England, and to accommodate himself to that inevitability:

> We decided we could not go to live in Spain under those conditions ... All the things that we took for granted in this place just didn't exist in Spain. It was like going back one or two generations. More or less until then, we had considered the possibility.

That was in 1957 and he admits 'we had more or less burnt our boats by then already, because we had bought a house'. Like British citizenship, obtaining a mortgage was often seen as the final severing of any private hope of a return to Spain. Some who did were criticised by their friends, as if acquiring a house was not simply a private action, but also a public admission that their political aspiration for a new, reformed, Republican Spain was equally forlorn. Not surprisingly, therefore, many delayed making that decision, and continued to live in rented accommodation. Valeriana recalls that it was years before she and Rafael considered buying a house:

> We never thought about it because our idea was to return to Spain. So we didn't spend money on buying furniture either. It was very, very rudimentary what we had in our homes. We used to get orange boxes from the market-place and put a piece of cloth over them. That was our furniture for a long time.

Yet, in the five years from 1945 to 1950, about 150 of the children who had been stranded by the onset of World War II did leave Britain.[3] The majority went to be reunited with relatives who were themselves exiled in France or South America; and a few made the journey back to Spain, despite the prevailing social and political conditions, their fears of persecution, and (for the boys) the prospect of having to spend their first three years in the army. Usually it was a plea from their parents which prompted the decision to return to Spain. For those who had then spent more than half their lives in England, such a request could become an agonising dilemma: a letter from one girl to the Basque Children's Committee reveals, as late as January 1949, just such a turmoil:

> Dear Miss Picken, I hope you had a very nice Christmas also a happy new year. I'm enclosing a letter from my father, hoping you'll be able to get it translated for me. You said in your last letter would I let you know if I still felt the same about going back to Spain. I'm afraid I do ... I should like to see my parents but I know I could never be happy in Spain. I should like to settle down in England and marry but I don't see how that can happen without quarrelling with my people. I'd much rather avoid that. Can you advise me on what to say?

It is difficult to overstate the tireless efforts Miss Picken made on the children's behalf in the post-war years. She appeared to be intimately familiar with the circumstances of most of those still in England and was the friend of many, especially the younger ones who had been taken in, and looked after in private English homes. She kept in regular touch, by letter and by visits; she arranged for the translation of countless letters which passed between parents and those children who had lost their native language during the long years of separation. Like all who knew her, Feliciana remembers her with great affection:

> After the Carshalton colony closed I was in hospital with T.B. and Miss Picken came to visit me each week. She was a lovely lady, small, and the smile lines were always around her eyes and her mouth.

Largely because of her concern and energy, each case of possible repatriation was examined with immeasurably greater care than had been possible in the fearful haste of 1939, and the children were advised of the domestic circumstances to which they would return. 'They were still careful, even in 1945 and '46', says Juanita. Indeed, it was on the basis of just such information that she decided to reject her mother's request and chose to remain in England. 'Reading between the lines,' she says, 'I could see that things were not right.'

In 1947, at the Consul's invitation, Miss Picken was able to recommend María Rosa, one of the Basque girls who had learned English well, to a post in the Consulate in Bilbao. She became, effectively, the agent for the Basque Children's Committee and communicated regularly with Miss Picken:

> At last we were able to go to Portugalete one afternoon this week. We went to see the mother of the boys you mentioned and explained the position. She doesn't quite know what to say, and for the present she feels her boys are better off there [in England] than they would be here. But as the oldest son is so set on returning, she thinks that perhaps it would seem to him as if he were not wanted at home if she said she didn't want him to return now. Besides, she wonders if he is unhappy where he is at present, and that is making him want to come home ... It would seem, Miss Picken, that the only thing to do is to let them come back if the eldest continues to be so anxious to do so; they will probably regret it but there you are.

It was, of course, not a matter of letting them come back: that decision no longer rested with the Basque Children's Committee. In this particular case María Rosa's prediction was to prove sadly accurate – the boys did come to regret their decision – but now it was the children's prerogative.

Some of those who eventually made the return journey were to resettle happily, although their subsequent letters of thanks to the Committee indicate their initial difficulties – the strangeness of a country they barely knew, relearning their own language, and rediscovering parents they had not seen for ten years or more. 'Life is very eventful for me over here,' wrote one boy, after returning in October 1947. 'Everyday I find a new friend and they all seem very pleased to help me in any way they can in the Spanish language.'

Others, however, were quickly to regret the impulse that had taken them back. Their letters speak of their loneliness, the loss of friends in England, of the poverty they encountered on their return to Spain and the difficulty of earning a living, and their sense of estrangement from a homeland made foreign by years of separation. Two sisters who had returned, in response to their widowed mother's appeal, wrote resignedly to Miss Picken: 'We are still a bit English sick but we know we have to make the best of it.' And another girl confessed:

You ask, Miss Picken, if we are better here. Telling you the truth –
I would return now. I long for my dear 'aunty'. People here are so
different ... I hope things are alright in dear England.

Even María Rosa, despite the relative privilege of her job in the British Consulate, wrote to Miss Picken, explaining her intention to return to Britain:

I don't seem to be able to settle down here at all. Everything is so
very strange. At first I thought that with time, I should get used to
being here, but it is difficult. Ten and a half years is a long time to
be away.

The saddest cases of all were the few who came deeply to resent their mothers who, in their loneliness and widowhood, had implored them to go back. Amelia knew one such instance – a brother and sister who had been in the same Cambridge colony as herself:

Unhappily and reluctantly they returned, although my mother tried
to dissuade their mother. 'You cannot provide for them here,' she

said. The boy escaped over the Pyrenees; the girl was sent out to sell newspapers. She was most unhappy and she came back to England, many years later. She hated her mother then. 'Why did she bring me back to sell newspapers?' she said.

In a letter to one of those English families who had looked after a Basque girl for many years, Miss Picken asked the same question and, perhaps, answered it:

> I find it difficult to understand the reason why her mother asked her to return (I realise, of course, that she wanted very much to see her after so many years of separation) but there is nothing, except perhaps a small piece of land, for [the girl] to interest herself in.

That particular girl, like a number of those whose repatriation in the late 1940s was to turn into a bitter disappointment, had appealed to Miss Picken to arrange for her to return to England. Naïvely confident that this would not present any difficulties, she had even specified the date on which she would prefer to travel. In fact, the obstacles were all but insurmountable: the British immigration authorities were extremely reluctant to grant anything other than short-stay visas and even a one-month visitor's visa was worthless if the Spanish authorities refused a passport on which it could be endorsed. 'I wish I had known all this before', she wrote to Miss Picken some months later, sadder and wiser.

Although the return to Spain usually proved irrevocable, a few did secure a way back to England. Some attempted the clandestine route, passing without papers through France. It was not difficult to avoid the border guards in the Pyrenees and, even if caught, they could often be bribed – the going rate in 1949 was said to be 1,000 pesetas – but arriving at an English port, without passport or papers, ensured scant chance of being allowed to enter the country. One boy did succeed in this desperate venture: he had served in the Merchant Navy during the war and had always punctiliously reported to the police during his shore-time leave. They knew him well and, fortunately for him, it was they, rather than the immigration authorities, who detained him when he arrived in England illegally. They explained his case to the Home Office and he was permitted to remain in England. He was an exception, however, and no doubt his wartime record helped.

The only secure way back was for a British national to apply to the Home Office on the Spaniard's behalf. That is how Alvaro returned to Wales in

1947, sponsored by a family who had befriended him during the year he spent in the Brechfa colony. They had hoped he was going to remain in Britain – he had not been reclaimed by his parents – but he was among those who were hastily repatriated just before the war. He had arrived back in Spain to find his brother and brother-in-law in concentration camps, and 'the hardship was horrendous because only my father and I were working and I, only a small little kid, was getting seven pesetas a week'. But he always remained in contact with the family from Carmarthen:

> When I came back to Spain, we kept in touch all the years, years and years, and then they came to my home for a holiday, at San Sebastián. That was after the war. And we talked about it, and they said, 'Would you like to come back to Carmarthen?'

Alvaro said yes, on the spot. He had already made a number of unsuccessful attempts to leave Spain illegally. Once, he and a friend had managed to get aboard a British cargo boat, bound for Cardiff, without passports, in the poignant belief that once in Cardiff they would get in touch with the people they had known in Carmarthen, and that 'they will have us with open arms like, you know':

> We wanted to escape, you see. We had met some of the sailors in San Sebastián. We were having a chat and a drink, and we explained that we wanted to come – we had friends in Wales and all that. But whilst we were in the boat, they asked us for money – they wanted money to bring us to this country, you see. And we didn't have money, so they said, 'Out you go!' So we were chucked out at two o'clock in the morning; we were very lucky we weren't caught. But I remember being in that boat. Oh, we're going to Cardiff, now! And then, at two o'clock in the morning, they said 'You're out!' Oh, it was cruel.

Earlier still, during the war, the two of them had endeavoured to enlist in the British forces:

> In those days, there were open offices to join the Blue Division, where they were fighting for the Germans. So we went to the British Embassy and we said we wanted to join the other side. And he told us we had to go to Gibraltar. Well, how can we go from San Sebastián to Gibraltar? Oh, it was most disappointing.

Finally, when his Welsh friends made the offer, he did not hesitate. He arrived with a one-month visa and before the month was out he had applied for an extension. His visitor's visa was extended to three months, then to six months and then to twelve months. Finally, it was made indefinite and with that came a work permit from the Ministry of Work. Throughout this time he lived with the family who sponsored his application and the man who had been the Secretary of the committee supporting the Brechfa colony gave him his first job in the garage he owned. Ten years previously, this was the colony which had earned so infamous a reputation in the popular press.

Of those children who remained in Britain, some were to discover that British immigration policy could be far more intransigent. Once they acknowledged that there was no likelihood of returning to Spain, a few sought the help of the Basque Children's Committee in obtaining permission for their parents to join them in exile in England. That would be no easy matter, the Consul in Bilbao explained, in reply to Miss Picken's enquiry in February 1947:

I agree that it is unfortunate that members of these Basque families should be separated from one another for so many years. Everything possible is done to assist local residents desirous of joining relatives in the United Kingdom in making out their applications for visas; but the final decision as to whether or not they may be allowed to enter Great Britain rests with the Home Office to whom the applications are referred through our Embassy in Madrid. Experience has shown that only in very rare instances are such visas granted.

Antonio had already known something of that experience after months of frustrated effort trying to obtain an entry visa for his mother. The day the Cambridge colony closed and the five children were dispersed about the country, he had set himself the ambition of one day reuniting the family. By the end of the war he had partially succeeded: he and his brother had said farewell to their itinerant crop spraying, and were working in Cambridge, and all three of the girls were then back in the town. But bringing his widowed mother there, from her exile in Lisbon, had proved far more elusive:

I'd been going backwards and forwards to the Home Office about getting a visa for my mother. And when you're only a small fish they say, 'Oh, yes, we'll let you know.' But, you don't make any headway.

By this time both the brothers were playing football for Cambridge Town FC and, after one training session, Antonio informed the club Secretary that he would not be available to play on the following Saturday. He intended to make yet another excursion to the Home Office, he explained, to see if he could make any progress with his mother's visa. But the secretary proposed a better idea: the MP for Cambridge was coming to watch the match that Saturday, as a guest of the club, and, if Antonio could play, he would be able to meet him:

> He came, he saw the match and after that we met him in the bar. He said, 'I hear you're trying to get your mother over here.' He took my name and several particulars, and I should think that within seven days he got a visa for us – there you are.

In 1947 the flight from Lisbon cost about £27 and Antonio was earning less than three pounds a week, but he had enough money saved to buy her a single ticket, and to hire a car so that all five of her children could meet her at Northolt:

> I think the plane was due in at about 6 o'clock in the evening and we left Cambridge – I think we were up there by half past eleven, fidgeting about the airport. And I always remember the policeman coming up there and talking to us. 'You're waiting for your mother then, are you?' I says, 'Yes.' 'How long since you've seen her?' I said, 'Ten years.' 'Oh, dear,' he says. 'You know my advice to the five of you? Go to Harrow,' he says. 'Have something to eat. Then there's a nice cinema there,' he says. 'Go in there for about four hours, because otherwise,' he says, 'you're not going to last until the flight comes!'

María Luisa, the youngest of the five, remembers that they followed his advice, but it was still 'a very emotional meeting – lots of tears'. In the ten years since they had bid each other farewell, their mother had fled from Bilbao to Paris and from there, after its capture in 1940, she had travelled back across Spain to Lisbon. The family she was then working for had promised to take her with them to Mexico, but in Lisbon they abandoned her. There she had remained for the last six years, working for an Italian Countess. Then, in 1947, she was in Cambridge, with her children, and Antonio's project was realised:

My mother always said those were the most peaceful times she had in her life, living in Cambridge. The most relaxed, peaceful. She worked for nearly ten years in Pye's, the radio people. She got on the line there ... And my brother was with the Gas Board, and any of the gas meter readers, if they were working around our area, would say, 'Let's go and see the Spanish lady.' She was well known in Cambridge; she was known as 'the Spanish lady'.

For María Luisa, too, then sixteen, these were happy times: with the arrival of her mother she felt she had a home at last and the chance to invite people to it:

We had a small place; it might not have been very good or anything, but you had that freedom, you know? 'Come home. Have a cup of tea.' You might not have had very much but whatever it was, you were quite free to offer – which is a very great thing.

This was the happiest of reunions, but there were others where parents and children were unable to surmount the gulf of those years of separation. 'We were complete strangers when we did meet', says Fausto. His parents had come to join him and his brother in London, in 1947:

They were very disappointed and sad that I'd grown up without them. They were absent at a time when you needed your parents most – a ten year gap. It was very sad for them. They expected us to live with them, but we'd already made our own lives by then. Really, we only lived together for three years.

It was much the same for many of the children whose parents came to England for a few months to visit them in their new life: establishing a relationship did not necessarily come naturally. Elvio had said farewell to his mother in Santurce when he was nine years old; he was 22 when he next saw her:

It was emotional. I mean, I didn't know how to take it. There was I, a grown-up person, as opposed to the little boy leaving her. That sort of affection and love which you have for your mother doesn't – it's not apparent straight away. It must have been upsetting for her, I would think.

Through those years of separation this must surely have been what their parents most dreaded. Yet, however painful it must have been for them, it is scarcely surprising that their children, who had grown to adulthood without them, should find it difficult to discover within themselves the filial affections which they so obviously longed for.

Often, parent and child scarcely recognised each other. Fausto remembers their mutual surprise when they first saw each other on Victoria Station: his mother seemed so little, while his parents appeared to be expecting to meet a little boy. Similarly for Ascensión: she had waved goodbye as a little girl of six in 1937 and when next she saw her mother, at Bilbao railway station, she was a married woman of 21:

> And the first thing my mother asked me to do – because she didn't recognise me – she asked me to show her my finger. And she said, 'Yes.' By that, she knew I was her daughter.

Half of that finger was missing – it had been accidently severed by her brother, Leno, chopping firewood, not long before they left Spain. And, with that gesture, her mother knew that this young woman, who spoke no Spanish, was the daughter she had not seen for fifteen years.

This was 1952 and in the previous year the Basque Children's Committee had finally been dissolved. Almost its last act was to appeal to the Home Office on behalf of two brothers who had entered Britain illegally in October 1950. They were two of that family which María Rosa in the British Consulate had visited, after their return to Bilbao three years earlier. As she had foretold, they had come to regret their decision. At first their mother had been able to report to Miss Picken that her sons appeared to have settled. They were relearning Spanish (although in the house they still spoke English) and they had found jobs. But, she had continued:

> As you see, they work too many hours, and yet we can't live well, though our home is a happy one. My children are good and kind, and are satisfied with everything except to be told they will not return to England. I quite understand it, they were so young when they went.

After learning their trade and completing their military service, she explained, they hoped to return to England. Apparently, they decided not to wait that long. They stowed aboard a ship, slipped the immigration officers at the port and, having visited one of their English foster families, arrived on the doorstep of the Basque Children's Committee. Miss Picken persuaded them to give themselves up and, a week later, from Brixton prison, they wrote to her:

> After having been in the police station for two days, we were brought here at about 10 o'clock on Saturday morning to wait and see whether or not they would arrange our papers. But I think that if there is nobody who will help in any way, I doubt that the response will be favourable. I have begged a thousand times for them to intervene, but according to what they have told us, it remains in the hands of the Home Office. Again I ask you, please try to do something for us.

She did, but her appeal, and her assurance that the foster family would be willing to accommodate them, failed to move the Home Office: both boys were deported. A month later Miss Picken learned that the two parcels of clothes and packets of cigarettes she had sent to the prison never reached them. 'The young men had not requisitioned for them', explained the prison governor in reply to her inquiry.

Thus the Basque Children's Committee ended as it had begun, confronting the hostility of government departments and agents, or their casual indifference. But, through the voluntary effort and generosity of countless individuals and families, and the selfless endeavour of its staff, the responsibility that the Committee elected to undertake, thirteen years earlier, could be said to have been honoured. Of the *Habana*'s original cargo of 4,000 children and 200 adults, some 270 were still living in Britain in 1951. For them, now all in their late teens or twenties, 'only three months' was beginning to look more and more like a lifetime.

8 MAKING OUT IN BRITAIN

*Adversity can bring out the best in individuals, provided it isn't so
great that it completely crushes.*

In the last days of the colony at Carshalton, Herminio was sent out to work
in a small local shop repairing electrical goods. Seeing few prospects for
himself there, he left for a farm near Colchester. But there wasn't much
future there either and, after a year, he returned to London:

> Coming back from Colchester to the East End, there was just nobody
> you could turn to. I tried. I went to the Youth Employment; there was
> no help there. The point was – you had to be self-sufficient.

Self-sufficiency is the common requisite of all those who are to survive
exile and, young as they were, the Basque children were no exception. As
they came to acknowledge there would be no return to Spain within the
foreseeable future, that their own displacement was perhaps irrevocable,
the message became clear: now they would have to fend for themselves.
'We had no shoulder to cry on', says Virgilio:

> The fact was that you've been taken away from your surroundings,
> your parents, from everything, everything that you know. Lack of
> education, of course; we didn't have any education. All those things.
> We've had to make our way 'the hard way'. Nothing's been easy.

Yet, with remarkably few exceptions, they have made their way. They
were to discover the determination and the resilience that the moment
demanded. Today it remains a source of some pride to them that, despite the
trauma of their exile – growing up without parents in a foreign land,
sometimes living in the shadow of rejection which comes from unresolved
departures, as well as the practical hardships that had to be endured – they
have survived to become mature, well-adjusted adults. Those familiar
correlates of exile such as poverty, mental breakdown and alcoholism are
almost entirely absent among them. Enriqueta attributes all of this to their
upbringing:

The Basque country always was a very prosperous place and, although we came from only working-class people, our parents encouraged us and taught us how to survive – and the value of things. I believe that's what it is, you know: it was inculcated in us to such an extent that as soon as we found ourselves in a position where we had to either sink or swim, we swam. We are extremely hardworking. I worked hard all my life.

Hard work is the constant motif. When they look back over their life in England and what they have made of it, hard work is invariably the explanation they offer. 'We did it without thinking about it', Jesús maintains. 'I never remember anyone complaining about their lot or being out of work.' The fact of being a foreigner was, for some, an additional spur. 'It's never easy to be a foreign person in a foreign country', insists Rodolfo. It bred in him a self-consciousness whereby he always felt obliged to 'do a little extra':

In my own mind, I always had to be better than anyone else because I was a foreigner. Wherever, I've always worked hard. I was at Lockheed for 30 years and not once did I start my tea-break before the bell went; not once did I go to wash my hands before I was due to. At the end of the day I worked till the bell; I never left before. I was always there ten minutes after everybody. The only time I was late was if there was snow and I couldn't get through. It was always because I had to – I felt I had to – be beyond reproach. I didn't want people to say, 'That foreign bloke!'

Javier tells a similar story: for 28 years he had worked as a setter-operator on the production line at Reynolds Trucks in Luton. When the firm was contracting its work-force and the management invited volunteers for early retirement, his request was initially refused. It is not difficult to see why:

I hadn't been sick for twenty years. I hadn't had a day off and I was never late. Sometimes I'd been to the doctors and he'd said, 'take a week off', and I'd destroyed the certificate, because I'm that type. You have to be a certain type to take time off and I'm not that type. I have always worked hard.

There was no shortage of jobs in post-war England – Javier can count as many as 22 before he settled at Reynolds Trucks. In that respect, they were all fortunate, but many saw their employment prospects constrained, none the less, by the severe disruption to their education. Joseba's case is typical:

> I lost my schooling, you see. I was just at the age and I was pretty good at school, pretty good at learning. And that's what happened at the beginning: we lost the schooling. Came here and we couldn't carry on with it.

There is no doubt that they were disadvantaged, most especially by their lack of any English schooling. And yet, the regret which many of the children express for their lost education, and the fierce determination with which a few subsequently pursued it, seems to go beyond the purely instrumental concern for the occupational chances that were thereby forfeited. Articulate, well-read and self-taught as many of them are, they speak of a more generous conception of education. It is such a vision that brightens Palmiro's recollections of his father:

> My father never fought in the war; he was an intellectual, really. He was good; he had good qualifications ... I very much regret not having had an education. It all finished when I was ten. All the reading I do: I read *The Guardian*; I read the newspapers, all the books, the interest I've taken – on international affairs especially – is something that came about probably because of the environment I lived in in Spain.

When he speaks of him in that way, you hear not only the sad fondness of his memory, but also a regret that the circumstances which stranded him in England were to deprive him of the same opportunities. Education is something he prizes, but for him it was only ever a promise.

Some, it should be said, were luckier: there were a few who, even at an early age, revealed a particular talent which attracted systematic adult guidance and support that lead them into distinguished careers. First encouraged by Pepe Estruch, when he was in charge of the final colony at Carshalton, Firmín Aldabadetrecu was eventually to become a principal dancer at Covent Garden; José Alberdi became an internationally renowned sculptor; Emilio Aldecoa played in the First Division of the English football league, first at Wolverhampton Wanderers and later with Coventry City. There were also those who, even if not without a struggle, benefited from the Juan Luis Vives Trust: thus Amador became an architect, Caireles a commercial artist, Luis a company secretary to a firm of importers. But the majority of the older children ended their formal education before leaving Spain and that proved a handicap they always had to carry. Several of them had been apprenticed into skilled trades in the early part of World War II; many others, even without apprenticeships, were able to become skilled craftsmen in due course. Their expectations were modest and the first jobs obtained for them by the Basque Children's Committee were, in many cases, to determine for ever the horizons of their working lives.

Those who were a little younger were denied even these opportunities and, for them, 'making it the hard way' invariably demanded not only hard work, but also patience. The stories they tell are frequently punctuated by the eventual intervention of a supervisor, or an employer, who had the insight to recognise the natural talents that lay beyond their conspicuous diligence and propensity for hard work. In Palmiro's case, it was a tanker captain:

> After the war, when the 'essential work order' finished and I could move jobs, I was offered a good job by the skipper of one of the Shell-Mex and BP vessels to come and work with him. He had always been impressed by the way I worked, you know. And he said, 'When there's a vacancy here, that's the one I want.' Actually I was away at the time and when I came back to Gloucester, there was a message waiting for me: Skipper Armstrong wants you to join him. Better job, better pension. That was the making of me really because when you work for a good company, they treat you like staff. I worked for them right through, from 1946 to when I retired.

This was the boy who had started work on a Devon farm at the age of thirteen. It was those of his age, ten or eleven years old when they arrived in England, who were perhaps the most disadvantaged. Their limited schooling in Spain was the sum total of their formal education. When their colony closed they were out to work and out to live, often in poor lodgings, inadequately prepared, speaking little English, and frequently with no one to turn to.

Like Palmiro, when the 'essential work order' restrictions were lifted, Antonio was free to change his job and say goodbye to crop spraying. He was recruited by a Cambridge wholesaler but, conscious of his own lack of schooling, he required a lot of persuasion:

'No, Mr Mathews, I couldn't,' I said. 'I'll tell you what,' he says. 'You come and work for me. There's any trouble, I'll take full responsibility for it.' So I went and worked for him. I worked for him for 27 years.

Even then, long after he had become the firm's most successful salesman, he still felt the same inhibitions when Mr Mathews sold out to a larger company:

I wasn't very keen on going [to the new firm] because I never had much confidence with – I mean I never went to school in England, so I never had much confidence with writing. But Mr Mathews said, 'As far as you thinking of yourself as not a proper salesman, you can forget it. You can go there with your eyes shut.' And I did and I always got on very well. I did another twenty years with them.

Some lacked that necessary patience, or perhaps it would be more accurate to say they were simply denied the fortuitous personal connection which might have led them to work that was more commensurate with their abilities. Oscar, for instance, alone and out of contact with any other Basque children, worked on a succession of West Country farms after he had left the colony in Street:

And you go to bed and you say, 'What am I going to do tomorrow?' And you'll do the same – more labour work. And the years go by quick.

Energetic and ambitious as he was, he took himself to London, and to a job in the British Library. That, he thought, would lead somewhere, but all it did, he says, was teach him how to make tea and tie string round parcels. Finally, in 1948, he decided to chance all and return to Spain. The chance paid off – he was to become a successful businessman – but the disillusion is still apparent in his voice, even now: 'England forgot about us':

When you are in a place, and the landscape for you is very small and you don't see how you can do anything there, because there you are considered a refugee, or because the people don't realise that you had to do something else, you have to take a risk. Leno, my brother, was lucky – he had something.

Leno was, in fact, one of the lucky handful of children to be adopted by a wealthy family and given a private education. Yet, as he was to discover, there could be a cost to be paid for the material comforts and educational advantages he enjoyed:

> One of the problems that one has in growing up as an evacuee and living with a family like that is that you feel you don't fit in. And when you know that, you're never relaxed; you can never be yourself, at whatever age.

After his one near-fatal venture as a merchant seaman, he had gone to Millfield School, but had refused the place that was later offered him at Loughborough College. Instead he was persuaded to work at Clarks shoes, where his guardian was a director. Despite a successful career in their design department, he insists 'It was a foolish thing to do, for there is no substitute for doing what you really want to do.' Only much later in life, after he had left the Clarks for voluntary work with the probation service and the Nature Conservation Trust, did he feel that he was at last doing what he really wanted to do: 'I never really took the bull by the horns; I should have had the courage to do that much sooner.'

But he is unduly severe with himself. Exile, it is said, is the most profound test of internal freedom and several of those younger Basques were to confront that test, more fully, perhaps, than the older ones whose destiny had been securely shaped by the jobs they had been forced to take at the outset of the war. The experience of an exclusive English education might have opened up more options but isolation, not simply from Spain but from other Spaniards in England, deprived them of the connections and all the familiar points of contact that would have helped them determine the direction of their lives. As it was, some, like Leno, were to discover that making their way in England was a process that could take many years.

Elvio came to the same realisation. He had been supported through boarding school by the Cadbury's Trust and when he left he took a job with the company. It was a temporary measure, as he saw it then, 'just to help me find out what I really wanted to do in life'. It took him ten years to make that discovery when a chance invitation led him into the wine trade; he speaks now of having wasted all those years.

Mario was in a similar position when he left the Beltane School. With no idea as to what he was going to do with himself, he joined the Friends' Ambulance Unit:

It was voluntary – they paid you just ten shillings a week pocket money. So if you smoked, you didn't smoke. But they gave you your food and a uniform. You had to join for two years and it was a commitment, complete.

By turn he was a telephone operator, a breakfast orderly, a cook; he was lent to the Salvation Army to pack up clothes for Germany and to decorate an old people's home in the East End of London; finally he was sent to work in a Church of England school for orphans and delinquents. Still at a loss when his two years were up, he stayed on for another year until one of those chance personal connections – which played so significant a part in the lives of many of the children – took him to an engineering training school in Gloucestershire. But that was ultimately to prove a disappointment: after eighteen months, working by day and studying in the evenings, he was refused the day release he needed to complete the HNC course. Despite the pleas of the personnel manager, he resigned:

'What do you expect?' I said. 'Here I am, somebody wanting to do more, and get on, and you block me. And it doesn't cost you anything.' There was no question about leaving – I was lonely anyhow – there was no point in staying.

So, another year, in another engineering firm in Bristol, until at last he could feel he was getting somewhere. 'Up there on the balcony was the drawing office and it was the goal' – but that goal was never realised either: the vacancy in the drawing office had been promised to him but it was filled by the son of the firm's director, just down from university. Mario was not prepared to wait. This time he left not only the firm, but engineering itself, and returned to London, into a bohemian milieu centred around some of those friends from the Beltane School. It was to be several more years before his life assumed a settled pattern:

By then, I wanted a home and a solid set of parameters. I had done all the jumping about. I had travelled this country from top to bottom. I wanted settlement.

Herminio is another who speaks of being 'still unsettled even when I was 21'. By then he had had several jobs and, more significantly, had embarked upon an educational quest. This, too, had to be pursued the 'hard way', over many years of evening institute study, for, when he returned to

London from his year on the farm, the funds of the Juan Luis Vives Trust were totally exhausted. He began at the Working Men's College in Camden, and from there moved to a technical college to study for City and Guilds:

> I approached my employer and said, 'Look, I don't mind how little I earn, so long as I can survive, but I want one day off a week to go to college.' That way I started at Poplar Technical College, one day and three evenings a week. At one stage, I had a room in Shepherds Bush. I used to cycle to work – I was in a workshop in Battersea – clock-in at eight o'clock; finish at six; clock-out; cycle right through the City, down the Mile End Road to East India Docks to the college; have a cup of tea and a bite; go to evening class – half past seven to half past nine; cycle all the way back, through the East End, the City and West End to Shepherds Bush – a good hour; have a bite to eat; to bed. Three nights a week. It was a dreadful existence. I did it.

He did, in three years, what was normally a five year course, then discovered that his City and Guilds enabled him to train to become a teacher. Two further years at Shorditch Training College and he qualified. Even then his educational ambitions were not finished – through the same routine of evening study at Birkbeck College, he later completed a degree – but an aspiration that had originally been fired during his period of temporary adoption was fulfilled:

> I first remember thinking about teaching, funnily enough, when I was at the school in Leicester. I loved school and I remember thinking – I must have been thirteen – 'Wouldn't it be lovely to work as a teacher.'

Two sisters, Marina and Carito, also became teachers, but somewhat better fortune had smiled upon them: they were picked out by the exiled Dr Camps during the time she spent working for the Basque Children's Committee. She brought them to the independent, progressive school at Dartington Hall; they completed their matriculation and then trained for teaching in the college attached to the school. Eventually they were recruited on to its staff, as in fact were several other Republican refugees. They laugh now because they say, 'there was a time when it seemed like you needed a Spanish passport to get into the village of Totnes'. Few of the other Basque girls, however, had that kind of opportunity: like the boys, most were handicapped by an education that had been irreparably interrupted and, unlike the boys, there had been no wartime apprenticeships for them. Only the luckiest, or the youngest, were able to pick up some of the threads in an English school. Ascensión, six years old when she arrived in Britain, was one of the youngest:

> I started [school] when I was ten. I'd still lost a lot of schooling, but – as I say – I learned to read, I learned to write, arithmetic, and I got a good job, I suppose. I was in the Co-op at the head office in Walsall. I was a typist there, in the Senior Secretary's office, so I suppose I didn't do that bad. But compared to my children and what they've done, you know, I would have loved a real good education. I would really. But I suppose I didn't do so bad.

None of them did 'so bad'. Pilar began as a junior in a London department store and ended her working life as one of their buyers, and, like most of the girls, combined employment with motherhood and building a home. 'We all worked hard', she says, in the same unimpressionable way that many of them recount their lives in England. Yet there seems to be something more to it than that: often, as these women speak, you cannot but detect a resourcefulness and an inextinguishable sense of humour; you glimpse an enterprise that goes beyond mere hard work. 'The Basque women are tough,' says Marina, 'and very independent and practical.' She regularly witnessed the grace of those qualities in the years after the war when she and Carito spent all their school holidays with their mother who worked first for the Spanish government in exile, and later for UNESCO, and who lived among the displaced Republicans in Paris:

> It was the women who resorted to anything – cleaning people's staircases, or anything - to bring home twopence for the children and their husbands. The Spanish men lost their personality, everything, once they left Spain; it was absolutely devastating for them.

Scarcely any of the Basque children were destroyed in that way by their exile in England. You sense, nonetheless, that it may often have been the girls who, in their hard-headed and enterprising way, had been able to hold everything together. Enriqueta, married at nineteen to an Englishman, lived with her in-laws for the first six years:

> Then we moved: we had a little cottage – two up and two down. I made a nice little place of it. It had gas lighting but we soon had in

the electricity; no water indoors, but we soon had water indoors. It was I that did that. I was always good at sewing; I made all my clothes and my daughter's clothes. Once I was in my home – it had a great big attic – in there went the machine, and I started taking in repairs and alterations for people.

When her younger sister, Carmen, died, she took in Carmen's baby son and cared for him for more than two years until his father remarried. Then, when her own daughter was old enough for school, Enriqueta was able to resume working as a clerk. Today, even in retirement, she continues to work, five days a week, as a volunteer in local hospitals.

Carmen had died of tuberculosis. It was a disease that was to claim the lives of a good number of the Basque children – the first within six weeks of their arrival in England. Another half dozen were to succumb in the colonies during the following two years and others during the war years. The annual report of the Basque Children's Committee for 1946 told of two more who had died of the same cause in the previous year; one of them was Joseba's younger brother, Iñaqui. Joseba had gone down from the farm in St Neots to meet his brother in London for the VE celebrations:

As I left him I said, 'You're not looking very well, son. Why don't you come and stay with me for a month, in the country, in the fresh air?' 'No,' he said, 'I'm alright; I'm alright.' He wouldn't give in. He liked his job – he was in the kitchen at the Savoy Hotel – but he worked long hours and he was unlucky because he had very poor lodgings. He used to help out at the Barnet colony, too; he never took much rest.

A month later a telegram came from the Basque Children's Committee: Iñaqui had been taken ill and was in Barnet hospital. Joseba went immediately but before he could see him on the ward, the doctor had taken him aside. 'There's no hope for your brother', he told him. 'He's actually got galloping T.B. and hasn't got more than a few months.' Iñaqui died at the beginning of November. 'It was two days after my birthday', Joseba recalls. 'I know he wanted to hang on long enough to wish me a happy birthday.' Even all these years later, he cannot hide his sadness.

But each one of the accounts the Basque children give of their life in England admits to losses – of family, sometimes of language and culture, even of memories, and always of all the familiar points of reference that once gave continuity and meaning to their lives. Many, like Palmiro, saw a parent or a sibling for the last time as they boarded the *Habana* on that May evening in 1937, yet they still talk of those bereavements with a tenderness and reverence. Enriqueta, for instance, can recount the fondly stored memories of the long weekend walks with her father and his friends in the mountains above Bilbao, or the excitement on the streets of the city on Republican day. Salomé's most affectionate recollections are also of the family, before the Civil War:

You see we had three or four cows; we had a donkey called Carolina; we had chickens; plus my father working. And we had a bit of land ... At weekends we used to sit, all of the children, around the table having supper and he would start playing the cucharas – the spoons – and start singing, and we used to sing, and – he was a wonderful man. Wonderful man.

Eliseo last saw his father as he pressed a silver duro into his palm on the quayside at Santurce:

When Bilbao fell he wasn't allowed to do any work; they took over our house and put some Italians in there. My father was forced to go round begging. He was picked up on the road in Bermeo – just lying in the gutter. Some nuns took him in; he was dying. They looked after him. For a while he seemed to get better and he was doing all the paper work, running the accounts, in the convent. He was a very, very clever man ... We never saw him again.

Mario has the stoical, dignified farewell letter that his father wrote on a scrap of paper in his prison cell on the eve of his execution and he can recall, in exquisite detail, the scenes in the small-town café-bar that his family once ran. 'It was a centre where people of like minds gathered':

My father was an intelligent man, active politically, a 'man of the people'. People had great respect for him and he commanded a following. He had a political angle to his life which was very personal. He was a very soft-spoken, unhurried sort of person. He wasn't a militant, if you want, but he carried enough weight.

Marina and Carito's father died in Barcelona, eleven months after the fall of Bilbao, of a broken heart they say, and perhaps it was merciful, for they fear he could never have survived exile. Their mother did, however, and 30 years later Marina had the chance to walk with her once more through the streets of Bilbao:

> Suddenly somebody stopped her – one of mother's ex-pupils. And this woman simply said, 'Doña Caridad', and she cried and cried. It was a very moving experience: she simply could not say anything except, 'Doña Cari'. She symbolised to her everything that was Spain, that was Bilbao before the war – decency and honesty. Yes, and what might have been.

They are all mourning an individual death, of course, but also the ending of so many hopes and expectations, and the sense of connectedness embodied in those relationships. The death betokens a greater loss – the loss of all that might have been.

But life goes on and, if it is not to be bereft of purpose, the broken strands of continuity with the past have to be rewoven such that they can once again give meaning to the present, and to whatever the future might contain. Failing that, they must be abandoned altogether and the links with the past consciously obliterated. That is precisely what some chose to do, but for others it seemed too bleak a prospect. Juanita remembers one boy – still only in his teens – who was brought down from the Scottish croft, where he'd been living, to one of the early post-war reunions of Basque children in the Hogar Español:

> The Committee brought him back to find out what kind of life he was leading in Scotland and he spent about two weeks here, with some Basques – he stayed with them. And every evening he was in the Hogar. I always remember this boy because he had such a strong Scottish accent. I got into conversation with him because I thought, 'He's like me – not much Spanish.' And he said, 'This is not me. I'm a shepherd.' He was a shepherd up in Scotland and he said, 'My family are up there. This to me is nothing. It would break my heart to leave my family in Scotland.' The Committee offered to help him visit Spain, but he wouldn't; he was really adamant about it. He said, 'I'm staying the two weeks here because I said I would, but I'm not interested.' He stayed the two weeks out of politeness to the Committee, but he was not tempted. And it stayed in my mind because it upset everybody – terribly. It really did.

The boy was one of the youngest; it was the older children, tied more securely to their past by lengthier and richer memories, who were so profoundly disturbed by this repudiation of all his Spanish attachments. They could not do that even if they wanted to; for them, the past always beckoned more strongly. It still does, says Caireles, and he contrasts his own feelings today, with those of Feliciana, his wife:

> I mean, Feli – she was only six; she doesn't know anything about Spain. When I start to romanticise about my childhood in Spain, she can't do any of that because she was only a baby.

Others point to younger siblings and maintain that 'it was easier for them; they assimilated better'. Pilar, for example, speaks of her youngest sister as 'the most British of the lot'. She married a Welshman and now speaks more Welsh than Spanish :

> She doesn't think a great deal about Spain; she hasn't got the same sentiments towards Spain. What happened, happened. There was nothing she could do; she was only six.

To assimilate can mean to relinquish the threads that bind one to the past, so as to face the future afresh, and that was always more likely to happen to the youngest. Their memories were shorter, their links more tenuous. María Luisa, for instance, was also only six when she arrived in England; little now remains for her beyond faded images of the family's flat in Rentería, and blurred recollections of visiting her father in prison. Furthermore, these younger children were the ones who were likely to have been adopted into an English family or to have known the Anglicising experience of some English education; they were also more likely to have married an English spouse.

But to assimilate can mean something different and age is not everything. Herminio was also one of the youngest, and for three years had been taken away into an exclusively English environment, but chance brought him back to the last remaining colony at Carshalton, and into the orbit of the Spanish community in London. Years later he embarked upon an MA degree in Spanish Studies:

> I had this need to establish some sort of roots, intellectual roots, and to find myself. I needed to have a background.

The older children had a background. If they were not to obliterate it, their need was to preserve it from loss, to retain all that was important in their Spanish past and reformulate those memories in order to give meaning to their future, even as they assimilated into English life. This was why so many attached such importance to maintaining their connections with each other: it went beyond the practical help they could offer each other, valuable though that was. In isolation, exile can be a slow but inexorable forgetting, a relinquishing of the past in a new country in which that past no longer holds any relevance. But together, in each other's company, they were constantly able to revisit that past and revivify their memories of it.

Sometimes the memories have probably been reinvented: it is possible, for instance, that the boy who recounts, so movingly and exactly, an eye-witness account of the landing of those long-awaited, long-promised fighter planes flying into Bilbao, and the collective agony of despair as two of them crash landed, never actually saw them. Desperately needed, as they were, for the defence of the city, they had risked the long and perilous direct flight over Nationalist-held territory finally to arrive in Bilbao. But that, according to Steer, was on 22 May 1937 – two days after the *Habana* had set course for England.[1] Yet their arrival, and the emotions which accompanied it, are as vivid and secure within his memory as if, only yesterday, he had actually been standing on the edge of the cinder runway.

The fact that he may never have been there is not important: it is the story itself that is material and the ability to retell it all these years later. It serves the same poignant purpose as each one of those precise recollections of their childhood before the Civil War, and their accounts of their parents' courage and self-sacrifice during the war, and their stoicism through the years of retribution that followed. Whatever their *mélange* of memory and hearsay, hindsight and myth, all these narratives work to prevent their own history, and the value they attach to it, slipping away amidst the everyday routine of making out in England. To harbour and protect those memories is not simply a matter of honour: they are necessary because they illuminate and give meaning to their lives; they help to define who they are.

So, after more than half a century of living in England, how may these people be defined? Are they Spanish or are they English?

> I don't know what I am – neither one thing, nor the other – and I think practically everyone will tell you that too.

Enriqueta is right; most do say exactly that: 'We feel a foreigner in both countries'; 'We're English when we're in Spain and Spanish when we're in England'; 'To tell you the truth, we're misfits in both places.' And so it goes on. 'It's sad when you think about it', says Helvecia and even her brother, Elvio, who maintains he is 'more pro-England than most of my English friends', to the extent that he would refuse to buy a 'foreign' car, hesitates to call himself English:

My ways are English ways, but I can never be an Englishman. I'm naturalised, but I'm still a foreigner really. I don't feel it till people start talking seriously about nationality, then I realise England is an adopted country for me.

In England, their residual Spanish accent marks them indelibly as foreign; in Spain, they are known as 'los inglesitos' and 'we are like fish out of water', says Feliciana. However fluently they have retained their own language, there is always what Jesús refers to as that '¿Tú no eres de aquí, no?' ('You don't come from here, do you?') because the acquired English intonation cannot be disguised, or they speak too slowly or, as Luis has discovered, their conversation is punctuated with English conventions of politeness:

I say 'please' or 'thank you' too often. My sister gets annoyed when I say 'thank you'. 'What's the matter with you?' she says.

Nor is this ambiguity of identity simply a matter of how they are viewed by others and how they are spoken of in the two countries. They carry the same uncertainty within themselves wherever they travel and it reveals itself in numerous ways – the equivocal use of the word 'home', for instance: home is Bilbao or London, San Sebastián or Warwick, according to the context, and with whom they are in conversation. Eliseo talks of his home town of Baracaldo and then immediately speaks of those times when he has returned to Leamington Spa:

For years and years, as soon as I landed – a pint of bitter. Till I had that pint of bitter, I wasn't back. Always the first thing to do. Pint of bitter – now I am home!

The same ambiguity shows in the paintings of Basque hillsides, with their patchwork of small fields, or the spectacular colour photographs of the bay of San Sebastián which adorn the walls of many of their English homes. It shows in the animated exuberance with which many describe their visits to the Basque region in recent years. London is undeniably home for Helvecia and yet:

I still get excited when I'm travelling and I'm getting near the Basque country and I start seeing the lovely green hills or the caseríos [mountain houses]. You get real excitement inside you.

And once, travelling in another part of Spain, she was delighted to have her accent recognised as Basque: 'I was so happy inside me. I thought, "fancy that"' – that most English of phrases.

Some try to make sense of this ambivalence by distinguishing between emotional and practical attachments. 'The practical part of me is very British', says Jesús:

I've been in this country so many years, how can I help it being anything else? I earn my living here, I live here. But from the sentimental side – going to Spain and talking to anybody in the street, which you don't do here, takes me back. Jumping on a bus or a train: 'Hola! Buenos días.' That sort of thing doesn't happen in this country.

It is the same with Joseba:

England has been my country for – oh, such a long time. Mind you, Spain is still here, in the heart. You understand that?

And so too with Pilar and Tony. 'Home is here', they say emphatically, gesturing around them; their house in Barnet is just a mile or so from where they met, in the mock-Elizabethan mansion that once housed the Barnet colony – 'This is home; there's no question about it.' They speak, too, of having a 'British mentality' and of their complete familiarity with British ways, such that if illness were to strike, even if they were in Spain at the time, they would want to take the first plane back home to England: 'Here, we could cope with anything that happened to us.' But sentiment? That, says Pilar, with equal emphasis, is a quite different matter: 'Oh, Spanish. Oh, the sentiment is very Spanish. I just can't describe it.'

Most find that sentiment impossible to describe and the attempts they do make seem scarcely able to do justice to its abiding force, and can, at first glance, appear trivial: watching any old Spanish film; tuning the radio late at night, when the air waves are clear, to pick up a Spanish programme; arresting the tears that are suddenly pricked by the strains of Spanish music. 'If there's something on TV about Spain you want to watch it,' says Pilar, 'because, whatever it is, you love it.' It is a love which is touched upon by each of those illustrations, an inexpressible longing for the landscapes of their childhood and for an inheritance which they know is theirs: 'Can you call it "homesick" after all these years?' asks Ascensión. She has assimilated as fully as is possible into English life and, in the process, lost her original language, and almost all her Spanish connections. And still she speaks of a sentiment that defies description:

> I know I shall not be buried out there, but there's a feeling of, well, 'I started there and I want to go back there'. It's a strange pull, I'm afraid.

There are times when that love transcends any practical attachment which has derived from being lodged, for however long, in a corner of English life and, perhaps, as some admit, it increases with the years: certainly, in recent years, a few have returned to live permanently in Spain. The death of Franco first opened up that possibility; before then it was never more than a dream. Carito remembers her umbrage towards those first English tourists who could cross the border at will, seemingly without thought or feeling:

> I resented them: why do they go to Spain? Spain is much more mine than theirs, but with Franco there they can go and I can't.

All that was to change in 1975, but at that time most were irresistibly tied to England, by their jobs, by their children's education. Any presumptions they may have been harbouring about returning had, therefore, to be deferred, relegated to their retirement. Now, in their retirement, a few have returned, although not to the Basque provinces, but rather in the manner of retired Britons, to the Mediterranean coastline. 'There is a community of about 10,000 English people there', Virgilio remarks, conscious of the irony.

For José Mari, returning was the eventual realisation of a hope that had never evaporated, but the decision was also governed by the realistic considerations that he and his wife would be able to live on their pension more comfortably in Spain: it would be cheaper, especially in the winter. That has been Virgilio's thought, coupled with other attractions:

> Also in Spain, in the winter, life goes on a long time. You can walk in the streets at ten o'clock at night and still people are about. Here, after six o'clock, there is not a soul; Leamington dies after six o'clock.

For the majority, however, any thought of going back – a prospect to which they may once have held fast – has long since ceased to be one they could seriously entertain. Others, while they still retain it, have simply lived in England for far too long; they have changed and so too has the Spain to which they would return: 'I would be a stranger in my home town in Spain', says Mario. 'I could never go back there to live.' 'Transplanted', is how Caireles puts it: 'Like a tree that has been taken from one field and put in another, the tree has been acclimatised to those new conditions.' Spain might still be in the heart, but the heart is ruled by another set of considerations: 'We could not fit in there, now', is the view that many express. Uprooting the tree once more is not easy, as Feliciana explains:

As I grew up, I had this sentimental idea that I would be going back to Spain one day … It's rather tragic, you know, because until I retired, four years ago, I still had that thing – 'Oh, well, when I retire, when I retire.' I retired and went back for about three months, but it was pathetic. I could see that I was completely lost there. I was very downhearted. So, you know, I'm still here and still don't know what to do.

Perhaps if she had been younger it would have ben easier? That's a thought that Rodolfo has considered:

If I was a bit younger, perhaps I might have considered going back to settle in Spain. I don't know. But the thought of starting all over again? No, no.

There is a further reason, and a more deeply ironic one, that fastens most of them ineluctably to England – the urge not to be separated from their children as their own parents were from them. 'I think if it were not for my children and grandchildren I would settle in Spain', says Palmiro; but his children live within walking distance. Even as he is making this assertion – if it were not for my grandchildren – they have emerged from the local school and are arriving at his house for lunch, just as they do nearly every weekday. It is the same for Jesús: 'I wish I was twenty years younger,' he declares, 'then I'd go back to Spain and say, "Sod it – let's take a chance".' But he can no more do that now, even though his children are adults, than he could have done twenty years ago. The roots he has put down are not merely those of practicality; there are also sentiments that bind him to England:

Go to Spain, like some have done, and leave the kids here – all the time, year in and year out – and see them maybe once a year? No, we couldn't.

In one direction or another most have resolved that tension within themselves: the pull of ancient Spanish attachments against the ties that connect them to England. 'You have lived to see another generation', explains Salomé. 'You have come through.' For a few, however, it appears a permanently unresolved issue. 'We're still here and we're still not sure', says Luis:

> We were never sure, not really. Although I suppose, once we were married we must have known, but we were never really sure, not really. We always thought we might go back ... We're still not sure.

The uncertainty seems always to have remained throughout all the years, the indecision, so unlike that of the sixteen-year-old boy who acted so conclusively by running away into the New Forest to avoid the repatriation boat. But now, as he indicates, there is a further complication:

> I have three families: there is my family in Spain; there is my family here – my two children; and there is another family – our friends in London, the Basque brothers and sisters.

He is not alone in speaking of those enduring ties among many of the Basque children as 'a family'. Undoubtedly, in the early years of their displacement, those connections had to compensate for their losses, especially, perhaps, for the youngest ones. Now, for all that they have integrated into English life, it is those attachments, built upon a shared and unique experience, that, for many, form their most valued friendships. Palmiro speaks of a 'love' among them which has survived into late middle age:

> We were like a family, you know, like brothers. I can go and visit them, and know I would be welcome. I can call on my English friends and they will say, 'Hello, Palmiro, how are you? What can I do for you?' The others – the Basque children – would open the door and open their arms, and say, 'Palmiro! Of course! Come in!'

Dita, an immigrant herself, who married one of the Basque boys, acknowledges that solidarity:

A lot of them went through a lot of hardships and a few went under, but very few. In most of them it brought out the best in them and I count myself as being very lucky marrying into all that. I'd never have had that community otherwise. Really, I did well.

And these young Basque exiles themselves did well: they did not freely choose those hardships, but in most cases they have surmounted them. 'We have done well', they tell you and then add, with apparent modesty, 'although none of us has become very wealthy'. But it is a false modesty: it cannot disguise the fact that wealth is not their criterion. They have seen how easily an entire world can be lost to be seduced by its material vanities. When Mario says 'Our needs have been met by a lot of work, very little money and a lot of ingenuity', he is speaking for most of them. In one way or another, he maintains, they have come through: they have survived the early traumas and the subsequent adversities, and it is this which has shaped them. Herminio says much the same:

I feel that adversity can bring out the best in individuals, provided it isn't so great that it completely crushes. I think this is why so many of us feel, in a sense, fulfilled.

Exile exacts its sacrifices, but it provides a unique angle of vision and surmounting its obstacles can furnish a perspective which appreciates all that comes from having inhabited two worlds, especially when, as Marina insists, 'they were both such rich worlds':

We never earned a lot, but it didn't matter: the life was rich, nevertheless, and we were aware of that – that it was a good life.

9   'WE DID NOT COME: WE WERE SENT'

My life has been an interesting experience.

In 1987 the fiftieth anniversary of the evacuation of so many thousands of Basque children and their dispersal across half of Europe was celebrated with a reunion in Euba. Some 2,000 were there, 'arriving in an uninterrupted flow of buses and private cars from all corners of the province', reported the local newspaper, *Deia*, and 'emotional scenes carried on throughout the morning as old friends met each other again after half a century of separation'. The majority of the middle-aged men and women who attended had returned home to Spain as children, but there were also contingents from those who had remained in Britain, France, Belgium or Russia – in whatever country had offered them a temporary haven so many years before – and for them the three-day celebration of the anniversary probably had a somewhat different meaning. 'Certainly our heart has always been here, happy in your triumphs and saddened by your disappointments', said Helvecia, speaking for the British delegation, in a brief address to the reunion:

> It is an emotional experience to find ourselves once more in Euskadi because, in spite of time and distance, we have never forgotten our homeland, not for one moment.[1]

The peculiar poignancy of the occasion was not lost on another who had spent 50 of his 59 years in England:

> I listened to the speeches in the Town Hall welcoming us back and I thought what a waste it all was. Our lives were completely turned upside down. For what? 'You are the lucky ones that got away', they said and I thought, 'little do you know'.

It is not difficult to imagine why those who suffered the full three years of the Civil War and its appalling aftermath might describe these particular evacuees as 'the lucky ones'. After all, they had been removed from the immediate dangers and the deprivations in Bilbao, and spared the subsequent

205

horrors encountered by those who remained. Poor though many of them were after the colonies had closed, and however hard they needed to struggle during their first years of independence in England, they knew nothing of Spain's post-war poverty – the years of acute hardship and famine when wages (for those who were allowed to work) dropped to nineteenth-century levels.[2] Many of the Basque children would concede the truth of that assessment. 'Of course we were lucky', insists Eliseo:

> You hear the stories of those who stayed behind or those who went back. And what my mother and sister went through – moving from one place to another, one place to another one, machine-gunned across the Pyrenees in the dead of winter. They went through hell.

And, in England, they were at least safe from the prolonged retribution that Franco's repressive regime continued to inflict upon the defeated for many years after the end of the war. 'The way things turned out,' says Palmiro, reflecting on his luck, 'I probably would have suffered in Spain in the same way as my brothers and my sisters.'

But luck can be double-edged: their lives *were* turned completely upside down. The way things turned out was so very different from what anybody envisaged, 50 years earlier, during the frantic few weeks of 1937 when the evacuations were being organised. The expedición a Inglaterra was to be for three months; it was to provide a brief respite from the bombing; it meant food for hungry young mouths; it promised temporary relief to anxious parents. That was what everyone believed. No one sending their children to the safety of a foreign land imagined that they were committing them to a lifetime's exile and themselves to years of separation. Who would have put their children aboard the *Habana* if they could have seen beyond the tear-stained, optimistic goodbyes in the gloom of Bilbao station, or on the quay at Santurce, to the irredeemable finality of that decision? The reunion of some of those children, 50 years on, was an inevitable reminder of that ironic miscalculation and must have prompted them to question the wisdom of the entire enterprise.

This question is unlikely to carry the same kind of significance for those who made the return journey back to Spain. A year or two of separation can certainly be an inordinately long period of time for any child, especially when they are pursued by anxieties about the safety of their parents, and there is no news from home even of their whereabouts, yet their memories of that period are, for the most part, extremely happy. One of the girls who returned had lived in the Theydon Bois colony; this was the colony run by

Miss Leah Manning, who, in the spring of 1937, had worked so tirelessly in Bilbao to ensure the evacuation took place:

> She was a fabulous lady: she gave us such love and did so much for us that it would be impossible to forget her.

She speaks of those days as being the happiest of her life and given the opportunity, she, like many, would have retraced her steps back to England for the abrupt return to Spain was traumatic. 'It left an indelible mark upon us', comments one of the boys who arrived back in Bilbao in December 1939:

> Then we realised how difficult it was going to be, not only adapting to the new life with our parents, but living in the atmosphere of repression which existed. It was not the atmosphere of liberty to which we were accustomed; it was a strange mixture of fear, uncertainty and anxiety.

There still persists an extraordinary affection for England in the hearts of those who returned to Spain as children and most especially for the generosity of the English people they encountered during their time in the colonies. However, all of that was a lifetime ago and now it must seem like a mere interlude. It was an important and memorable one to be sure, but not one that prevented them from picking up the threads of their life in Spain again, albeit in a very different Spain to the one they had left.

For those who were to remain for ever stranded in Britain, however, the question of whether their parents had been wise to send them away has a different significance altogether. It is one they have all asked themselves, probably many times over and if, as they are inclined to speculate, nostalgia increases with the years, it is not surprising that it still remains a live issue. María Luisa, for instance, finds herself facing it more now than ever before:

> I do wonder, I really do. In fact, more so as I get older. It's probably always been there but perhaps I never allowed it to come to the surface. Perhaps as I've got older I've felt safer in myself, with my husband and children, and I can investigate what I really feel.

What do they really feel? Mostly, their feelings are mixed: there are few answers which are not qualified by ambiguities and the inevitable accompanying sighs seem to reflect all their ambivalence. There is never any means of knowing for certain what might ultimately have befallen them had they remained with their families in Bilbao or if they had trailed behind them in their flight from the city, perhaps into exile elsewhere. Nor is there any ready calculus by which they might assess the balance of gains and losses which they now know followed in the wake of their parents' decision. Even the certainty of their good fortune can be tainted, however unreasonably, by the persistent sense of guilt that sometimes lives with the survivors of any human disaster. It is not something that is easily admitted but, occasionally, as the Basque children weigh the benefits and costs incurred by their exile, there is an unmistakable hint of self-reproach, as if their evacuation had been tantamount to a conscious desertion. 'We did not suffer as they did', confesses one of the girls:

> There is a gap between us. We are not as close as we would have been if we had gone through all the miseries and shortages that my brother went through.

Yet, if pressed, most feel sure that the measurable benefits have outweighed the costs. 'It was definitely the right decision,' insists Josefina, 'because mother could not have supported us: there was no widow's pension for those who had fought on the Republican side.' Similarly, any lingering doubts that Elvio might have entertained as to his mother's actions – persuading him aboard the *Habana* on the promise that she would soon be joining him in England – were dispelled by the evidence of his own eyes during the first return visit he made in 1950. If the regime was still as repressive then and life still marred by such bleak austerity a decade after the war had ended, what, he asked himself, must it have been like in its immediate aftermath?

Antonio says the same: 'One year after the Civil War they were nearly dying of hunger.' For him it is the proof that his mother made the right decision and he has before him a direct comparison: the life he was to lead in England set against that of his two cousins. Their names, just like his, had been put down for the evacuation, but, in the very final moments, their mother could not bring herself to part with them:

> That was the biggest mistake my aunt ever made. She said so herself afterwards. She could have put them in with us because we were all together in the hostel in Bilbao. But, no, she didn't want to let go her children and they begrudge her. They do.

Also, for some of the children, living in England, even living the life of an exile, conferred blessings upon them which they readily acknowledge: there were opportunities which would not have been available to them had they never been signed up for the evacuation or if, like the majority of the Basque children, they had returned to Franco's Spain. This is perhaps especially true for the girls. Valeriana, for instance, is certain of that: 'My life has been more fulfilled than it would have been in Spain, where the role of women was very different', she insists.

None of this, however, negates the reality of all that was irredeemably lost, which is unquantifiable. That, too, is part of their fate, for it was hardly of their choosing. It would be astonishing, therefore, if there were never moments of acute sadness for the blindness of chance that has so conspicuously attended their lives. In such a moment, Rodolfo expresses the confusion of those emotions:

> Our youth, our education, our upbringing – everything we knew –
> had all been taken away from us. I don't blame the parents. They did
> what they thought was the best thing for us, what they knew was best
> for us. The decision was wrong, but they were right to make it.

There is no blame: the one certainty which every one of the children who was later to be marooned in Britain acknowledges is that their parents' decision was prompted by an immediate and pressing concern for their safety. The bombs that were then falling daily upon the unprotected city, the repeated wail of the sirens and the frantic dashes to the *refugios*, the endless queues for every meagre morsel of food, the ever-tightening pincers of the Nationalist army, and the fear of what might ensue from their triumphant entry into the city were the existential stresses that impelled the parents to send them away. Some, who were never reclaimed, perhaps came to feel they had been abandoned, but all admit to the intolerable anxieties to which their parents were subjected throughout the bitter spring of 1937. Events subsequently interceded to thwart every anticipation of their return, but that is another matter and can only be judged by the unhelpful wisdom of hindsight. They recognise – most have children and grandchildren of their own now – the elemental responsibility of all parents to protect their offspring, to remove them from situations of imminent danger. It is that fact alone, says Oscar, which explains and justifies their decision:

> I think they decided wisely. In the Civil War they didn't know how
> Franco would behave towards them – 'Rojos', as he called them –

so they were afraid. And when people are afraid, the first thing they do is safeguard their children. They can't risk them and say, 'No, we're not going to send them because probably we won't see them again, or probably this or probably that.' No, no, no. The future you cannot forecast and cannot foresee.

They would all concur with that: their parents had acted in good faith, driven by concern for their safety. Yet there is a competing principle which states that, in situations of great peril which threaten each member of the family, the family should remain together. Thus, whatever fate befalls one, befalls them all. They confront the dangers and the uncertainties together, but never the havoc of separation, and dispersal. Coming, as all the children do, from a culture in which the virtues of family ties are so deeply ingrained, one might anticipate it to be a view which would carry some weight among them. It does with José Mari:

> I think, actually, if I had that choice with my son and my daughter, I would say, 'Look, if we're going to suffer, we suffer together. Let's see this through together.'

Then comes the inevitable reflection on the anguish of his and all their parents, and, after a pause, the weary acknowledgement that principles may need to be tempered by the exigencies of the moment. 'I don't know', he admits. 'It's very easy for me to say that now, but then the bombs were falling.' And falling bombs have scant respect for the value of family cohesion: they kill indiscriminately.

Had all this occurred just a few years later, when, throughout Europe, the bombing of mothers and children had become commonplace, and entire cities could be destroyed without moral scruple in a single night, the parents in Bilbao might have made a more sanguine calculation as to the risks of keeping their children by their side. But this was the first encounter with that strategy. From then on it would be the way by which modern warfare was conducted, but, at that moment, Guernica still burned in the memory, its terror kindled by the escalating rumour of General Mola's threat to visit upon them the same savagery. How would any parent live with that possibility and not secure the safety of their children? That was the implicit question with which Feliciana's father answered her, many years after, when she told him that, in similar circumstances, she would not part with her children. It was a moment born of extreme sadness for all the losses and a moment that was immediately regretted:

210

I was very sorry as soon as I'd said it because he said, 'Well, if you were in the situation we were in, with the children perhaps going to be killed, you would. Of course you would.'

How difficult was the decision to part with the children, even at that time of imminent danger, we can never know. 'It must have been an awful sacrifice for my mother', says María Luisa. Within a matter of months she had lost her husband and then seen her five children depart from her. But many were prepared to make that sacrifice. 'Take our children away; save them at least from the horrors of this war', was the repeated plea that the two Quaker observers heard throughout beleaguered Bilbao.[3] Twenty thousand children were delivered by their parents into the mercy of foreign hands and, undoubtedly, many more would have been if that option had been available. Time, it could be said, was also on their side, since there was so little of it. The decision had necessarily to be made in great haste – sometimes in a matter of hours – so there was not the drawn-out time that might have led them to dwell upon, and agonise about, all the possible consequences. And there was always the official reassurance, and comforting belief, that the evacuation would only be for a brief period. Perhaps, then, if the alternative was unthinkable, it was not so difficult to make the choice. This is rather what Marina seems to be suggesting:

I don't think it is so awful when it is so clear that you have to do it. Then you go and do it. It probably was very clear to them and they were determined that we should be safe.

But Carito, her sister, protests: 'Oh, but they were so fond of us.' Marina can only agree: 'Yes, Cari, but that's why – if you are so fond of somebody.' All the clarity with which their parents saw their duty could not lessen the pain of its execution; their determination to ensure the safety of their children provided no immunity from the sorrow of separation: it was the very cause of it.

Some, of course, were never to see each other again; others were to meet, ten years or more later, almost as strangers. Lives that had been entwined had become separated, relationships unravelled and many of those disrupted attachments were never fully restored. Several of the parents, so their children report, were to rue the choice they had made. How often we take decisions which lead to roads we had no intention of following; the best of intentions are ambushed by events over which we neither have any control nor could reasonably have foreseen. There were widows, especially, who, as they went their lonely way, came to judge the subsequent balance of gains and losses somewhat differently to their children. And some, like Mari's mother, were haunted by a persistent sense of guilt:

> My mother felt guilty all her life. She felt she had let us come here and had abandoned us. But I never felt that.

Parents do not expect anything in return from their children, except perhaps to be remembered, hopefully with affection. Throughout those empty years of separation, those who had unwittingly dispatched their children into exile must often have feared that they had been forgotten or wondered how much lingering resentment their children harboured. Juanita is certain her mother did:

> My mother told me, years afterwards, 'I shouldn't have let you go – two girls like that. I should have kept you – and taken a chance.'

As it was, she did take a chance: she let them go and took a chance for, in the midst of civil war, there is no line of action that excludes risk, or the interventions of fortune. 'Who is to say what would have happened if I'd stayed?' Juanita asks, knowing she can answer with no more certainty than her mother could forecast what would happen if she let her go. In the end, she took her own chance. Sixteen years old at the time, she said to herself: 'To hell with everything. I'm going to try and make it here.' And she succeeded.

There are moments of heartache, of course, for all that was forfeited in the process; there is some bitterness, too – at the indifference of a British government which never wanted them here in the first place or at the vengefulness of a Spanish government which always wanted them back – but rarely do you hear bitterness spilling over into self-pity. On the contrary, most seem somewhat contemptuous of those few among them who persistently bemoaned their life in England. More often, the pity they have is reserved for others who have been similarly afflicted. Their own experience, suggests Tony, has equipped them particularly well to sympathise with those who have also known what it is to be uprooted and dispossessed:

> When I think of the upheaval today, all over the world, people who really don't know where to go, then I can understand them and I get annoyed with some people – it's just a matter of principle: you ought to be thankful.

Most of the Basque children do speak of their own luck, with the overtones of thankfulness which Tony would applaud. Ascensión, for instance: 'I don't know what I have done to deserve such luck'; Elvio: 'I've been lucky: most people have been good to us.' Over the years, some have had to confront the 'bloody foreigner' jibe; others say they have never faced any form of xenophobic animosity from the British they have encountered. But, however much those experiences have varied, every one of the Basque children who remained behind will willingly cite the numerous acts of spontaneous kindness, made when their command of English was inadequate to express their gratitude, and made more precious now by memory. When, for instance, the Barnet colony was damaged by a German land mine and some 60 children were forced to camp for a week in the village hall, one local lady, her name long forgotten, ensured that every one of them had a bath in her house:

At the time, it meant nothing. Perhaps you even grumbled – a bath! It's only now that you recognise the generosity and regret that you were not able to thank them.

They speak of those kinds of experiences as a privilege: 'It's a privilege to have encountered such good people.' Enriqueta's voluntary work, five days a week in the local hospitals, is, in its undemonstrative way, a silent expression of her gratitude – 'a way of giving back something of what Witney gave to me'. And, similarly, Señorita María sent her savings to the miners of Aberdare during their strike of 1984, 'because I had such good memories'. More than 40 years earlier, during the time when she was working in the Consulate in Cardiff, she would regularly visit the families where a number of the Basque children were still lodged:

Weekends, I used to go visiting the families that had Basque children – very poor families, miners and poor. But kind? I will never forget the kindness of those people. They didn't show you money, but the kindness. They helped you with what they had.

But the gratitude they show goes beyond a simple recognition of their debt to those who helped them when they were in greatest need. Some speak of their entire lifetime in England – the three months that have stretched out beyond half a century – as having been a 'privilege'. In this context, it is a word which takes you wholly by surprise and, only on reflection, do you begin to realise its implication. It expresses more than thankfulness for the sanctuary and whatever other benefits were afforded them by the 'luck' of their enforced exile in England; it suggests a view on life itself. 'I've been around', says Palmiro; 'my life has been an interesting experience!'

The dislocation, the times of acute loneliness and all the wandering have not been in vain. Prised too early from their childhood, their lives were turned completely upside down, but they have been lived fully. F a c i n g their misfortunes and assimilating their losses demanded courage, energy and a collective generosity, and they live now in the secure knowledge of what they have come through. It leaves its mark, in the self-respect they display and, as Mario expresses it, in the pride they have in each other:

> When I look back, I think it was extraordinary that, given the pain and the suffering, and the anxiety, and all that happened to these children, that they survived happily and became on the whole, stable and level-headed people.

Without doubt, their lives have been the answer to that extraordinary remark of the Secretary of the Save the Children Fund, in May 1937, that he would 'sooner see them die in their own land than rot slowly in exile where they would deteriorate physically, morally and mentally'.[4]

If exile, the flight from political terror, has been one of the most poignant motifs of the twentieth century, the systematic and rationally calculated bombing of civilian populations has been its most horrific. These Basque children have known both: they were amongst the first to feel the chilling fear of aerial bombardment, and they were the first of many whose parents, in their dread at its indiscriminate peril, dispatched their children to any place that offered the promise of safety. 'We did not come: we were sent', they say, and thereby their lives were changed irrevocably. Yet, even as they speak of it, their voices still richly resonant with the imprint of their original Spanish, they seem not to be soured by that ironic working of fate. Meeting them, you sense people who have achieved a contentment with who they are, rather than what they are; you are made aware of both the seriousness of their concerns and their capacity for joy.

And what of those who were not sent, but who volunteered to accompany the children? Laureana, a twenty-one-year-old, newly qualified teacher, with no pupils because the Civil War had closed the schools, answered the appeal for adults to go with the children. Now, among her few treasured possessions is her Alien's Registration Book, issued shortly after her arrival in Britain; she had to plead with the immigration officer to be allowed to keep it when she became a naturalised British subject. It documents her movements, from one colony to another, during those first two years – from Tottington to Redhill, to Margate, to the convent in Hammersmith – and, later, all her wartime employment. In the attached photograph the dark hair is cut short and swept severely back, but it is the eyes that fix your attention, looking steadily out at the camera as they were to look upon life itself. Despite its youth, it is the face of indelible resolution and, yet, in the slight curve of the mouth, there is the suggestion that at any moment it might dissolve completely into smiles.

The same look greets you today: serious, attentive and full of warmth. 'I never cried so much in my life [than] on the day Guernica was bombed', she tells you, adding, in a whisper, 'all those things remain there'. But, then, a moment later, with a laugh of sheer delight, comes a quite different recollection: 'My mother would have fought Franco face to face, she was such a character', and you know she must be her mother's daughter. Declared a 'traitor to the state' and denied a visa, she was not able to return, but perhaps it didn't matter:

I was happy here. I'm always happy. They all say that – all the old ladies round here. I'm one of life's optimists.

She worked in the same clerical office for 28 years, taught Spanish in the evenings and was a governor of two schools for handicapped children. Now she lives on her pension in a small flat in south London. Its walls carry the familiar pictures and reminders of the Basque country; on the table are Amnesty International newsletters, Labour Party posters, and a pile of United Nations Association envelopes waiting to be addressed. Her optimism has not deserted her, nor has her vitality and abundance of energy. Her needs are few, beyond the need for friendship: 'You can't do without friends, can you?' she asks. 'You need friends all the time, my dear.' And, of these, she has many.

England provided her with a home, but England has benefited from her work and by her presence, just as it has from those children she escorted, and taught. They came for three months and stayed for a lifetime:

Yes, we all thought we were coming only for three months. Fifty odd years and it seems like yesterday.[5]

NOTES

Chapter 1
1. Eden, A., *The Eden Memoirs; Facing the Dictators*, p. 412
2. Steer, G. L., *The Tree of Gernika*, p. 159
3. Ibid., p. 167
4. Eden, op. cit. p. 443
5. *The Times*, 28 May 1937
6. Public Records Office (PRO): FO 371 21291
7. There, 'they caused some embarrassment, the Foreign Office regulations concerning Diplomatic Bags making no provision for the despatch of such genuinely inflammatory material'. In Cable, J., *The Royal Navy and the Siege of Bilbao*, p.100
8. Eden showed Stevenson's report to the Portuguese Ambassador on 7 May 1937 and 'assured him that the author was a well balanced person, impartial and without any inclination towards the Reds'. In Southworth, H. R., *Guernica! Guernica!*, p. 211
9. Hansard, vol. 322, col. 1712 (20 April 1937)

Chapter 2
1. Steer, op. cit. chapter 24 provides a particularly vivid account of the final exodus from Bilbao
2. Manning, L., *A Life for Education*, p. 130
3. PRO: FO 371 21379
4. PRO: FO 371 21292
5. PRO: FO 425 414
6. *Unidad*, 10 May 1937, quoted in Alonso Carballés, J. J., 'La prensa franquista de Guipúzcoa frente a las evacaciones por mar de refugiados vascos (mayo – junio, 1937)', in *I Encuentro de Investigadores del Franquismo*, 1992
7. PRO: FO 371 21371
8. PRO: FO 371 21370
9. Ellis, R., 'Four thousand Basque children', in *The Lancet*, 29 May 1937
10. Ibid.
11. Lloyd-Williams, B. and Gee, L. M., *The Friend*, 23 April 1937, p. 373,
12. Ellis, op. cit.
13. PRO: FO 371 21370

14. PRO: ADM 116 3516
15. Ellis, op. cit.
16. PRO: FO 371 21370
17. PRO: FO 371 21371
18. PRO: FO 371 21290
19. Steer, op. cit., p.260
20. *Southern Daily Echo*, 14 May 1937
21. Ibid., 15 May 1937
22. Ibid., 17 May 1937

Chapter 3

1. The personal papers of the late Wilfrid Roberts MP (Roberts papers), now held in the Modern Records Centre, University of Warwick
2. National Union of Boot and Shoe Operatives, Monthly Report, June 1937
3. Letter, Hunter to Roberts, 20 September 1937 (Roberts papers)
4. *North London Recorder*, 28 May 1937
5. *War Cry*, 12 June 1937
6. Ibid., 3 July 1937
7. *North London Recorder*, 18 June 1937
8. Details of the Cambridge colony are drawn from Stewart, J. (ed.), *'Recuerdos' – The Basque Hostel in Cambridge*,Eastern Daily Press pamphlet, 1939
9. Printed in *'Recuerdos'*
10. Buchanan, T., 'The role of the British Labour Movement in the origins and work of the Basque Children's Committee, 1937– 39', in *European History Quarterly*, vol. 18 (1988), pp.155–174
11. *Peace News*, 5 February 1938
12. Vulliamy, C., 'East Anglia through Spanish eyes' (publication unknown)
13. Brockway, F., *Inside the Left*, p. 322
14. Reprinted in *'Recuerdos'*
15. C. and J. Clark Ltd., Museum and Archives
16. *Peace News*, 7 April 1939
17. *The Yarmouth Mercury*, 15 January 1938

Chapter 4

1. *Manchester Guardian*, 21 June 1937
2. Steer, op.cit. pp. 330–331

3. The following account is drawn substantially from Yvonne Cloud, *The Basque Children in England*
4. *Eastern Daily Press*, 21 June 1937
5. *Manchester Guardian*, 21 June 1937
6. Minutes of the meeting of the Basque Children's Committee (BCC minutes), 5 July 1937 (Roberts papers)
7. *Peace News*, 10 July 1937
8. *Manchester Guardian*, 21 June 1937
9. BCC minutes (Roberts papers)
10. Glasser, R., *Gorbals Boy at Oxford*, p. 22
11. *Manchester Guardian*, 27 July 1937
12. *Sunday Dispatch*, 25 July 1937; *Daily Mail*, 24 July 1937
13. *Carmarthen Journal*, 30 July 1937
14. Reprinted in *'Recuerdos'*
15. BCC minutes, 28 July 1937 (Roberts papers)
16. *Catholic Herald*, 21 May 1937
17. *The Tablet*, 19 June 1937
18. *Catholic Herald*, 25 June 1937
19. PRO: FO 371 21374
20. BCC minutes, 31 August 1937 (Roberts papers)
21. Letter to BCC, dated 26 August 1937 (Roberts papers)
22. Letter from Fr Gabana to Duchess of Atholl, dated 28 September 1937 (Roberts papers)
23. Alonso Carballés, J. J. and Mayoral Guíu, M., 'La Repatriación de "Los Niños del Exilado": un intento de afirmación del régimen Franquista, 1937–1939', Congreso Internacional, Madrid, Mayo 1994
24. *Catholic Herald*, 17 September 1937
25. Letter from Macnamara to Roberts, dated 1 October 1937 (Roberts papers)
26. Letter from Canon Craven to Roberts, dated 5 October 1937 (Roberts papers)
27. Letter from Roberts to Woodruff, dated 19 October 1937 (Roberts papers)
28. BCC minutes, 28 October 1937 (Roberts papers)
29. PRO: FO371 22606
30. *Spanish Relief: Bulletin of the National Joint Committee*, No. 11, March, 1938 (Roberts papers)
31. *The Times*, 7 February 1938

32. Letter from Chloe Vulliamy to BCC, 18 March 1938 (Roberts papers)
33. Letter from Tewson to Miss Vulliamy, 23 March 1938 (Roberts papers)
34. BCC minutes, 22 June 1937 (Roberts papers)
35. BCC minutes, 5 February 1938 (Roberts papers)
36. Letter from Tewson to Miss Vulliamy, 23 March 1938 (Roberts papers)
37. Reported in *Manchester Guardian* and quoted in *Spanish Relief: Bulletin of the National Joint Committee*, No. 11, March 1938 (Roberts papers)
38. *Daily Herald*, 24 May 1937
39. Feiling, K., *The Life of Neville Chamberlain*, p. 394
40. PRO: FO 371 24148
41. *Peace News*, 19 May 1939
42. PRO: FO 371 24148
43. Record of interview between Mr R. A. Butler, MP, and members of the Basque Children's Committee, 28 September 1939
44. Record of interview between Mr R. A. Butler, MP, and members of the Basque Children's Committee, 16 November 1939
45. Letter from Roberts to Butler, 3 November 1939 (Roberts papers)
46. Letter from Roberts to Señor Lizaso, 6 November 1939 (Roberts papers)
47. Letter from Butler to Roberts, 16 October 1939 (Roberts papers)
48. West London Basque Children's Committee: appeal letter, dated 20 November 1939 (Roberts papers)
49. Translation of letter received by teacher from daughter in San Sebastián, (Roberts papers)
50. BCC minutes, 19 July 1939
51. Thomas, H., *The Spanish Civil War*, p. 577. *The Joint Letter of the Spanish Bishops*, published in Britain by the Catholic Truth Society, was probably written on Franco's instigation, suggests Thomas
52. Letter from Canon Craven to Bishop of Southwark, dated 28 December 1937 (Southwark Cathedral Archives)
53. In a 67% poll, 11,808 voted for Mr William Snadden, the Conservative candidate, and 10,495 for the Duchess of Atholl.
54. Hetherington, S., *Katharine Atholl, 1874–1960*, p. 218

Chapter 5
1. BCC circular, May 1939 (Roberts papers)

2. NJCSR appeal letter (Roberts papers)
3. *Fundación Juan Luis Vives: Report on its Work 1942–1947*, courtesy of Mrs Helvecia Hidalgo
4. Basque Children's Committee Archive, housed now in the Fundación Universitaria, Madrid
5. *Fundación Juan Luis Vives: Report on its work 1942–1947*, p. 11

Chapter 6
1. BCC archive, Fundación Universitaria, Madrid
2. *Carshalton Basque Home News*, 1941, courtesy of Mrs Helvecia Hidalgo
3. Letter from Plymouth Basque Children's Committee (Roberts papers)
4. Courtesy of Mrs Feliciana Martínez
5. *Peace News*, 28 July 1939
6. BCC archive, Fundación Universitaria, Madrid
7. *Fundación Juan Luis Vives; Report on its work 1942 – 1947*

Chapter 7
1. See Preston, P., *The Politics of Revenge*, especially chapter 2
2. BCC archive, Fundación Universitaria, Madrid. All the letters quoted from and referred to in this chapter are from the same source
3. BCC archive, Fundación Universitaria, Madrid

Chapter 8
1. Steer, op. cit., p. 280

Chapter 9
1. *Deia*, 25 May 1987
2. Preston, P., *The Spanish Civil War, 1936–39*, pp. 170-171
3. Lloyd-Williams and Gee, op. cit., p. 373
4. PRO: FO 371 21371
5. Laureana Puerta died a week after this final chapter was written

BIBLIOGRAPHY

Alonso Carballés, J. J., 'La prensa franquista de Guipúzcoa frente a las evacuaciones por mar de refugiados vascos (mayo–junio, 1937)', *I Encuentro de Investigadores del Franquismo*, Barcelona, 1992

Brockway, F., *Inside the Left*, Allen and Unwin, 1942

Cable, J., *The Royal Navy and the Siege of Bilbao*, Cambridge University Press, 1979

Cloud, Y., *The Basque Children in England*, Gollancz, 1937

Eden, A., *The Eden Memoirs: Facing the Dictators*, Cassells, 1962

Feiling, K., *The Life of Neville Chamberlain*, Macmillan, 1947

Fyrth, H. J., *The Signal Was Spain*, Lawrence and Wishart, 1986

Glasser, R., *Gorbals Boy at Oxford*, Pan Books, 1990

Hetherington, S., *Katharine Atholl, 1874–1960*, Aberdeen University Press, 1991

Manning, L., *A Life for Education*, Gollancz, 1970

Preston, P., *The Spanish Civil War, 1936–39*, Weidenfeld and Nicolson, 1986

Preston, P., *The Politics of Revenge: Fascism and the Military in Twentieth-century Spain*, Unwin Hyman, 1990

Southworth, H. R., *Guernica! Guernica!*, University of California Press, 1977

Steer, G. L., *The Tree of Gernika*, Hodder and Staughton, 1938

Stewart, J., *'Recuerdos' – The Basque Hostel in Cambridge*, Eastern Daily Press, 1939

Thomas, H., *The Spanish Civil War*, Penguin, 1965

Watkins, K. W., *Britain Divided: the Effect of the Spanish Civil War on British Political Opinion*, Nelson, 1963